Indian Country
Essays on Contemporary Native Culture

≪ • ≫

Indian Country
Essays on Contemporary Native Culture
≪ • ≫
Gail Guthrie Valaskakis

ABORIGINAL STUDIES SERIES

Wilfrid Laurier University Press
WLU

This book has been published with the help of a grant from the Canadian Federation for the Humanities and Social Sciences, through the Aid to Scholarly Publications Programme, using funds provided by the Social Sciences and Humanities Research Council of Canada. We acknowledge the financial support of the Government of Canada through the Book Publishing Industry Development Program for our publishing activities. We acknowledge the Government of Ontario through the Ontario Media Development Corporation's Ontario Book Initiative.

Library and Archives Canada Cataloguing in Publication

Valaskakis, Gail Guthrie
    Indian country : essays on contemporary Native culture / Gail Guthrie Valaskakis

(Aboriginal studies series)
Includes bibliographical references and index

ISBN 0-88920-479-9

    1. Indians of North America—Canada. 2. Indians of North America. I. Title.
II. Series: Aboriginal studies series (Waterloo, Ont.)

E77.2.V34   2005   305.897'071   C2005-902019-9

© 2005 Wilfrid Laurier University Press
Waterloo, Ontario, Canada N2L 3C5
www.wlupress.wlu.ca

Cover photograph: Margaret Gauthier in the ceremonial dress she gave to the Smithsonian Museum in the late 1920s. Photograph courtesy of the author. Cover and text design by P.J. Woodland.

Every reasonable effort has been made to acquire permission for copyright material used in this text, and to acknowledge all such indebtedness accurately. Any errors and omissions called to the publisher's attention will be corrected in future printings.

∞
Printed in Canada

≪≪≪≪≪≪≪≪≪≪≪≪≪≪≪≪≪≪ ● ≫≫≫≫≫≫≫≫≫≫≫≫≫≫≫≫≫≫

Table of Contents

≪ CONTENTS ≫

≪≪≪≪≪≪≪≪≪≪≪≪≪≪≪≪≪≪≪ ● ≫≫≫≫≫≫≫≫≫≫≫≫≫≫≫≫≫≫≫

List of Illustrations

≪≪≪≪≪≪≪≪≪≪≪≪≪≪≪≪≪≪ ● ≫≫≫≫≫≫≫≫≫≫≫≫≫≫≫≫≫≫

Acknowledgments

I thank the Social Science and Humanities Research Council of Canada for a publications grant in support of this book; Concordia University for the Administrative Research Grants that allowed me to present conference papers and publish articles during the years in which I was vice-dean and dean of the Faculty of Arts and Science; and the Aboriginal Healing Foundation for the privilege of serving as Director of Research. I am grateful, too, to Jacqueline Larson, Carroll Klein, Beth McAuley, and the staff of Wilfrid Laurier University Press for their support, insight, and skill throughout the processes of editing and publishing this collection of essays.

I am also indebted to the distant teachers, whose writing weaves through these essays; and to the close companions, whose generosity, curiosity, and knowledge are woven into my daily life: Stan Cudek, Gregg Guthrie, Ion and Paris Valaskakis, Lorna Roth, Miriam Van Buskirk Guthrie, and, most of all, my father, Ben Guthrie.

The essays in this book have been written or rewritten during a decade of cultural struggle between Natives and newcomers and Native people themselves. In these years, my reflections on contemporary Native culture have been reworked and updated. Essays that draw upon the material in this collection were originally published in the following:

"The Chippewa and the Other: Living the Heritage of Lac du Flambeau." *Cultural Studies* 2, 3 (1988): 267–93.

"Partners in Heritage: Living the Tradition of Spring Spearing." *Journal of Communication Inquiry* 13, 2 (1989): 12–17.

"Rights and Warriors: First Nations, Media and Identity." *Ariel: A Review of International English Literature* 25, 1 (1994): 60–72. Courtesy of the Board of Governors, University of Calgary.

"Rights and Warriors: First Nations, Media and Identity." In *The Mass Media and Canadian Diversity*, ed. Stephen E. Nancoo and Robert S. Nancoo. Mississauga, ON: Canadian Educator's Press, 1996. 110–23.

"Postcards of My Past: The Indian as Artefact." In *Relocating Cultural Studies: Developments in Theory and Research*, ed. Valda Blundell, John Shepherd, and Ian Taylor. London: Routledge, 1993. 155–70.

"Postcards of My Past: Indians and Academics." In *Between Views and Points of View*. Banff, AB: Walter Phillips Gallery and the Banff International Curatorial Institute, 1991. 31–35.

"Indian Country: Negotiating the Meaning of Land in Native America." In *Disciplinarity and Dissent in Cultural Studies*, ed. Cary Nelson and Dilip Parameshwar Goankar. London: Routledge, 1996. 149–69. Reproduced by permission of Routledge/Taylor and Francis Books, Inc.

"Sacajawea and Her Sisters: Images and Native Women." *Canadian Journal of Native Education* 23, 1 (1999): 117–35. Reprinted with permission.

"Sacajawea and Her Sisters: Images and Native Women." In *Civic Discourse and Cultural Politics in Canada: A Cacaphony of Voices*, ed. Sherry Devereaux Ferguson and Leslie Regan Shade. Westport, CT: Greenwood, 2002. 275–94. Reproduced with permission of Greenwood Publishing Group, Westport, CT.

"Sacajawea and Her Sisters: Images and Native Women." In Marilyn Burgess and Gail Guthrie Valaskakis, *Indian Princesses and Cowgirls: Stereotypes from the Frontier*. Montreal: Oboro Gallery, 1995. 83 pp.

"Sexual Difference on the Frontier: Cowgirls and Indian Princesses," by Gail Guthrie Valaskakis and Marilyn Burgess. *C Magazine: Contemporary Art Quarterly* 36 (1993): 11–16.

"Dance Me Inside: Pow Wow and Being 'Indian.'" *Fuse Magazine*, Special Issue on Cultural Appropriation 16, 5–6 (1993): 39–44.

"Blood Borders: Being Indian and Belonging." In *Without Guarantees: In Honour of Stuart Hall*, ed. Paul Gilroy, Laurence Grossberg, and Angela McRobbie. London, UK: Verso, 2001. 388–94.

"Parallel Voices: Indians and Others—Narratives of Cultural Struggle." Guest Editor's Introduction. *Canadian Journal of Communication* 18, 3 (1999): 283–94.

Introduction:
Approaching Indian Country

Duke Redbird (Hughes 1967) tells a story about a non-Indian who is driving through a maze of unmarked reservation roads, searching for the road to the Duck Lake pow wow. He sees an old Indian piling wood. He rolls down his car window and calls out, "Where's the road to the Duck Lake pow wow?" Without looking up, the old man answers, "Don't know." The man in the car rolls up his window, muttering, "Dumb Indian." The old man looks at the stranger and says, "I might be dumb, but I'm not lost."

For five hundred years, the social imaginaries of the dumb Indian and the lost white man have travelled together on distinct historical journeys. The trip has been arduous and eventful, and the destination is still uncertain. Shackled to one another in cultural conflict and political struggle, Natives and other North Americans have lived different social realities. The chain of histories and heritages, of images and experiences that divides Natives and newcomers is linked to the popular culture and political protests that mark the social landscape of this continent. This is Indian Country, land that was occupied by ancient Indians and colonized by the ancestors of other North Americans. The encounters between Indians and Others are etched into the cultures of Canada and the United States, where they express narratives of struggle that nurture friction between each other and conflict among themselves.

Today, Natives and newcomers are engaged in conflicts over land and treaties, stories and stereotypes, resources and policies, all interrelated issues that arise in collapsed time and continuing discord. The threads of this discord are formed from dissimilar memories, images and meanings, each strand knotted in contention and contradiction, each string entangled in struggles over territory, history, and ideology.

Indian Country has always been absorbed in encumbered discourse. Indians and colonists met as unequal companions, adversaries who

frightened and fascinated one another. For five centuries, Indian cultures have been the objects of studies and stories, but the voices of Native
people themselves were elusive. In the years when Indians were silenced
by commission or omission, newcomers wrote hundreds of books
describing tribal history and culture, detailing the impact of colonialism and telling about life among Indians. The legacy of Native culture
was recorded by non-Native explorers and traders, anthropologists and
historians, photographers, artists, and novelists. Even in recent writings
on traditional practices and contemporary Native cultures, we know
less from Indians themselves about the meaning of the cultural intrusion
of foreigners, little about how the transformations of Indian cultures are
understood and expressed and enacted in the everyday lives of Native
people.

For Native and other North Americans, unravelling the past in the
present—personal, political, and cultural—can begin to make sense of the
struggles over difference that characterize both the nation-states of
Canada and the United States *and* the Native nations, whose subjugation
has accommodated these national formations. In current conflicts over
power and identity, the Indian past is often perpetuated in a historicized
myth of parallel voices, expressions of a relationship symbolized in the
Two Row Wampum Treaty between the Iroquois Confederacy and the
Dutch, negotiated in 1645. Written into the beads of a treaty belt, it represents a pact of partition between Indians and immigrants in two discrete lines of blue beads that run across a sea of white, never intersecting,
never imposing upon one another. Natives and newcomers are portrayed as co-habitants in a respectful relationship of separate nations, one
nation travelling in an Indian canoe, the other in the settler's sailing ship.

If the voices of Indians and Others were once parallel, they are not
parallel now. Today, the expressions of non-Native academics, writers,
and artists compete or blend with Native voices that recall oral tradition or express current culture. The conflicting perspectives that some call
the narrative and the counter-narrative, actually overlap and intertwine
in stories and ceremonies, art and artifacts, studies and statements. Even
absorbed in the politics of difference, Natives and newcomers are bound
together in the web of representations that emerge and transform to construct who we are and our relations with others.

In discourse that interweaves historical experience and current practice, Natives and other North Americans negotiate the relationships of
dominance and resistance that thread through popular culture. Old nar-

ratives emerge in new forms that spiral into personal and political struggle, repositioning, transforming, or displacing traditional Indian knowledge and practice. The result is a mélange of Native images and texts that circulates in a cultural terrain filled with blind spots and pitfalls. Each account or analysis is part of an ambiguous mixture, a particular voice that can only be understood in the context of other voices that are sometimes absent, mystified, or ignored, and always incomplete. The partiality of personal, academic or artistic accounts blends with a mixture of local and national narratives that are riddled with stereotypes and tricksters in the stories we tell, stories that we remember, borrow, and create.

Narrative Voices

As the first Native person to give Canada's prestigious Massey Lecture, Thomas King (2003: 2) tells us, "The truth about stories is that that's all we are." Indians have always known that stories are important. Kiowa author N. Scott Momaday (in Swann and Krupat 1987: 566) says, "We are what we imagine"; and Lenore Keeshig-Tobias (in Slapin and Seale 1992: 985–99) writes, "Stories are not just entertainment. Stories are power. They reflect the deepest, the most intimate perceptions, relationships and attitudes of a people. Stories show how a people, a culture thinks."

Academic writing has long recognized narratives as a window on who we are, what we experience, and how we understand and enact ourselves and others. But resonating with the words of Thomas King, recent writing on literary, artistic, and ethnographic practice, reveals a more complex relationship between written or visual narratives and the formations of identity, community, and the alliances of power that construct our social lives. In particular, writing in cultural studies suggests that we actually construct who we are through a process that involves our individual identification with the cultural images and narratives that dominate our ways of seeing and representing the world.

Culture is the shared experiences and signifying practices that build social relations, and, in the lived experience of our daily lives, each person is a "'thing-which-is-becoming,' as opposed to a 'thing-which-is'" (Ross 1996: 101). Our identities are formed not in internal conceptions of the self, but in the adoption of changing representations and narratives that we generate and express in our individual and social experience.

Identity is continually contested and reconstructed in the discursive negotiation of the complex alliances and social relations that constitute community. Built in the ambiguous representations of visual and verbal stories, our communities are not cemented in unity and belonging, but in a dynamic process of change and difference that Stuart Hall (1986; 1989) describes as "articulation."

In an interview with Lawrence Grossberg (in Morley and Chen 1996: 141), Hall explains that articulation refers to linkages between different elements of discourse and social forces that under certain historical conditions can, but need not necessarily, be connected. These linkages unify dissimilar experiences, practices, narratives, and meanings in structured relationships that are neither determined, absolute, nor constant. In the continual shift of social forces, relations of dominance and subordination build "unities" through the linkages of particular discursive expressions, historical conditions, and social realities. These "unities" dissolve and emerge, constructing identities and ideologies that are continually changing. Our experiences, practices, alliances, and narratives are connected, decoupled, and realigned in the unstable processes of linkages that forge our identities, our relationships, and the meanings that we enact and express.

Considered from this perspective, stories are not just the cultural glue that holds communities together or transports them over time. Stories express the dynamic cultural ground in which individuals and communities are formed through a continual process of adopting and enacting allied or conflicting representations and the ideological messages they signify. In North America, the icons and ideologies expressed in Indian communities—and articulated to different elements of history, heritage, and everyday life—became more visible to others in the 1960s and 1970s through the widespread circulation of pivotal Native narratives.

For Native Americans and Canadians, 1969 was a critical year, a marker for events that those who are unaware of the tenacity of indigenous knowledge consider a Native cultural and political renaissance. In 1969, Alcatraz Island in San Francisco Bay was occupied by "Indians of All Nations" in a move that was a forerunner to the conflicts years later in Akwesasne (Ontario) and Oka (Quebec), and to the 1970s occupations of the Bureau of Indian Affairs in Washington and Wounded Knee in South Dakota. The angry protests of those years were influenced by the politics of the times and empowered by the newly discernible voices of Native intellectuals. In 1969, Vine Deloria, Jr., published *Custer Died for Your Sins*; N. Scott Momaday became the first Native American to win the Pulitzer Prize for his book *House Made of Dawn*; and Harold Cardinal published *The Unjust Society: The Tragedy of Canada's Indians*. The narratives of those who Stan Steiner (1968) called "the New Indians" nurtured Native cultural and political activity on both sides of the border. Tentacles of what became known as the "Red Power" movement in the United States spread north in the 1970s; but in Canada, more significant battles were fought in the courts and over negotiation tables, particularly after 1969, when Jean Chrétien, then minister of Indian Affairs, issued the *Statement of the Government of Canada on Indian Policy*.

Known as the *White Paper on Indian Policy*, it called for the abrogation of the Indian Act, the elimination of the special status of Aboriginal people entrenched in legislation, and the abolition of Indian reserves. This new narrative of displacement and acculturation recalled the establishment of Indian boarding or residential schools in the United States and Canada in the late 1800s, and the episodes of Indian removal, relocation, and reservation terminations in the United States. In Canada, renewed voices of cultural and political self-determination resisted the federal government's move to absorb Native people into common Canadian citizenship, and Native voices resonated with expressions of protest south of the border.

The counter-attack on the White Paper was led by the National Indian Brotherhood, later renamed the Assembly of First Nations. This alliance of Native nations adopted what Indians called the "Red Paper," a treatise that spoke about indigenous presence and Aboriginal rights, declaring registered Indians as "Citizens Plus." In the years since, the public voices of Native Americans and Canadians have increased in number, volume, and significance, expressing narratives of cultural and political struggle that merge with pan-Indian discourse and the voices of Others.

One of the new Native narratives reconstructs the public representation of the term "Indian," replacing this misnomer with "First Nation" in Canada and "Native American" in the United States. Today, the inaccurate and sometimes disparaging term "Indian" grates against the sensibilities of many indigenous people, some of whom reject colonial collective idioms altogether and assert the respective names of Aboriginal nations. This book of essays attempts to negotiate the pitfalls of competing narratives, adopting the word "Indian" to mark historical, communal, traditional, or stereotypical references to indigenous people; and adapting "Native" to serve as an inclusive term referring to contemporary First Nations and Native Americans.

Native Trajectories

Native narratives, of course, are no more monolithic than Indians themselves; and as Thomas King (in Perreault and Vance 1990: xii) tells us, being Native doesn't impart "a tribal understanding of the universe." The cultures, languages, and environments of Native America are wide-ranging, relevant, and real, and generalizing involves the dangers of essentializing. But common cultural currents run through the mosaic of Native nations that constitute Indian Country, expressing similar representations of land, spirituality, and governance that grind against the dominant discourse of North American culture. In the mixture of voices—culturally specific, pan-Indian, and Other—that circulate in artistic approach, anthropological method, cultural appropriation, and Native reappropriation, we can trace the trajectories of contemporary Native culture and current practice.

My voice is here, too, recalling the understandings and experiences of an Indian "insider-outsider," lived, remembered, and imagined. I am forever joined to Lac du Flambeau, where one of my paternal grandfathers signed the treaty that established this reservation that is my home; but I also live the heritage of a maternal grandfather, an East Coast sea captain and Dutch immigrant, who sailed commercial vessels along the colonial coast. I walk with a moccasin on one foot, a shoe on the other, allied to Indian Country and a mix of border zones, academic, urban, and social. My voice joins others that assert, contradict, and confront. Through a blend of conjoined voices, we can begin to unravel the meaning of Native experience and approach the points of connectedness between Natives and other North Americans.

The eight essays in this book reflect on treaty rights and land, media warriors, Indian princesses and squaws, pow wow, museums and art, researching Indian culture, and Native nationhood, land, and membership. The work forms a "literary kaleidoscope" in which each essay stands on its own, focusing on a specific expression or experience of contemporary Native culture. Taken together, the essays reveal different facets of a common theme. Adopting the vocabulary of cultural studies, they draw on concepts that orient the writing of Native and other academics to penetrate the prismal voices that express personal and collective memory, tribal and national events, real and imagined representations.

Maggie Hodgson (1990), former director of the Nechi Institute in Edmonton, tells a story that speaks about the significance of multiple perspectives. The narrative she tells is a long and wonderful story, which I've borrowed, and then shortened and reshaped in the retelling. The story is about a wolf, a trickster who ignores a promise on his journey through life and loses his sight. Hungry and blind, he comes upon a mouse in his travels. He pleads with the mouse for his eyes, and the mouse finally agrees to give him one eye. The wolf thanks him and continues on his way. But with his small mouse eye, he can only see one tiny bit of reality at a time, one person, one drum, one rock. Then he bumps into a buffalo. He pleads with the buffalo for his eyes, and the buffalo finally agrees to give him one eye. The wolf thanks him and continues on his way. With his big buffalo eye, the wolf can see the complex alliances of families, communities, and nations in which he lives. And so the wolf proceeds on his journey through life, now able to see with both his mouse eye and his buffalo eye; his sight reveals interrelated realities: individual and collective, past and present, Indian and Other.

With the sight of our mouse eye and our buffalo eye, we can begin to probe the complex experience of being Native in North America today.

≪ • ≫

Living the Heritage of Lac du Flambeau: Traditionalism and Treaty Rights

Englishmen! You ask me who I am. If you wish to know, you must seek me in the clouds. I am a bird who rises from the earth, and flies far up into the skies, out of human sight; but though not visible to the eye, my voice is heard from afar, and resounds over the earth! Englishman! You wish to know who I am. You have never sought me or you should have found and known me.

> Keeshkemun, Crane Clan, hereditary chief
> of the Lac du Flambeau Chippewa
> (in Warren 1885: 373)

Since the earliest days of anthropology, ethnographers have tried to access the experience of the researched through biography. This is reflected in the range of writings about individual Indians, the study of whose cultures has long been at the heart of ethnography. But biographies have always been marginal to cultural analysis, an interesting annex documenting individual memories, feelings and beliefs. Unlike language, kinship systems, or social structure, narrative has not been valued as a source of scholarly analysis or as the lived experience of collectively constructed cultures.

Recent discussions about the practice of culture in everyday life have restored the value of narrative. Writing in cultural studies has reconceptualized culture itself as everyday action, discourse, and events: lived experience and public text. And ethnographers have considered anew the significance of the relationship between personal experience and authority, accuracy and objectivity, between narrative and understanding (Pratt, 1986). Academic work in the past three decades represents a tentative move away from the notion of the narrative Other as an object, reified through time-distancing in writing that reflects an "ethnographic present" (Fabian, 1983: 80), or research that is embedded in structures abstracted from action through anthropological analysis. Current literary, artistic, and ethnographic writing moves toward what Native North Americans have long incorporated as lived experience: culture in the present woven with a kaleidoscopic past of intertwined experiences, representations, signifiers, and boundaries; history as heritage, living traditionalism.

In the writing of outsiders, Native traditional practice is often misunderstood as feathers and fantasy or, worse, as oppressive reification of the distant past. But Indian traditionalism is neither of these; nor is it lost in transformation or revived as a privileged expression of resistance. Traditionalism is an instrumental code to action knitted into the fabric of everyday life, the "lived historicity of current struggles and the interminable intertwining of past and present" (Walkerdine 1986: 182). It is cultural experience, "contested, temporal and emergent … Representation and explanation—both by insiders and outsiders" (Clifford 1986: 19), which situates the social field of current practice. Traditionalism is experienced collectively and individually as heritage, a multivocal past, re-enacted daily in the ambiguous play of identity and power.

Today, as in the past, Indian heritage is linked to other North Americans in cultural struggle. One of the central arenas of this struggle is treaty rights, a site in which traditionalism is enacted, transformed, and contested in the enveloping cultural distance between Natives and newcomers. Treaties are not an artifact of historical policy or practice. Treaties assert the rights of indigenous heritage, remembered and lived, communal and personal. In the always-incomplete process of reconstructing traditional heritage and the "collective reflexivity" (Fabian 1983: 92) of lived cultural experience, biography is central to an ethnography that recognizes the extent to which "notions of the past and future are essentially notions of the present … an idea of one's ancestry and posterity is really an idea of the self" (Momaday 1976: 97).

Being Chippewa

We were very young when we began to live the ambivalence of our reality. My marble playing, bicycle riding, king-of-the-royal-mountain days were etched with the presence of unexplained identity and power. I knew as I sat in the cramped desks of the Indian school that wigwams could shake with the rhythm of a Midéwiwin ceremonial drum, fire-balls could spring from the whispers of a windless night, and Bert Skye, the son of the medicine man Anawabe, could (without warning) trans-form himself into a dog. I knew that my great-grandmother moved past the Catholic altar in her house with her hair dish in her hand to place graying combings of her hair in the first fire of the day, securing them from evil spirits. And I knew that I was yoked to these people through the silence of ancient actions and the kinship of the secret. Later I real-ized that we were equally and irrevocably harnessed to one another and to this Wisconsin reservation land through indigence, violence, and ulcerated exclusion, recoiling among outsiders and ourselves; and that I was both an Indian and an outsider.

This land was reserved for the Lac du Flambeau band of Lake Supe-rior Chippewa in the Treaty of 1854. The treaty didn't become a con-tested charter in our daily lives until a century after its signing; but we have always known that this is Chippewa land. We are Anishinabe, known to Others as Ojibway or Chippewa, one of the Three Fires. We, with the nations of the Potawatomi and the Ottawa, are shot with the sacred Mégis shell in the secret ceremonies of rebirth that signify the Midéwiwin, a way of life "more powerful and impressive than the Chris-tian religion is to the average civilized man" (Hoffman 1886: 356). Together we followed the Mégis shell as it appeared above the water to direct our slow migration from the east. Around 1300, we separated at the interface of Lake Superior and Lake Michigan, each nation moving inland to forests and lakes, which we held in trust through our respect for the grace in sighting an eagle and our fearful anxiety of the bear's appearance. We who followed Keeshkemun, chief of the interior Chippewa, were here at the heart of the Flambeau Trail, the trade route south from Lake Superior, when the black-robed Jesuits came in the early 1600s (Warren 1885: 114, 192). They came in consort with French fur traders, who became partners in our heritage through their practices of naming, commodifying, drinking, and taking Indian women as country wives. Our daily lives became entangled in the interchange of furs and souls, of consumption and resistance; but our realities remained separate, bounded. François Malhiot, Northwest Company post manager at Lac du Flambeau in 1804 and 1805, wrote in his journal: "As a rule they [the Savages] possess all the vices of mankind and only think they are living well, when they live evil lives" (Malhiot 1910: 204). Our understanding is stated in the words of a Métis historian, "It was prophesied that the consequence of the white man's appearance would be, to the An-ish-n-aub-ag, an 'ending of the world'" (Warren 1885: 117). And these attributes of the foreign intruder and the unknown savage, encased deep within the prism of Chippewa experience, are reflected in the representations of who we are and the nature of Others.

We are known as "Lac du Flambeau" because fur traders, arriving at night during the spring spearing season, isolated this ageless custom and attached it to us forever. They were awed by the sight of torch-lit canoes moving silently along the shallows of the lakes, silhouetting Indians poised to spear fish. We have identified with their romanticized image of a "Lake of Flames" from that day to this. We were always Waus-wa-im-ing, "People of the Torch." But between 1640 and 1835, one and sometimes two and three trading posts at Lac du Flambeau were sites of exchange, defining us as traditional trappers, endlessly attracted to the sociability of rum: the humour, the quarrels, the deadening silence (Bokern 1987). Now we are Lac du Flambeau, known to each other through reconstructions of the past and Christian names, many of which are French transformations of our Ojibway language, and pronounced today as English. Our names, like this land, were claimed in Chippewa blood when the trading period forced alliances through inter-tribal warfare. We fought for ourselves, for the French, and, refusing the demands of the British, we fought for the Americans.

In 1737, the Chippewa, the Fox, and the Dakota Sioux began 150 years of dispersed, desperate battles to hold this land with its intrinsic resources and its trading empires. When the Fox were driven south in the mid-1700s, we fought the Dakota (Bokern 1987: 11, 14). The last memorable battle between the two tribes took place in Lac du Flambeau in 1745, and we are forever pierced by what we experienced. After days of scattered fighting, the Dakota were driven to Strawberry Island in Flambeau Lake, just as evening fell. The Chippewa regrouped, waiting for the dawn's final attack. Surrounding the island at the first light of day, we found the enemy had vanished, leaving a presence more powerful than bodies, scars on the land, or worldly artifacts. Near the Dakota campsite stood an enormous rock, a panoptic gargoyle, white in its newness, confronting the Old Village across the water with the ambiguity of our spiritual heritage.

Like the violence that spawned it, Medicine Rock became involved in the migrations of newcomers, Indians, and Others, who found their way to Lac du Flambeau. My great-grandparents were among the first to stay, thirty years after the reservation was established in 1854. They were Christian half-breeds living near Chippewa Falls, where my great-grandfather was an interpreter for a French fur trader. They married in 1883, and came upriver at the urging of Ke-nis-te-no, my great-grand-mother's grandfather, who was a signatory of the treaty that, in 1887, enrolled the Lac du Flambeau band and granted land to tribal members. The practices signified by my great-grandparent's religion and bloodlines set them apart as the Indians' struggle to defend their presence shifted to the inner arena of community. It was two years before my great-grandparents were allowed to approach Medicine Rock, and they never left the customary tobacco there. This difference conceived in experience was fixed by a policy of appeasement. When individual Chippewa were granted land through the Allotment Act, disgruntled full-bloods were given 160 acres and disclaimed half-breeds, 80 acres. Our family's posterity was preserved when my great-grandmother's name, written on the tribal roll of 1895, was omitted as the membership was read aloud to the old full blood chiefs.

My great-grandfather's land was allotted at Lac Courte Oreilles reservation; my great-grandmother's sister was enrolled in the Bad River band. We were a region of Chippewa even then, clans and cousins of the Anishinabe nation, gathered and restricted from a migratory cycle of hunting to the south in winter, moving north in summer to gather maple sap and wild rice and to fish. We were called a "timber people" (Hoffman 1886: 149); but this land, so attractive to outsiders for its cover of white pine, lacked underbrush to support large game. Especially here, where "the Pokegama arm of the Lac du Flambeau ... abounds with fine fish, which the Indians take in great numbers in gill-nets and with the spear" (Owen 1852: 280), our lifeblood was sustained in the nurture of spring harvesting and the presence of Gitche Manitou, the Great Spirit.

The Treaty of 1854 created six Chippewa reservations, small, irregular configurations of land reserved from territory ceded or sold to the United States in 1837 and 1842, when treaties became ritualized means for the extraction of copper, iron, and timber. A fur trader wrote: "To my certain knowledge the Indians never knew that they had ceded their lands until 1849, when they were asked to remove therefrom" (Armstrong in Bartlett 1929: 68). We remained sutured to this land through the starved silence of the abandoned fur trade and two government removal orders before the reserve was conceded. Little Bee, the Lac du Flambeau chief, walked with Chief Great Buffalo of the Red Cliff reservation on the footpath of resistance, worn down by the delegates sent to Washington in 1852 to protest the order to leave Wisconsin, and in 1862 to petition for a larger land base on the new reservation and the promised annuity payments (Bartlett 1929: 74, 82). Our Elders witnessed the starvation of the Chippewa who marched west to Minnesota. We from Lac du Flambeau did not move, and, finally, letters to the president broke the stubborn stillness. One was from the Wisconsin legislature requesting reservations, for "Chippewa Indians are peaceable, quiet and inoffensive people" (Rutlin 1984:16). In 1854, our Elders signed in relief, framing the heritage of our traditional practices: "The privilege of hunting, fishing and gathering wild rice upon the lands, the rivers and the lakes included in the territory ceded is guaranteed to the Indians, during the pleasure of the President of the United States" (Klapper 1904: 492).

When the Chippewa were enrolled as tribal members, the quiet indifference was shattered by the boom and bust of sawmills. Loggers began to cut timber from land allotted to individual Indians in 1887 and, when we were decreed competent to sell our allotments in 1910, Lac du Flambeau stood at the epicentre of the logging era. We who had always dreaded the anxiety of confronting a mythical, flesh-eating Windigo, a bear, or a stranger, now encountered a town, magnetic in the bustle and brawl of work and whisky; repulsive in the corruption and control of agency and enterprise. In 1909, when the Senate Committee on Indian Affairs came to Lac du Flambeau, one after another—Headflyer, John Martin, Louise Chapman, Ma-kwe-gon, John Wildcat, my great-grandmother, and many others—told Senator Robert la Follette of their problems with land allotments, payment of timber annuities, and credit at the company store. My great-grandmother testified that she (like Headflyer) had a licence to start a store, but

> Mr. Herrick [the mill owner] said that anybody that went into business like that, that he would starve them out.... He also said that no one could start a store here, that he was the "Rock of Ages" in this place, and that frightened me, and I thought that it would not be very well to go against him. (Senate, 1910: 775)

Loggers brought settlers, outsiders from a distance who came to stay. In the acrimony of this intrusion, we drove the first Protestant missionary off the reservation in 1886. But the Catholic and Protestant churches, which now stand staring at each other on opposite sides of the road

between the Old Village and the new town, emerged in the ambivalence
of the last decade of the century. We from the clans of the Crane, the
Snipe, and the Marten wrapped the Midéwiwin drum in white cloth
and secured it in Jim Bell's house-of-the-keeper, in the shadow of Medicine Rock. We incanted the hymns and prayers of Christian rebirth
through the typhoid epidemic of 1887 and the smallpox epidemic of
1902. My great-grandmother witnessed five hundred baptisms: each
name inscribed in the ornate frames on the walls surrounding the
Catholic altar in her house. Like the names, we were suspended between
Christian ritual and Chippewa custom, including the newly incorporated practice of drinking. But we never surrendered the secrets of the
Mégis shell, with its dreams and fasting and sweats for "pimadiziwin,
life in the fullest sense; life in the sense of health, longevity and well-
being" (Hallowell [1955] 1967: 294).

In 1895, a government boarding school in Lac du Flambeau folded
new generations of Chippewa into the discipline and distance of acculturation enforced through English, farming, and contact with children of
foreign tribes. Flambeau grew as a construction of Others between 1908
and 1934, when the Indian Agency centralized the bureaucratic power
of written policies and Indian wardship in a compound of white-frame
buildings. But, long after, my great-grandfather told of Old Man Sky in
Odanah at Bad River who could shake three wigwams at once; my great-
grandmother took my father to the drumming of the Midéwiwin, wearing her cross; and, when the medicine man Anawabe died, the fear of his
power was immobilizing. Four days passed before his women dressed
him and buried him in the intercession of night.

My great-grandparents moved closer to the new town, consigned to
loggers in sawdust and sweat, to those invited or non-Indian. There they
learned English, witnessed the disruption of development, and eventually built a rambling structure of yearly additions for the mill owners.
They sent their only child to a Catholic school in Saint Paul, Minnesota,
when she was seven. She never came back to the reservation except in
summer, and, like her children and their children, she married a non-
Indian. My father was a Lac du Flambeau Chippewa during the summer,
a student in Minneapolis during the winter. He chose the ancestry of
his Indian name, Kenisteno, when he came to Lac du Flambeau during
the Depression of the 1930s; and he stayed, first for his grandparents, then
for himself. He remained here to the end with my mother, who came to
Lac du Flambeau as a tourist from Chicago at fourteen and lived here for

sixty years. Like many others since, my brother and I are living boundaries between the city and the reserve, the Chippewa and the outsider.

In 1912, the judgment of Gitche Manitou settled upon the deterio-
rating reservation. The sawmills closed, the owners left, and a giant,
flesh-eating Windigo bellowed a cyclone that destroyed the Old Village.
In the silence that followed, the young and the mixed-blood were the first
to move into the deserted mill houses of the new town. The Old Village
and the families of the full-bloods that remained were designated forever
traditional.

Our land was largely stumps and cut-over brush, meandering among
150 lakes within the township of Lac du Flambeau, decreed by the state
in 1900. The new underbrush now supported deer; but it was the lakes
and the fish of our spring spearing grounds, which, through the log-
ger's legacy of alienated land, now attracted outsiders. In 1897, the same
year that liquor was forbidden on the reservation, the Chicago and
Northwestern Railroad snaked through Lac du Flambeau, at first to carry
logs out, then to carry tourists in. Chippewa land within our borders
became the currency of contact until land allotments and sales were
stopped for the last time in 1933 (McKinsey 1937: 2). By then, almost
half of our reserved lands were privately owned, mostly by non-Indians:

> The most desirable and valuable portions of lands along the lake shores
> have practically all been alienated [from Indians] by white owners
> and much of the remaining land, owned by Indians, is swamp lands,
> cut over or burned over timberlands and for the most part is of little
> value. (McKinsey 1937: 1)

We still brood with the burial mounds on Strawberry Island, now owned
by a businessman from Chicago who has never dared to disturb the
spirits there.

In 1913, my great-grandparents began building a new hotel, a beacon
for city fishermen and city families, which spawned into cottages, boats,
and a bar. During the next two decades the new Lac du Flambeau
unfolded in integrating structures: roads, stores, a day school, a Depression Civilian Conservation Corps (ccc) Camp for Indians from across
Wisconsin, and our now venerable fish hatchery. By the late 1940s, there
were one hundred resorts installed next to one thousand summer homes
on the reservation, and summer came to mean tourists. Chippewa spearers were transformed into fishing guides, specialists of the storm warning, the brush pile, and the shore lunch. And women, the hearth of our

Big George Skye with Ben Guthrie (age six), standing in front of the trading post built by Ben and Margaret Gauthier on the Lac du Flambeau reservation, Wisconsin, 1914. Ben Guthrie collection, George W. Brown, Jr. Ojibwe Museum and Cultural Center, Lac du Flambeau, Wisconsin.

culture pursued for their bodies or their souls, now sold beadwork and domestic service. We lived in the ambiguity between the new town, where we were baptized, educated, sometimes employed, and often drunk, and the vestiges of the Old Village.

There were outsiders who valued the passing objects of our presence: the walking-stick plug-chewing elders, the floral beadwork, the fishing friendships. But, in fear of the foreign, the dark, the drunk, few tourists followed the rutted road to the gathering grounds of our pow wows at Bear River. There, the Lac du Flambeau drum sat beside visiting nations and Chippewa cousins surrounded by moving images of the identifiable: beaded buckskin, appliquéd ribbon, silver bullet cones. But the drums of the Old Village, the covered graves, and the ceremonial Round House continued to represent the Indian as Aboriginal Other:

Across Lac du Flambeau, you will find it, strange and picturesque, this ceremony of the aborigines with rhythmic tum-tum of drum and pound-

> ing of moccasined feet in lengthening sunbeam through western win-
> dow.... Perhaps you will have an opportunity to snap your camera and
> gain a coveted picture of aboriginal costume, smiling squaw or quaint
> papoose—perhaps not. Most of those of the older generation retain their
> primal aloofness and decline to be subjects for the Kodak. (*The Septem-
> ber Outer's Book* 1917: 178)

With the curtailment of our seasonal harvesting that was intertwined
with migration, fewer families gathered wild rice or maple sap, and
fewer trapped. But we always hunted, and each spring was marked by
spot-lit spearers, now women and men, inching wooden boats and canoes
along ancient shorelines in the Lac du Flambeau night.

In disregard for our sovereignty, we were declared citizens of the
United States in 1924. Two years after the Indian Reorganization Act of
1934 had established bureaucratic tribal government, the inheritance of
Keeshkemun was reified with the whispered name of Jim Grey, our
hereditary chief, and the election of a new tribal council. Eighteen chair-
persons have led the enigmatic restoration of tribal empowerment,
always discussing and deciding in isolation from the town board, first
elected in 1901, which governs private property owners. We have moved
in seventy years of process from silence, through the rosary of resentments, to decisions on housing and working, to controlling and living our
lives in Lac du Flambeau, all in the shadow of the government of Others, and always angry. We are still often angry, with imposed policy and
decided practice, with non-Indians and other Indians and with one
another. And this anger erupts into violent events of word and body:
fighting, gossip, and accidents, which cut into the substance of our efforts
and ourselves. We are only partly the image of earthy nobility etched in
the artifacts of others; but we are much less the relics of integration
described in the written ethnography, which proclaims: "At Flambeau,
a high level of acculturation conceals a psychological skeleton" (Hallowell 1967: 366).

In the 1940s and 1950s, there was an assumption of acculturation in
Lac du Flambeau. One hundred and fifty Chippewa left the reserve to
fight in the Second World War. Those who returned brought fragments
of other experiences, other people, and images of the military masculine, all still present here, along with the interests of agency:

> Education at Lac du Flambeau has been inadequate to meet the needs of
> local Indians. Transition from Indian to White has been slow. Indians

have not learned what is proper social intercourse according to white standards. Maintenance of law and order has been rotten. Some untrained youths on the reservation are unaware of right and wrong. Men and women have not acquired the trait called, "Stick-to-it-iveness." Many are poor employees and cannot be depended upon. Many live too much on a today-tomorrow philosophy. Many cannot plan. Many cannot save. Many expend foolishly and are poor. (Great Lakes Agency 1944: 1516)

The attractions of the town expanded to include the communities of Minocqua and Woodruff, hosting non-Native bars and banks, shops, and services several miles to the southeast. The road manoeuvred past the sign "You are leaving the Lac du Flambeau Indian Reservation," alive in the sight of some lone old man walking home, rusty reservation cars labouring the load without a muffler, and the whiz of wary tourists. We still joke about finding our way home in the deep night by following the lights that lined the road, a Flambeau Trail of reflecting beer cans; but going home is important. We travel to these towns for groceries and clothes and televisions, for court and high school and hospital, always as outsiders and never very comfortable. The more Minocqua and Woodruff merged into a Disneyland of riding stables and water-ski shows, movies and McDonald's, the greater our felt distance from these constructions for the touristic consumption of Others, and the more urgent the economic necessity of our participation, forever clouded by the need to "compete, eliminate or reduce the bad publicity we get relative to hunting and fishing out of season ... the neighboring public keep attention focused on the reservations all the time" (Gauthier 1938: 4).

Our summer town, too, was flush with tourists when, in 1951, the Indian Bowl was built as a monument to our shared discontinuity. This gentle amphitheatre, carved into the lakeshore where the sawmill once stood, remains a tribal landmark celebrating the disjuncture of pow wow for profit. Sometimes we still sit on cement steps with the Others, haunted by beached canoes and dancing bonfire silhouettes; Bob Link's playful tales of super-smart Indians, and George Brown's ponderous voice welcoming the carnival crowds to experience all this. Over the summers, spotlights were larger and dancing was faster. Pow wow became a pan-Indian mélange of the no-longer identifiable western, Woodland cultures: bustled fancy-dancers with roach headpieces, slim-skirted shawl-dancers, all whirling in rhythm around the mincing movements of buckskinned traditionals. Even before the twice-weekly festivals-of-the-foreign upstaged the gatherings at Bear River, an anthropologist wrote: "The younger people at Flambeau seldom join in the Indian dances given as exhibitions, even for fun. Many of them do not know the Indian steps" (Hallowell [1955] 1967: 342).

The perception that we were being absorbed by the Other brought ethnographers to Lac du Flambeau, just as muscatel wine became legal for those whose daily lives were regulated by the practice of its rituals. In 1952, we were decreed equal under state law through the legal sale of liquor, a manoeuvre of federal disengagement under President Eisenhower, who, in 1965, stood on the scaffold of our heritage and became an honorary member of the Lac du Flambeau band.

The anthropologists who came to Lac du Flambeau were never interested in my great-grandfather. His memories were too eye-twinkling and slow-paced and droll for them to extract the factual from the interpretive. It was my great-grandmother, now called Grandma by everyone, who attracted ethnographers. She acted as interpreter and sang songs recorded on wax cylinders for Frances Densmore (1910, 1913), and gave her ceremonial dress to the Smithsonian for exhibit (Densmore 1929). She puzzled over Rorschach inkblots as Barnouw (1950) and Hallowell (1967) studied the personality of the Chippewa; talked about health for Ritzenthaler (1953), and about buckskin and beadwork for Hunt (1954). No one asked about her hair dish or her altar, about the ambivalent and binding power in the unspoken meaning she assigned to Medicine Rock, Bert Skye's transformations, the Midéwiwin, or spring spearing. No one asked about her father, who died in Andersonville prison during the Civil War; her daughter in Minneapolis and the other children she raised; or my great-grandfather's occasional disappearing binges. No one asked about the heritage, historical and recent, Chippewa and Other, ambivalent and prescribed, from which she acted. No one asked who she was.

My brother and I were raised at my great-grandparents' resort in the heart of town, climbing trees and fishing through the pier in the city that is Lac du Flambeau summer, walking to school in the unpredictable winter, sometimes being Indian, sometimes white. My great-grandmother was ninety-seven when she died a willed death in the calm of the Indian summer of 1958, a decade after my great-grandfather died, when the resort was sold and my father built a summer-season restaurant and liquor store filled with antiques and artifacts, material representations of his endless interest in Great Lakes Indian history. His vocation has always been avocations, school boards, town board, tribal committees, and proj-

Margaret Gauthier in the ceremonial dress she gave to the Smithsonian Museum in the late 1920s. Photograph courtesy of the author.

ects, all bridges between Indians and outsiders built in reverence for the past and impatience with the present. My mother taught high school English in the removed environment of Woodruff as my brother and I left, he for university, the Marine Corps, and eventually the ministry, I for school and city—all other places to Chippewa, who are rooted together in the reality of returning home. In 1973, my brother wrote: "I chose to be an Indian. That is my right. The right my grandfathers have given me" (Guthrie 1973: 1). He moved back to Lac du Flambeau, just as tourism and our fragmented collective experience began to change.

Being Home

To the new generation of two-week tourists, laden with children, motoring north to McDonald's, Indians were less exotic and more dangerous. Reservations represented the unromantic warriors of Indian protests at Wounded Knee and Rosebud and Alcatraz. The visitors drove quietly through Lac du Flambeau, no longer stopping to ask, "Where are the Indians?" attributing their distance as outsiders to an exaggerated sense of our violence among insiders. The drums of the Indian Bowl echoed in the abandoned night, and Lac du Flambeau receded into the 1970s behind the boarded windows of empty shops as protests arose in Indian Country.

But the raised fists of the American Indian Movement were never welcome here. Sympathizers of the movement confronted the binding conventions of Indian heritage and the encrustations of our political process. Lac du Flambeau is defined by an interpretation of parentage that implodes from the government definition of Indians as people who can prove one-quarter blood. We are distinct, bound through common Chippewa grandparents rooted to this place. Generations of intermarriage with Winnebagos, Oneidas, Potawatomis, and Menominees have lodged other Indians here who float as timeless members of their tribes, alike in daily life and the government's prescription, but untransfixed to Lac du Flambeau. They are here, but do not possess this place. Unlike tribal members now living in the city, they cannot come home and hunt or fish or run for office. And there are band members who live on the border like my brother, an enrolled Indian who served on tribal council before a referendum ruled that Indians without one-quarter Lac du Flambeau blood could not hold office.

Other Lake Superior Chippewa are acknowledged for the common experience of cousins and causes; but they too are removed. Red Cliff, Bad River, Lac Courte Oreilles: the names conjure up the friends and fights of projects and parties, pow wows and politics. This delicate membrane that holds in Lac du Flambeau by keeping others out is honeycombed with ancient strategies to redefine power in the present. Colour, language, custom; schooling, dress, bloodlines; religion, craftsmanship, residence: all contribute to effervescent definitions of who is an Indian now. Patricia Manor has experienced the transparent bell jar that is being Indian:

> We got talking and stuff and I mentioned something about being Indian. And he goes: "Don't tell me. Your grandmother is a Cherokee princess." Oh, I was so mad. I said "No! No! ... I'm a Chippewa, from Lac du Flambeau, Wisconsin"... and then, I finally showed him my tribal ID and I said: "See. I'm Indian. I'm Indian." I don't know why sometimes it seems like it's so important for other people to know that. (*Wausau Daily Herald*, 1 November 1987: 9)

Political constituency in Lac du Flambeau appropriates identity and fragments of community in the endless, all-consuming contest that is Indian politics. Our Red Power is elected wearing the armbands of family, carrying the shotguns of government grants and Indian jobs. The overpowering dynamic of tribal politics emerges from the daily sustenance that depends on short-term grants: daycare, and Head Start and federal housing; the clinic, the new fish hatchery, and elderly support programs. Politics is the framework for scholarships and business loans, tourism, tribal jobs, and tax-free cigarettes, all of them strategies against poverty, all of them supporting the income-producing projects of the tribe: the old land leases and the new casino. We have moved toward anchoring our economic independence, sheltered by revenues from gaming. We probe for tribal power beyond the Indian Self-Determinism Act of 1975, which allows us to administer local programs (Handrick, 1987: 39–40), and we are partners in a process linked to other reservations through the Great Lakes Inter-tribal Council. The politics interwoven with all our actions is grounded in articulations of self-determination and Indian control, treaty rights, and traditionalism.

In the spring of 1980, Strawberry Island released a relic of great age in the form of a twenty-four-foot dugout canoe. This *mitigo-jiiman*, with its carved turtle bow and metal tools of 150 years of travel and trade, embodied a silent recollection of our heritage. At first preserved in the quiet of the Ben Guthrie Public Library, "our prized white pine dugout canoe" (*Soaring Eagle*, 1986: 40) became the heart of a growing collection of birchbark and beadwork, photographs and artifacts housed in the tribal museum, alive in the personification of the present through the past. In 1983, the drums at Bear River echoed the renewal of our collective recognition at Lac du Flambeau. Our annual pow wow is now part of a circuit of Indian socialization reconstructed in 1974, when Chippewa drummed "Honour the Earth" at Lac Courte Oreilles reservation. The Bear River Pow Wow represents the range of identification, Indians in buckskin or Bermuda shorts, all here or home for the honour song of our traditional present.

Our transforming sense of who we are is represented in a range of ambiguous power, mysterious actions, and concrete strategies in the struggle with alcohol and self-sufficiency, community, and self-determination: weekly socials at the Round House of the Old Village; Wisconsin Indian Artists' shows; the re-emergence of the Big Drum Society and the Midéwiwin; sobriety pow wows; the new tribal ownership of Simpson's Electric Company; and the recurring interest in a Lac du Flambeau high school. The road to the Old Village has been widened and resurfaced. Fewer Indians drink in the cool of the trees near the historical marker facing Medicine Rock. There are more "Indian-abish," a twinkling acknowledgment of the young and ageless who place tiny teepees on the ice for winter spearing, or sew a hundred shells upon a pow wow dress, or search out the silent spirit of the Bear River. These representations are reflected in a television program entitled *The Enduring Ways of the Lac du Flambeau People* (Slabbaert 1988), which became a three-year process of rediscovering the traditional in the 1980s. In these years of renewed and reconstructed Chippewa practice, our heritage (Indian and Indian-abish) became involved with outsiders in the whirlwind of a new Windigo: treaty rights.

Treaty Wars

In the circling seasons of 1974, two Chippewa from Lac Courte Oreilles were arrested for spearing fish through the ice on a lake near this reservation. Like the discovery of the dugout, their fish exposed our permanence and sparked a disagreement over political positions that is as old as the naming of Lac du Flambeau. With the arrest of Fred and Mike Tribble, six tribes filed suit against the county, the state, and the Department of Natural Resources for violation of Chippewa treaty rights. During a decade when Indians remembered and tourists forgot, the case meandered through the courts. In 1978, the Wisconsin District Court ruled in favour of a hundred years of policy restricting us to reservation harvesting. Then in January 1983, the United States Federal Court of Appeals reversed the rights, pronouncing in the *Voigt* decision what we have always held within our heritage: we the Chippewa nations in Wisconsin, Upper Michigan, and Minnesota kept our rights to hunt, fish, and gather wild rice when we deposited our lands in trust through the treaties of 1837 and 1842. In a concession to the times, the court affirmed the power of the state to regulate within the supersession of Chippewa treaties should we become a threat to natural resources, and referred the definition of our rights to the District Court. When the United States Supreme Court declined to overturn the state's appeal, "the Chippewa eventually won, and the victory touched off a conflict that a decade after the Tribbles incident still is crackling through the North Woods like a forest fire" (*Milwaukee Journal*, 14–17 October 1984: 3).

The fire began from friction, caused by the worry and racism of outsiders pressing against the spreading empowerment among Indians. Tourist towns surrounding Lac du Flambeau and Lac Courte Oreilles began a battle cry with images of excess: "Wisconsin—a Wildlife Wasteland—the Chippewa Can Do It" (*Milwaukee Journal*, 14–17 October 1984: 2). Discourse swelled across the boundaries of heritage and history, icons of overkill playing upon the genuine concern for lifestyles and livelihood built upon a base of lakes and trees, fish and deer. In Lac du Flambeau's Vilas County, where 26 percent of the residents work the rounds of tourism, treaty rights represented open-ended dispossession:

> I fear the loss of our deer herd in the North ... the Indians will be shooting at everything—does, fawns and bucks. The Indians will be able to spear on the four largest lakes on the Manitowish Waters chain. We might be catching muskies around here now but wait 'till the Indians start spearing. (*Milwaukee Journal*, 14–17 October 1984: 9)

Protest privileged numbers, yearly takes of fish and deer judged in isolation from the experience of our emerging practice. Every year the rhetoric rose along with the tribal harvest ratios, figures that ignored the vast open-season harvest of fish, or the estimated thirty thousand deer killed each year by cars (*Milwaukee Journal*, 14–17 October 1984: 8). Deer became a symbol of tribal visibility, building on fear of the drunk and the dark embedded in a heritage that has positioned us through representations of the noble or the savage, or in the studied, systematic constructions of the Aboriginal Other: "Some resort owners, prompted by bar talk of armed Indian hunters gone wild, warn customers not to walk in the woods" (*Milwaukee Journal*, 14–17 October 1984: 2). Winter was rife with signs of unambiguous hostility: bumper stickers that read Kill an Indian Save Twenty-Five Deer; signs of Save a Deer Shoot an Indian, and Open Season on Indians, Bag Limit Ten per Day. The season moved toward spring with slogans on fishing hats like Save a Walleye, Spear an Indian (*Milwaukee Journal*, 14–17 October 1984: 1–2). Spears became the Other's effigies of a pagan past, as Indian families slid aluminum canoes and boats along the darkened shorelines, children spearing next to bifocalled uncles and couples keeping company. Miner's hats spot-lit spawning fish protected only by the deceptive depth of water. First for nine and then for fifteen days, we speared in retribution for identity or community, for food or just for the fun of it, surrounded by the resentment of outsiders articulated in a code of overkill attributed to Indians.

Throughout the seasons, we sat within the shadow of our elders negotiating this practice of contested culture with the state, our lawyers talking to their lawyers. We allocated eight thousand deer in twenty-nine northern counties to Chippewa on six reserves, disallowed shooting from cars, and restricted hunting to a seventy-one-day season. We agreed not to gill-net fish on inland lakes beyond the reservation, nor to harvest fish in state refuges, and imposed a six-tribe limit of five thousand pounds of walleye (*Milwaukee Journal*, 14–17 October 1984: 6). We agreed to harvest on selected lakes and to observe quotas; and then some Indians stood in determination: "We're not going to hide anymore.... We are not going to take the back roads to our fishing sites. We'll go right through the middle of Woodruff and Minocqua if we have to" (*Milwaukee Journal*, April 17, 1987: 3B).

The fire spread, articulating other issues linked along the trail of treaty rights. Minocqua became an epicentre of argument packaged in the liberal lobby of Protect Americans' Rights and Resources (PARR). PARR became the password for a range of smaller groups like Totally Equal Americans and Equal Rights for Everyone, all appropriating constructions of Others that focused on the heritage of Lac du Flambeau:

> The Lac du Flambeau ... are skilled aggressive fishermen. Last year the band turned out 115 fishermen. They speared ... more than 80% of all Walleyes and Muskies speared by Chippewa bands.... Perhaps because of the Lac du Flambeau band's fish kill record or maybe because they do not mix very well with the white community, public hostility to Indian treaty fishing is most intense here in north central Wisconsin. (*Milwaukee Journal*, 14 April 1987: 1, 10)

The perception that we were rejecting outsiders brought rounds of reporters to Lac du Flambeau to write about the currency of confrontation; and some anthropologists (Cleland 1985; Handrick 1987) researched the historical patterns of resource use among the Chippewa. But amid the clash of cultures, ethnographers never found their way to Lac du Flambeau to ask about the modern meaning of practice transformed through time and treaty rights. No one asked about the confirmation of walking to hunt in woodlands ceded by the thumbprints of our grandfathers, or our romanticized image of Lac du Flambeau's "People of the Torch," stitched in ambiguity to Strawberry Island and Medicine Rock, Bert Skye and the Midéwiwin. No one asked about the impact of accidental deaths, of fighting, or family living in the city; the beer cans rusting in the water at Boy Scout Beach; or the traditional heritage of Lac du Flambeau's Christian churches. No one asked about the maze of tribal membership and politics; the empowerment of inter-tribal process; or the social act of spearing with a formerly feuding cousin. In those years of protest, no one asked about the purpose represented in nurturing the fish hatchery, or about the practices through which Flambeau became "the center of winter spearing," or the thirty-three out of seventy-nine Wisconsin carvers in a book on fish decoys who were Lac du Flambeau Indians (Kimball, Kimball, & Kimball 1987: 180–84). No one asked about the heritage, experienced and imagined, Flambeau and foreign, tentative and transforming, from which we act. No one asked us who we are or what it signifies to hunt and spear through treaty rights.

PARR raised protest rallies, invoking sign-carrying settlers and enclaves of drumming Indian spearers. The organization urged politicians to stop the practice of our treaties, adopting two Indians (one from Lac du Flambeau) who spoke in the exclusionary language of our heritage:

> Congress is derelict in its duties to abrogate the treaties which were made for full-blooded Indians.... There are no longer full-bloods, the treaties should be abrogated because they no longer apply. Indians with very little Indian blood are receiving benefits because of ultra-liberal interpretations of the treaties in recent years. (*Daily News*, 27 April 1986: 1)

Then, in February 1987, the District Court ruled upon a preliminary definition of our treaty rights: "The Chippewas have a right to harvest all natural resources used at the time of the treaties; a right to use methods both traditional and modern; and the right to extract a modest living from the sale of the harvest " (Great Lakes Fish and Wildlife Commission, n.d.: 7).

At the union high school located in Minocqua, our students were drawn into spearing before the season started, through the printed distribution of a poem that "contained sexually, socially and economically derogatory remarks about Indians and their treaty rights" (*Milwaukee Sentinel*, 20 April 1987: 5). In the aftershock of Indian accusations that "racial slurs have become a way of life," Jerry Maulson, then our tribal planner, spoke for those in Lac du Flambeau who stand between resignation and revenge: "There is a lack of knowledge, a fear of the unknown ... people don't understand the reservation" (5). His brother, Tom Maulson, then our tribal judge and spokesman for our spearers, began the season counting quota through the night, spearing with his son:

> Stocky like his father but blond-haired like his mother, Fred is a high school freshman who already has his own car and intends to join the Army after graduation.... "He's a good spearer," Fred's father said. "He's been doing this ever since he was seven." (*Daily Press*, 18 April 1987: 3)

Tom Maulson led the Was-wa-gon Treaty Association in opposition to the protests over spearing. The American Indian Movement was now more welcome here, accepted for their willingness to drum within the dark at boat landings and walk the paths of counter-protests. In the rhetoric of rallies and reporters, Maulson was called a radical by Others and some Indians. His stance was strengthened by white witnesses, who arrived in carloads from Chicago, Minneapolis, and Milwaukee to stand in solidarity with the spearers. On the shorelines of spot-lit lakes, a mélange of college students, committed souls, and people who were simply curious were caught within a purgatory between police protecting Indians and frenetic protesters. I remember Indians pressed together around the drum, separated from white witnesses and protesters by a human chain-link fence of strained police. We sang invocations to the past and warrior words of Wounded Knee in the escalating drumbeats of AIM involvement. But there were no Indian guns within these circuits of resistance. There were no fists or fights. As the numbers of white witnesses to racism grew in these explosive seasons of spring spearing, notebooks, flashbulbs, and video cameras became the weapons of Indians and their supporters.

PARR rallied against spring spearing; the twelve hundred people wearing protest orange reassuring us: "We don't blame the Indians, this

is a federal issue" (*Lakeland Times*, 28 April 1987: 4). "The event was fla-
vored with patriotism beginning with a pledge of allegiance and the
singing of the national anthem" (*Milwaukee Journal*, 26 April 1987: 2B). In
the now-familiar litany of protests, one PARR member carried a speared,
stuffed walleye pierced through the gut. Marching Indians pointed out,
"That spear's upside down" and "It's supposed to be in the back of the
head, not the belly," as non-Indians chanted Whites For Rights and Treaty
Rights Protect Us All (*Lakeland Times*, 28 April 1987: 9). Polarization
spread to Lac du Flambeau, and a petition accused the tribal judge of
"totally misrepresenting the tribe as a whole" (*Milwaukee Sentinel*, 29
April 1987: 1). As the season accumulated talk of quota violation and
gunshots aimed at Indians in the sullen darkness of the spearing grounds,
Butternut landing became a lasting symbol of the endless contestation
over treaty rights:

> Six hours of racial taunts and beer drinking marked a protest by non-
> Indians at Butternut Lake in Ashland County during the worst incident
> of the fifteen-day Chippewa spearfishing season Sunday night. The Lac
> du Flambeau Chippewa spearfishing there were far outnumbered by
> the protesters. Throughout the protest they remained in their boats, out
> of reach of the protesters straining against a police chain. (*Lakeland Times*,
> 5 May 1987: 1)

Four non-Indians were arrested, and in the constituted language of
repeated rallies the voice of PARR was answered by the Chippewa:

> Representatives from Lac du Flambeau and several other tribes marked
> the end of the 1987 spearfishing season with a show of strength, unity
> and ceremony at Butternut Lake in Ashland county. A heavy show of
> law enforcement also prevented many anti-treaty rights protesters from
> showing up at the landing. In the midst of questions of abuse of power
> by the tribal judge, protests at spearfishing boat landings, complaints
> about treaty rights comments allegedly made by a grade school aide,
> and adult and youth baseball teams boycotting Lac du Flambeau, there
> was a calm in the eye of the storm. Chippewa tribes from northern Wis-
> consin and the Upper Peninsula of Michigan returned Thursday to the
> scene of an ugly racial protest by whites to reaffirm their heritage.
> Approximately 200 tribal members from three states were there, includ-
> ing tribes from Lac du Flambeau, Lac Courte Oreilles, Bad River, Mole
> Lake and Red Cliff. Throughout the night the strong steady thread of
> the ceremonial drum knit the tribal people together in a show of unity.
> (*Lakeland Times*, 5 May 1987: 1)

My brother tells about the caravan of cars, 350 Indians of all ages wearing armbands of red, white, and blue, manoeuvring past jeering beer drinkers; the eagle sighted at the landing just before four boats slipped into the darkness, each spearing one symbolic fish from the waters, surrounded by racial reaction, and the differing realities of ourselves and Others expressed in treaty rights:

> I still remember what someone said to us, that it has taken us a hundred years to get back to this lake. That expressed the whole mood you could feel that night—that this was what our great-grandfathers did, and now it is what I'm doing. It became an identity thing and a rallying point. (McBride 1987: 17).

Negotiating Futures

We watched repeated summers swell this tourist territory, families on vacation uninterested in the underlying chant for change. On the Fourth of July, the season was pronounced "frantic" (*Lakeland Times*, 10 July 1987: 22), and a thousand people found their way to Lac du Flambeau's Wisconsin Indian Artists' Show. Almost inaudible above the motorboats dragging water skiers and fishermen along the lakes, a Republican congressional delegate from Milwaukee introduced a bill to abrogate the treaties. The question of abrogation was answered by Wisconsin's governor in 1985, who "told opponents of treaty rights ... that they were wasting their time trying to get Congress to change century-old agreements with Wisconsin tribes" (*Milwaukee Journal*, 12 January 1985: 1). As this political impossibility settled over PARR, politicians spoke in the timeless language of treaty negotiations everywhere:

> The tribes must recognize that they cannot expect members of Wisconsin's Congressional Delegation to support federal aid for tribal economic development or other tribal programs if they insist on remaining separate from the United States when it comes to hunting and fishing. (Kasten, 1987: 3)

We were sitting at the treaty table negotiating with the state when PARR produced a lasting symbol of the distance between ourselves and Others: "Treaty Beer." Cans in the Christmas colours of red and green on white depicted a walleye pierced through the gut by a five-pronged spear, bordered by burning dollars and the words "true brew of the

Indians from Lac du Flambeau marching in the Fourth of July parade, carrying "Indian Joe" flags, 1991. Photograph courtesy of the author.

working man" "equal rights," and "stop treaty abuse." In Minocqua, signs as big as store windows advertised the essence of our struggle since the arrival of the traders; radio ads played pow wow drums to underscore the message; and protesters marched with signs proclaiming Treaty Beer, Not Tribal Bingo. A guileless voice from Lac du Flambeau spoke about the boycott of our unique arena of openness to outsiders: "A lot of our customers come early to socialize.... Bingo isn't political. It doesn't have anything to do with the Voigt Decision" (*Lakeland Times*, 11 August 1987: 2). Summer deteriorated into fall with PARR announcing at a gathering in Illinois, "'It is now very possible that we could lose the whole United States to the Indians.' He [the PARR president] sees Indians fishing off homeowners' piers, bagging all the allowable game for themselves and gradually choking off everyone else's rights everywhere" (*Chicago Tribune*, n.d.: 2).

There have always been outsiders who valued the lasting distance of our presence: woodland skills and spirit-soaring pow wows, teasing humour that targets the too serious or self-important, mixed with the spiritual mystery of leaving tobacco at Medicine Rock. There are those who appreciate our past and praise displays of glass-cased artifacts; and some within our borders support the one-man movement entitled "White People Who Live on the Reservation and Wouldn't Live Anywhere Else." But we are still visible and disconnected, positioned through generations of shared discontinuity. Few fascinated outsiders persevere to pass the ambush of daily interaction that reflects inward isolation, the tests of toughness and motives, the sharing with others and laughing at yourself. Fewer still are interested in penetrating the concentric circles established in the grocery store, the restaurants, the post office, the tribal council meetings, arenas open to the daily contestation of discourse: a sharp raising of the head, a glazed stare, a frozen smile, all invitations to silence or to conversation. Immutable settlers and intermittent tourists tend to stay in compounds by the lake or drive in determination to Minocqua, never touching the experienced reality of Indian life in Lac du Flambeau or recognizing the daily signs of transformation. The casino brings outsiders here who never really see the reservation or speak with Indians; and we continue to feel uncomfortable in the unpredictability of tourist towns that have spread across our ceded land.

In this era of boom boxes and blaring radios, when protests are organized by email and websites, the quiet of the spearing grounds remains ambiguous. As the winter ice lifts off the lakes, we manoeuvre through the shallows, always listening for footsteps on a broken branch, always watching for car lights coming through the woods. In the spring of 2004, the Lac du Flambeau Chippewa continued to spear over twice as many walleyes and muskies as each of the other five Great Lakes Chippewa tribes (*Masinaigan*, Summer 2004: 2). The violent voices of PARR had faded in the succession of court cases and fines that emerged in the 1990s, when Chippewa spearers laid charges of harassment. But a group of spearers faced vulgar voices and slashed tires that spring (1), and there was talk of revived protest, and whispers of military militias and Aryan brotherhoods. Today the new umbrella organization called Citizens for Equal Rights Alliance (CERA) encircles a collection of active groups spread across Indian Country, each with names and acronyms that echo the protests against Indian treaty rights and traditionalism in the 1980s: All Citizens Equal (ACE), Protect Americans' Rights and Resources (PARR), United Property Owners of Washington (UPOW), Upstate Citizens for Equality (UCE), Proper Economic Resource Management (PERM), The Hunting and Angling Club (THAAC), Arizona Coalition for Public Lands, American Citizens Together, and Seneca County Liberation Organization.

There is now a coalition called Alliance for Freedom that has converged on congress to press for the termination of reservations and Native rights, and a charitable organization that issues tax receipts called Citizens for Equal Rights Foundation (*Masinaigan*, Summer 2004: 20). In the apprehensive silence on the spearing grounds, Indians and Others remain rooted in the crosshairs of conflicting futures.

For eight years after treaty rights became a way of life, our tribal chairman was Tom Maulson, the leader of the Walleye Warriors (Whaley with Bresette 1994) during the dangerous period of rally rhetoric. Since the turbulent 1980s, expanded tribal services in Lac du Flambeau have been housed in buildings named for past and present Elders, including the tribal council offices, the library, the clinic, and the fish hatchery. There is a new grade school for children of the town and tribe. Simpson's Electric Company is finally showing a profit, and there are other tribal enterprises: a grocery store, a gas station, and—the centrepiece of our economy—the new casino and hotel built along the beach where the old federal Indian school once stood. Everyone intermingles in this arena of commercial enterprise. Tourists crowd the blackjack tables and hunt along with Indians for open slot machines, and in this glittering enclave with no clocks and no windows, no one speaks of spearing.

Our town looks tattered in comparison to the new casino's flashing lights, but even that is somehow deceiving. Tucked into the hillside of the Long Lake bay, which is still called the "hot pond" in reference to the sawmill, is a beautiful museum, inviting tourists and Indians to learn the ancient art of Chippewa crafts, or hear the heritage of tribal territory, or search the growing archives of old images and objects for family photos or familiar works of art. Built by Indians and many others, the George W. Brown, Jr. Ojibwe Museum and Cultural Center is a living construct of reconciliation spearheaded by the tribe and my father, for whom "it has been a dream for so long" (Guthrie in *Lakeland Times*, 7 August 1987: 25). The museum brochure once said, "We have seen the future—and it is the past," a recognition of transforming practice affirmed in the words of a former tribal council chairman: "We have a growing revival of our precious cultural heritage here on the Lac du Flambeau Reservation, and I feel that revival is as important to the people here as anything we are doing" (Allen in *Soaring Eagle*, October 1986: 40). Today, in the precarious prospect of our future, the museum's letterhead reaffirms the words of Keeshkemun, our ancient leader, "Englishmen! You ask me who I am. If you wish to know, you must seek me in the clouds" (in Warren 1885: 373).

In Lac du Flambeau, some Chippewa still disapprove of spearing, declaring it a disaster for Indians that we brought upon ourselves. Other Indians, suspicious of the museum, the casino, and other economic enterprises, work to reconstruct the remembered traditionalism of the Old Village. We still battle with Others and struggle with one another over jobs and houses, over blood quantum, tribal elections, and resource revenues. Old jealousies, big families, new money, and urban influences push the pendulum of tribal power with new determination. There is recurring conflict over the distribution of meagre casino profits, disagreements over monies allocated for per capita payments to tribal members, or to social services, housing, and buying back private land within the reservation. But in the current era of old treaties and new traditionalism, every Lac du Flambeau Chippewa recognizes our reality. In the words of Jerry Maulson spoken in the 1980s:

> "The old ways are fading.... We are grasping at what is left or what we know of it." Although the controversy over rights has increased tensions with non-Indians, Maulson says there have also been positive effects. "People are asking questions now ... a lot more people have become aware of Indians, and we are more aware of ourselves." (McBride 1987: 9)

Treaty rights express a traditionalism that is embedded deep within the prism of Lac du Flambeau life, not as a form of resistance, privileged through some stereotypical reproduction of the past, but as a thread of transformation enacted daily among Indians and outsiders engaged in the arena of ambiguous identity and power that is fundamental to our enduring heritage. Traditionalism is the expression of a multivocal past of lived experience, of an Indian heritage that is "intricate with motion and meaning ... legendary as well as historical, personal as well as cultural" (Momaday 1969: 4).

≪ • ≫

Rights and Warriors:
Media Memories and Oka

Their past is sold in a shop: the beaded shoes,
the sweetgrass basket, the curio Indian,
burnt wood and gaudy cloth and inch-canoes—
trophies and scalping for a traveler's den.
Sometimes, it's true, they dance, but for a bribe;
after a deal don the bedraggled feather
and welcome a white mayor to the tribe.
    A.M. Klein, "Indian Reservation: Caughnawaga"
                (in Atwood 1972: 90)

Indigenous Nations, histories of resistance
we are clans, Nations, ever so strong
our roots, one with mother earth
this land, Turtle Island
Kaianerakowa, Great Law of Peace
ancient constitution of the Haudenosaunee people
history of survival, this is my history
I know who I am
      Donna Goodleaf, "Kahnawake" (1995: 26)

Even before the reserve near Montreal, named "Caughnawaga" by outsiders, took back its Mohawk name of Kahnawake, this community was entrenched in politics. In the book *Heeding the Voices of Our Ancestors*, Gerald Alfred (1995: 1) writes, "It is said that being born Indian is being born into politics," and, he adds, "being born a Mohawk of Kahnawake, I do not remember a time free from the impact of political conflict." Linked to the politics of Indian representation and cultural struggle, the experience of being Indian is shared and contested across Indian Country. But in the conversations and actions that construct

Indianness, being Mohawk or being Sioux encompasses a certain "something more."

Along the long trail of Indian resistance, there are two major watersheds in modern times: Wounded Knee in 1973 and Oka in 1990. For Indians, resistance is national, tribal, even local; assertions of cultural persistence expressed in petitions, court cases, demonstrations, and deaths that are remembered and reconstructed in the discursive struggles of today. For other North Americans, Indian resistance is movement, a progression forward or backward in incidents of action that are episodic explosions of political confrontation, which are ahistorical and unpredictable. These differing perceptions of social reality folded in upon one another at Wounded Knee, where the media became a player in redefining the representations of Indian resistance. Wounded Knee was not the first incident of national Indian protest, nor was it the first time that the media was drawn into Indian conflicts with Others. But at Wounded Knee, like Oka, the media mapped modern warriors onto the contours of Native resistance in representations of armed conflict and expressions of Indian radicalism that resonated across the deeply rooted borders separating Native and other North Americans. If the events at Wounded Knee have begun to fade from popular memory after thirty years, the echoes of Oka are still heard in Native voices and seen in media images of Indians today. For Native people across North America, Oka is part of a continually emerging "politics of remembrance" (Kroker 1994: 167).

Mohawk heritage is laced with a sense of political impatience that simmered long before the incidents that began in Oka. The discontent developed through three centuries of cultural and political displacement and territorial confiscation, most recently experienced at Kahnawake in the appropriation of Mohawk land for two bridges over the St. Lawrence River, a canal around the La Chine rapids, a super-highway into the city of Montreal, and a dump for urban refuge. Urban development reduced Kahnawake's land base from 44,000 acres to 13,000 acres; and as the population of the community grew to 8,000, they were separated from the river which has been "a focal point of Mohawk life for centuries" (Charney 1995: 117). The friction between Natives and newcomers, which intensified over years of land confiscation and enforced acculturation, finally erupted in the so-called Indian summer of 1990, when Mohawk "warriors" drew a line in the sand that led to what the media labelled "the Oka crisis." The Oka crisis was a sequential explosion of frustrations on two different Mohawk reserves—Kanehsatake and Kahnawake— with different historical experiences and different immediate grievances. But like the common culture and kinship that link these communities together and tie them to the conflict on the Mohawk reserve of Akwe-sasne, their struggles over control and community are, at the same time, similar and related, but local and specific. The confrontation that Ann Charney (1995: 109) calls "The Last Indian War" was actually a chain of incidents which, over time, stretched across the triangle of the three Mohawk reserves, struggling with each other and with Others over issues and ideologies that gave rise to barricades in 1990.

For non-Natives, the crisis at Oka began when the barricades were built. But for Mohawks, the crisis, which was rooted in centuries of dis-sension and exclusion, began many months earlier. The seeds of conflict were sewn when land claims were ignored in a move to extend a golf course into the grounds of an ancient Indian cemetery in Kanehsatake, a patchwork of Mohawk reserve land intertwined with the town of Oka forty-eight kilometres from Montreal. Women who were cousins or clan mothers sat in "the Pines" where the cemetery is located, through the media silence of a restless winter. Their vigil was vocal but peaceful, a statement of heritage and heresy voiced without the guns that attract media attention. Winter dissolved into spring and then summer. In June, when the weary voices of the women in the Pines became shrill, the mayor of Oka obtained an injunction against the protestors and sum-moned police to remove them. The women called upon Mohawk war-riors to defend their vigil, to resist their removal from consecrated land; and the festering wounds of Kanehsatake transformed from a campfire into a barricade.

The town of Oka's resolve and the media's reserve eventually led to Indian blockades in both Kanehsatake and Kahnawake. Confrontations between townspeople, police, army, and Indians focused on the imme-diate and local incidents of a gun battle between Indians and police that led to the death of a policeman; a highway blockade in Oka; a block-aded bridge between Kahnawake and the City of Montreal; the Canadian army's occupation of the area surrounding the reserves; and the histor-ical and national issues of Native claims to sovereignty and to land. When Mohawk "warriors" barricaded themselves inside an alcohol treat-ment centre at Kanehsatake, a standoff began involving reporters, police, army, and Indians that lasted for seventy-eight days—longer than the "Indian crisis" at Wounded Knee in 1973—and that deployed four thousand Canadian soldiers over the summer to support the police at barricades built in Kanehsatake and in Kahnawake, where for twenty-seven days Mohawks blockaded the Mercier Bridge to Montreal.

The "Indian wars" at Kanehsatake and Kahnawake were incidents that drew international attention. The army held two press conferences each day, providing "word bites" and "photo clips" for the media, even when there was no news; and the images of Indians that emerged in the turmoil of Native communities were appropriated by Indians themselves. In the heat of the moment and in the aftermath of Oka, many questions were raised about the role, nature, and function of the media in a democratic society—or in a military crisis. Like earlier inquiries into the media and the standoff at Wounded Knee, academics and journalists researched and wrote about the "Mohawk crisis" in relation to issues of news, reporting, and the media itself, examining the role of media events, tele-diplomacy, and reporters as participant-observers; the exigency of news backgrounding and historical context; the issues of censorship and propaganda; the impact of sometimes endless, unedited coverage of events and, at other times, the total shutdown of media coverage; and the role of differential reporting—French, English, and Indian—on the issues, the personalities, the armed standoffs, and the incidents of support and attack that sustained the crisis. But for the media, Quebec's Indian summer of 1990 was an uncontextualized link in a chain of isolated, militant Indian episodes. And like most academic writing on militant Indian events, the press misread or ignored the relationship between media representation, cultural appropriation, and the emergence and reporting of Native resistance.

In all the skirmishes, battles, and struggles across North America in the decades since the "Indians of All Nations" occupied Alcatraz Island in 1969, the representation and appropriation of Indians have been pivotal factors in the media coverage, in Indian activism and in the internal struggles of Native communities. Indians are an ambiguous presence in the narratives of popular culture that the media express and circulate, and, as Vine Deloria, Jr. (in Hazen-Hammond 1997: 289) writes, "Indians have always been politically savvy. What's changed is their resources."

Reading Warriors

The "Mohawk crisis" in Quebec is remembered in the startling media images of rock-throwing townspeople and scuffling Indians, staring soldiers and crying children. But in all the media coverage, one image emerged as salient: the image of the "warriors"—bandana-masked, khaki-clad, gun-toting Indians whose images dominated the news and were accompanied by headlines of "Rough Justice: After Oka Will the Violence Spread?" (*Maclean's*, 6 August 1990: 18–25); "The Fury of Oka: After the Showdown, Indian Leaders Promise a Violent Autumn" (*Maclean's*, 10 September 1990: 16–20); "Mohawk Militancy" (*Ottawa Citizen*, 15 September 1990: B1–2); "The Mohawk Warriors: Heroes or Thugs?" (*Toronto Star*, 24 November 1990: D1 and D5); and "The Making of a Warrior" (*Saturday Night*, April 1991). There was also Aislin's political cartoon of the "Mafia Warrior" (*Montreal Gazette*, 30 April 1990: B2). With few exceptions, the media's warriors were monolithic representations of Indian militants: the military masculine, criminalized through association with terrorism and epitomized in the ultimate warrior, Ronald Cross, code-named "Lasagna," who became the darling of the media and, in the words of one reporter, a "media slut" (Pindera 1990). Like the activists of the American Indian Movement before them, Mohawks on the barricades became both the media's rhetorical radicals and the Indians' "warriors of the headlines" (Vizenor 1984: 130).

In contrast to the majority of media images, when the Mohawk barricades came down on 26 September 1990, sixty people ended their occupation of the alcohol treatment centre at Kanehsatake: twenty-seven Indian men of various tribes and one non-Indian sixteen-year-old, sixteen Indian women (four from British Columbia), six children, and ten reporters. The Indians who were barricaded in the treatment centre—like the Mohawk women who sat in vigil in the Pines of Kanehsatake the winter before; the Mohawks who manned both sides of the barricades on the Akwesasne reserve in the spring; the Indians who blockaded the Mercier Bridge between Montreal and the Kahnawake reserve in the summer; and those who managed the warrior headquarters called the Mohawk Nation Office, or practised the traditional Longhouse religion, or spoke for sovereignty and self-determination—were yoked together as the media's Mohawk warriors. For the media, there has always been one dominant image of Indian struggle, one dominant narrative of Indian confrontation: warriors and the militant stories they tell.

Mohawk Warrior surrounded by reporters, Oka, 1990. Photograph by Robert Fréchette, in *Ciel Variable* 14, Hier 4, 1990. Montreal, Quebec.

It is easy to gloss over Mohawk warriors like the "Lonefighters" who protested a dam in Alberta, or the spearfishing Chippewa "Ogichidaw" and "Ogichidawquay" in Wisconsin, where "Walleye Warriors" (Whaley with Bresette 1994) speared spawning fish though turbulent spring seasons, exercising their treaty rights amid the deafening and dangerous protests of non-Indians. The common assumption is that Indian warriors are obvious symbols of violent claims to power, visibility, and identity. Edmund Carpenter (1970: n.p.) writes in *They Became What They Beheld*, "Violence offers immediate public recognition. This is especially true for 'invisibles' who thereby become—instantly—very visible.... Even the threat of violence is a powerful force in any quest for identity."

Violence, of course, attracts media attention and creates public visibility, and some Indians today use violence—threatened or actual—as a strategy to gain a voice in the enduring political struggles between Natives and nation-states. As Mary Crow Dog (with Erdoes 1990: 88) writes, "I learned that as long as we 'behaved nicely' nobody gave a damn about us, but as soon as we became rowdy we got all the support and media coverage we could wish for." But conventional writing on communication and identity linking violence and claims to power and identity, tells us little about the emergence, persistence, and meaning of warriors in Native popular culture and social formation, about what warriors mean to the political and cultural identity of Native people and their communities, or about the role media play in these processes.

Media images of violent Indians are, like other Indian cultural products that represent Native people, a double-edged sword for Indians themselves. Richard Wagamese (1996) writes in the guise of Indian humour:

> It's harder and harder to be an Indian in this country. Back in the good old days your average aboriginal could at least depend on existing stereotypes to amble though the rough spots. Nowadays, with Indians going prime time on a regular basis, you really have to work to be recognized as a bona fide Indian. In those days prior to the media explosion of the '80s, the general perception of Canada's Indians was that of guttural, welfare-dependent wards of the state with a charming romantic history. In tense social situations all you really needed to do was grunt a little, remain stone-faced and talk about your grandfather. (149)

From literary images of derelicts or renegades in dime novels and romanticized Plains warriors in films like *Dances with Wolves*, to the spiritual appropriations of New Age "Rainbow Warriors," Native people have struggled with who they are and the nature of their interaction with Others in relation to the Indian as the "Good Guy/Bad Guy" or the "Victor/Victim" (Atwood 1972: 91). Like the companion myths of the frontier or the pioneer, neither of these representations drawn from social imaginaries of the savage as noble or evil, lazy or militant, allows newcomers to identify Native people as owners and occupants of North American land, as sovereign nations absorbed in the struggle of their tenuous position within nation-states that were carved out in companies and constitutions, proclamations, and promises. If warrior images seem relegated to a past produced in western movies and dime novels and comic books, the 7 June 1999 issue of the *National Post* carried a large photograph of John Sharpe entitled "Big Warrior, Little Warrior," with a byline that began, "John Sharpe, an Oneida Indian, portrays a native warrior...."

For Mohawks, the incongruity of media representations of warriors is best expressed in James Fenimore Cooper's famous novel about the plight of the noble (and vanishing) Mohicans at the hands of the horrible Iroquois Mingoes, for whom "no act of violence or depravity is beyond them" (Atwood 1972: 91). In writing that erases the cultures, experiences, and communities of the Iroquois nations, "the basic formula in Cooper is the same as that in countless imperialist texts: savagery extinguishes savagery" (Brantlinger 1998: 19). The heritage of these constructed and contradictory images of Indians that are removed from the social meaning of lived experience in Native communities—and appropriated by non-Indians in everything from tourist brochures to the New Age "White Warrior Society"—is intrinsic to the media's coverage of the Oka crisis. Gary Mauser (1991: 12) writes, "The standoff at the Mohawk reserve in Quebec posed a basic problem for the media; who should be portrayed as the 'bad guy' and who should be shown as the innocent victim?"

But if media representations confuse the specificities of Indian culture, history, and heritage for outsiders, images of warriors pose even greater problems for Native people themselves. Warriors are "floating signifiers," representations which Rosemary Coombe (1996: 204) depicts as "endlessly reproduced and circulated by mass media, [and] they are identified by subaltern groups who use them to construct identities and communities, to challenge social exclusions, and to assert difference." Warriors are woven into the cultural texture of Indian Country, where they thread through the narratives of remembered heritage and emergent popular culture. For Mary Crow Dog (with Erdoes 1990: 74), "long black shining braids" were a sign of Indian pride that represented both the traditionalism and the resistance of the American Indian Movement. She writes,

> The AIM uniform was Sioux all the way, the black "angry hats" with the feathers stuck in the headbands, the bone chokers, the medicine pouches worn on our breasts, the Levi jackets on which we embroidered our battle honors—Alcatraz, Trail of Broken Treaties, Wounded Knee. Some dudes wore a third, extra-thin braid as a scalp lock. (76)

But in the humour of nostalgia, Richard Wagamese (1996) speaks of the discourse that Indian militants adopted in the 1960s:

> To fit that particular dimension you needed to sport long braids, turquoise, beaded vests, moccasins and various aboriginal accouterment. Your vocabulary needed to be spiced up with at least four derivations of the word "honky" (there are at least a dozen but four is a strong traditional number) and peppered with references to Che Guevara, revolution, broken treaties, the sanctity of the land and, of course, your grandfather. (149)

Rayna Green (1984) writes about more recent warriors in her poem, "Another Dying Chieftain":

> he was a braids-and-shades dog soldier
> aim all the way
>
> reduced to telling white women
> about counting coup
> in a hotel room
> late
>
> where they wanted his style
> and he wanted the reporters
> back again. (115)

But for Native people, these playful words about warriors are politically charged. The barbs of insiders that test and tease Indian warriors are always interwoven with memories of warrior power and pain. Even in 1990, when warriors at the barricades in Kanehsatake and Kahnawake wore khaki camouflage and bandana masks, Indian braids represented the history of policies and practices that forbade Indians from wearing long hair and signified the heritage of resistance. Braids recall the shaved heads of Indian residential schools, the flowing hair of Indian Elders, and the plaits of Plains warriors, who emerge in western novels and films and transform in the collective memories of Indian Country. Images that collapse time and place summon the ambivalent empowerment of Sitting Bull and Big Bear, Crazy Horse and Geronimo. Like Sitting Bull (in Ruoff 1991), who sang of his surrender in 1881, Indians remember:

> A warrior
> I have been
> now
> it is all over
> a hard time
> I have. (36)

Sitting Bull's experience threads through the narratives of pan-Indian heritage and North American histories in contradictory tales of loss and gain. The stories of warring nations are spliced with the ambiguity of shifting alliances. Indians were sometimes allies, sometimes enemies in the North American contests over commerce, resources, and sovereignty that remapped Indian lands for colonial settlement. Some Indians fought with the Americans in battles over British control in Canada, and other

Indians fought with the British in battles over American expansion. When the bloody struggle of the War of 1812 was finally over, the boundaries between the two countries were intact. Indians who had fought the enemies of Others were now the only adversaries. Undervalued and overpowered, they were moved West to reserves, where Indian battles eventually took on the policed policies of colonial control. In the years of struggle since, warriors weave through Indian heritage in the merger of contradictory calls to action. Warriors are allies in the wars that nation-states have fought abroad, and enemies in the modern wars that Indians still fight at home. Eddie Benton-Benaise (1998) writes:

> All of America's wars—World War I, World War II, Korea, Viet Nam, Desert Storm—have given us warriors. In equal status, so has Wounded Knee '73, the Menominee Abbey, the L.C.O. Winter Dam, the Wisconsin Boat Landings. In Canada, Oka, Gustafson Lake, Anishinabe Park, Kenora and other encounters have produced warriors. (17)

Grounded in the military masculine, the image of the militant Indian circulates among Natives today, reconstructed in the rhetoric of media's ageless warriors. From sports teams to images of Indians on "Indian Joe" flags and American Indian Movement armbands and berets, to icons of armed warriors at the barricades emblazoned on T-shirts and captured in photos of khaki-clad confrontation, warriors are recalled and reappropriated in the discourse of Native North Americans. As Native people struggle over claiming and disclaiming warriors, over the threats and promises of appropriated identity and power, the factionalism in their communities raises questions about the role these figures of popular culture play in the formation of Indian identity, community, and political activism. Who are these warriors, Lonefighters, spearfishing Chippewa? What do these images and the narratives they express signify to Native people whose identity is grounded in historical experience and current practice? And what role does the media play in the formation of contemporary Indian identity?

Until recently, our understanding of the relationship between communication and identity has emerged from writing in psychology and sociology. This work focuses on the bond between individual identity and the identification of social groups, analyzing how identity is constructed in conceptions of the self and the role of symbols in interaction. Recent writing in communication studies has begun to frame the relationship between communication and identity in the context of culture (see Carey

1989). Today, cultural studies links communication and cultural formation to identity through the analysis of lived experience and public text,
in the exchange of everyday action, discourse and events—individual and
collective, dynamic and diachronic, interactional and mediated—all inte-
gral to the formation of social subjects and all embedded in political
process. Particularly in the work of Stuart Hall (1985, 1986, 1989), this perspective moves toward an understanding of the relationship between
media representation, identity, and the political struggle of Native North
Americans.

The stories we tell in written and visual narratives have long been recognized as a window on who we are, what we experience, and how we
understand and enact ourselves and others. But as Hall writes (1989), stories are more than a window on identity. We actually construct who we
are in our identification with the discursive images and cultural narratives that dominate our ways of seeing and representing the world.
These narratives are reflexive and reflective. In the stories that move
and change in memory and community, we make sense out of history and
heritage, producing personal and social meanings and ideological positions. For Hall, identity is not formed in internal conceptions of the self,
but in the adoption of the changing representations and narratives that
we generate and articulate in our individual and social experience.
"Being" is always "becoming," and our identities emerge in "the continuous 'play' of history, culture and power" (Hall 1989: 70). Like the
context of social struggle in which stories are told, identity is continually
contested and reconstructed in the discursive negotiation of the complex relations and the hierarchical alliances that constitute community.
Like our discourse, our communities are not cemented in unity and
belonging, but in the transformation and difference that is constructed
in our ongoing struggle with power relations. The dynamic process of
building and rebuilding individual and collective identities centres on
conflicting social imaginaries and their ideological messages. As Marilyn Burgess points out, Hall's conception of social formation allows us
to speak of a politics of identity, of unities of difference with contingent
closures of articulation (Burgess 1990: 10). This approach, which locates
media representations and the construction of collective and individual
identities within the ideological struggle of power relations, points
toward the role and meaning of Mohawk warriors within the political
and cultural ferment of Indian communities today.

Old Roots, New Indians

Warriors have long been an important social force—and a contradictory presence—in Mohawk culture. Historically, warriors were peacekeepers, the men drawn from separate nations cemented in matrilineal clans and common experience, allied in the Iroquois Confederacy to protect against threats to "the Great Peace." The Iroquois Confederacy was formed by the political leader Deganawida and the orator Hiawatha in the fifteenth century (Hale [1883] 1972: 19); and "the Mohawks were the first nation to take hold of the Great Peace ... the founders of the League" (Wallace [1946] 1997: 46). Deganawida's constitution, known as "The Iroquois Book of the Great Law," was a compact between nations recorded in strings and belts of wampum beads, remembered in tribal oral tradition, and compiled or written in English at the turn of the twentieth century. In this powerful alliance, which "stretched to the four corners of the earth, [and] signified the extension of the Law, the Peace, to embrace all mankind" (35), all men became warriors under the leadership of an elected war chief, who acted upon the decisions of the political heads of state, the Confederacy chiefs. A.C. Parker ([1916] 1967) writes about the wars and the warriors encoded in the Iroquois Great Law, retelling what has become known as the "Newhouse Version" of the founding of the Iroquois Confederacy:

> When the Confederate Council of the Five Nations has for its object the establishment of the Great Peace among the people of an outside nation and that nation refuses to accept the Great Peace, then by such refusal, they bring a declaration of war upon themselves from the Five Nations. Then shall the Five Nations seek to establish the Great Peace by a conquest of the rebellious nation. When the men of the Five Nations, now called forth to become warriors, are ready for battle with the obstinate opposing nation that has refused to accept the Great Peace, then one of the five War Chiefs shall be chosen by the warriors of the Five Nations to lead the warriors into battle. (52)

Among the Iroquois, the Great Law situated the ways in which human beings related to one another. For Mohawks, confrontations with colonists that disrupted the Great Peace were breaches of the Two Row Wampum of the Iroquois Confederacy. This beaded treaty belt characterized the historical pact between Natives and newcomers in two discreet blue lines that stretch across a sea of white beads, never intersecting, never imposing upon one another in the exercise of a respectful relationship of separate nations represented by the Indian's canoe and the settler's sailing ship. Throughout the early history of Quebec, Iroquois warriors often engaged in battle to enforce the Great Peace. Inter-tribal warfare expanded as newcomers established the fur trade in eastern Canada, and "for most of the seventeenth century there was war between the Iroquois and the French" (Hall in MacLaine and Baxendale 1990: 21).

The Mohawk history of Kahnawake reaches back to the village of Ossernonen, which was known as the Eastern Door of an initial alliance of five Iroquois nations. This village, originally on the banks of the Mohawk River in what is now New York state, moved north to the St. Lawrence River in response to the growing pressure of settlers. Between 1667 and 1717, there were four new migrations, each moving the Kahnawakeronon, or Kahnawake Mohawk, further up river as war, Christainity, commerce, and settlement encroached upon Indian land and Indians themselves became embattled. In 1716, they settled in Kahnawake, or "On the Rapids," a site near Montreal's La Chine Rapids on the St. Lawrence River where, during a tumultuous period for Mohawks, Catholic Jesuits secured their sanctuary on forty-four thousand acres of land known as the Sault St. Louis seigneury.

The animosities and alliances between Indians and colonists—American, British, and French—rose and fell in waves, and there were periods of strained relations among the nations of the Confederacy. The Kahnawake Mohawks remained an active partner in the Grand Council of the Five (later Six) Nations Confederacy until 1694, when they moved to the status of "observers." French Jesuits held the deed to Kahnawake and, in the early years, French soldiers and farmers lived among the Mohawks. But the Iroquois allied with the British in battles that eventually established Quebec and positioned Canada within the British Empire, and this alliance established a legacy of historical tension that is sometimes expressed today. Mohawks and Quebec separatists voice competing claims to self-determination in the continuing political struggle over the borders of federalism and the boundaries of the Canadian constitution. From a Mohawk perspective, Quebec reflects both "a misplaced obsession with 'law and order' on Indian lands" and "a striking ignorance of Mohawk values and principles" (Alfred 1995: 100). More Mohawks speak French now, but virtually none identify as "Québécois." Although

French Canadians may feel affinities with some Native nations, their political relationships with Mohawks have been strained in the long struggle between Indians and Others over the imposition of foreign political systems, whether American or Canadian.

What are today the "Mohawk reserves" in Quebec were established through grants of land from the king of France to Catholic orders between 1667 and 1721, primarily for the purpose of harbouring Christian Indians drawn from the Six Nations Confederacy. Kahnawake, Kanehsatake, and Akwesasne (a reserve that straddles the borders between Canada and the United States and the boundaries between Quebec and Ontario) have long been historical sites of external strife with surrounding governments and internal struggle between conflicting religious factions: Catholics, Protestants, and those who follow two traditions of the Longhouse religion, one represented in Deganawida's "Great Law" that emerged in the mid-1400s, the other, a somewhat Christianized version of the Great Law that emerged under the leadership of Handsome Lake in 1799 and is called the "Handsome Lake Code." These Indian alliances based on spiritual practices were contentious and divisive because the two Longhouse traditions represented different strands of not only religious but also political resistance. Today, spiritual doctrine articulated to political ideology has spawned "three longhouses and several different factions in Kahnawake: the 207 Longhouse, the Mayo Longhouse and the Mohawk Trail which is a 'Handsome Lake Longhouse'" (Horn 1997: 13). All three draw upon the Longhouse teachings of Deganawida, but each is positioned by differing interpretations of "the old way" and different expressions of Deganawida's teachings, linked in articulation to the Iroquois Confederacy, the Warrior Society, and Christian influences. The 207 Longhouse embodies the Warrior Society and a para-band council organization called the "Mohawk Nation"; the Mayo Longhouse is a splinter group of the 207 Longhouse; and the Mohawk Trail Longhouse is allied with the Iroquois Confederacy, which endorses the Tree of Peace of the Great Law and what is known as the "Covenant Chain." This Chain represents an alliance of independent nations, Indian and Other, living together within a nation-state. For those who support the Iroquois Confederacy, the Great Law prescribes their relationship with other human beings, who live under the protection of the Great Tree of Peace and have no need for warriors. In the words of Jake Thomas (in Vachon 1993: 16), "Weapons of war and strife were buried under the Tree of

Peace, cast away forever." But the Great Peace envisioned by the Confederacy has never been easy to achieve.

In the late 1700s, both the United States and Canada established reservation systems of tribal residence on Indian lands that were treatied, ceded, or taken for the settlement and resource development of newcomers; and in the 1800s, both countries moved to assimilate Indians through "enforced legislation and the imposition of a foreign political system called the 'democratic elective system'" (Vachon 1993: 63). On both sides of the border, the process of imposing federal tribal governments in Mohawk territory was conflictual and embattled. The struggle over land, government, and religion on the Mohawk reserves is articulated to different historical dynamics and incidents, and each reserve has forged distinct political trajectories and formed localized social factions. But Kahnawake, Kanehsatake, and Akwesasne are sister nations, communities linked together in a common culture and in the tribally situated experiences of dominance and resistance.

All three Mohawk reserves were influenced by the Christian authority of their colonial formation. But on each of these reserves, a system of "traditional life chiefs" developed, producing leaders who were formally "condoled" in their positions by clan mothers and who then sat with the chiefs of the Iroquois Confederacy. This system of Indian leadership was disrupted as early as 1802, when the state of New York appointed three trustees to intercede with the traditional life chiefs in Akwesasne. In the years that followed, the relationship between the trustees and the traditional chiefs grew increasingly oppositional. By 1852, the government of the traditional chiefs in Akwesasne had retreated to the Canadian side of the reservation, leaving the trustee system of tribal government on the American side, where it became entrenched. American attempts to move Mohawks further west were unsuccessful; but by the late 1800s, residential schools, land allotments, and the imposition of federal law defined the dependency of Indian nations. In 1899, Thomas Morgan, the commissioner of Indian Affairs, wrote: "The Indians must conform to the white man's ways, peaceably if they will, forcibly if they must. The tribal relations must be broken up ... the family and the autonomy of the individual substituted" (in Vachon 1993: 65).

In Canada, Mohawks came under increasing pressure to assimilate. The government passed An Act for the Gradual Civilization of the Indian Tribes in the Canadas in 1857, followed by the Civilization and Enfranchisement Act in 1859. Ten years later, in 1867, the British North America Act pronounced the federal government's right to make laws for Indians and then, in 1876, the Indian Act was passed in Parliament. With the passage of the Indian Act, Canada had codified the nation-state's definitions of "Indians" and the nature of Native rights and benefits; and the focus of policy turned to tribal political process. In 1884, the Indian Advancement Act pressed "advanced" Indian reserves toward municipal status by imposing the elective system of tribal government upon traditional Indians, including traditional Mohawks.

In Kanehsatake, Mohawks were placed under the elective system of band councils in 1899, a move which they and Mohawks on other reserves repeatedly opposed. In Akwesasne, a man known as John Fire was killed in an incident involving tribal elections, and "traditional chiefs were arrested in 1899 and five held in prison for one year" (Hughes 1991: 3). Similar acts of political repression were repeated at Ohsweken, on the Six Nations reserve in Ontario in 1924. By 1959, Edmund Wilson (1959) wrote of Quebec's St. Regis reserve, which is part of Akwesasne Mohawk territory:

> You have at St. Regis the regular chiefs appointed by their clan mothers, who are supposed to be functioning in conformity with the provisions of the old constitution and upholding the claims of the Confederacy that derived from the original treaties. But you have also a board of three "state chiefs" or "elected" or "elective chiefs," as they are variously called, ostensibly chosen by popular vote but actually, according to the Confederacy chiefs, selected by the white authorities and subservient to white interests. The election of these chiefs took place in a Catholic Youth Center outside the reservation. Two candidates for each office were nominated, but there were only about twenty votes cast. These "chiefs" are, in any case, however, the representatives with whom the state deals. And there has also been a third group of chiefs—which is said to have ceased to be active—known as the Council of Twelve, who were originally set up by the French in the middle of the eighteenth century. This departed from the Iroquois system and followed that of the French nobility by making the rank of chief the inheritance of the eldest son in the patrilineal line. (92–93)

Mohawk resistance to the imposition of tribal government has a long history in Kahnawake as well. In 1890, Kahnawake women representing the matrilineal Mohawk political system of clan mothers wrote to the minister of Indian Affairs stating their intentions, then placed their own chiefs in office. The government moved to enforce elections in Kahnawake again in 1915, but none were actually held before 1945 (Vachon 1993: 70). Throughout this period, Mohawks protested tribal elections and Canada's government manoeuvred to counteract their efforts. As Geoffrey York (1990: 246) writes, "Indian activism has always been an annoyance to the federal government, and for most of the twentieth century Ottawa worked hard to suppress it. Every possible tactic, from financial pressure to police intervention, was used to block the development of Indian organizations." In 1924, the federal government established the elected band council in Kahnawake; but in the 1920s, Kahnawake Mohawks returned to full partnership in the Iroquois Confederacy.

If Mohawk warriors are historically situated in Iroquois narratives of heritage and resistance, they are also, to an equal extent, products of the struggle over Native self-determination and control that dominates contemporary Native political processes. For Mohawks, the move toward consolidated tribal action began in 1924, when band councils were established in both Canada and the United States, and the Indian Citizenship Act was passed, declaring that all Indians within its borders were American citizens. In that year, the Royal Canadian Mounted Police moved onto the Six Nations reserve to dissolve the Iroquois Confederacy and impose tribal elections. As the Mohawk communities battled an imposed political process and affirmed their alliances to the Iroquois Confederacy, free passage across the Canada–United States border became a new arena of conflict over federal jurisdiction and Mohawk sovereignty for those crossing the border, looking for work.

In response to the "boom and bust" pattern of economic colonialism, Mohawk men whose grandfathers and fathers were recognized as expert hunters, voyageurs, fur traders, and farmers, became employed as high-steel workers in the construction trade. In 1886, Mohawks began constructing bridges and buildings in the cities of eastern Canada and the eastern United States, where Kahnawake Mohawks forged the urban Indian experience that has marked the lives of so many other Native people. By the 1920s, the Kahnawake Mohawks living and working in Brooklyn, New York, had formed a "close-knit twelve-block neighborhood." This urban Mohawk community spearheaded "one of the first legal victories for modern Indian sovereignty—the legal right of tribal people to define themselves and to act as unique entities" (Deloria 1993: 388). Their legal case emerged from a culturally centred sense of nomadism that built communities based on shifting alliances and the common experience of home. Brooklyn Mohawks were sometimes "week-day warriors," sometimes "winter warriors," a teasing acknowledgment of the workers and their families who travelled between Mohawk communities on the reserve, and the reserve communities they reconstructed in the cities. In 1926, when Paul Diabo was arrested as "an illegal alien working without a permit," Kahnawake Mohawks living on both sides of the border fought the case in the courts:

> Diabo's lawyers argued that he was not, in fact, a Canadian but a Mohawk and that his rights to "free intercourse and commerce" across the border had been established in the Jay Treaty of 1794, and confirmed in the Treaty of 1796 and the Treaty of Ghent signed at the end of the War of 1812. (Deloria 1993: 388)

Mohawk resolve related to this incident led to the formation of the Indian Defense League of America, an organization that was active in Iroquois communities beyond the 1970s, when modern Indian warriors became leaders among those who were known as the "New Indians" (Steiner 1968). Changing cultural and political sensibilities emerged among Indian men and women in urban and academic communities in the 1960s and 1970s. In the United States, an amorphous group of vocal, angry, and sometimes militant Indians expressed their experiences of cities and prisons, sharing a blend of encounters—historical, lived, and imagined, tribal and pan-Indian. Mohawks like Richard Oakes, of Akwesasne, who led the occupation of Alcatraz in November 1969, were leaders among the "New Indians," (Steiner 1968) about whom Dennis Banks (in Crow Dog with Erdoes 1990) wrote:

> They call us the New Indians.
> Hell, we are the Old Indians,
> the landlords of this continent,
> coming to collect the rent. (73)

The occupation of Alcatraz, which lasted until June 1971, began with an alliance of urban Indians, mostly college students, who protested the Native plight in the name of "Indians of All Nations." But in Canada, the impetus for Native protest in the late 1960s did not come from urban or academic Indians. The rising voices of Native discontent emerged from reserves, and Indian voices grew stronger in response to the actions of the federal government.

In 1969, Canada's Department of Indian Affairs issued the *White Paper on Indian Policy*, which proposed the dissolution of Indian rights and reserves that are entrenched in treaties, in the Royal Proclamation of 1763, and in the series of Indian Acts legislated since the late 1800s. The White Paper was a volley in a new Indian war, a strike at the heart of assumed protections that shocked Indians into action across the country. As Native organizations solidified in opposition to this overtly assimilationist policy, Indian traditionalism and activism were gaining a foothold south of the border. In 1961, the American Indian Chicago Conference was organized, reinforcing a sense of national Indian collaboration across both countries. The Chicago Conference recalled the precarious pan-Indian efforts of the past: Pontiac's effort to rally allied tribes against the British in 1763; the inter-tribal warriors led by Tecumseh in 1809, and by Black Hawk in 1832; the formation of the Society of American Indians in 1911; the attempt to establish a continental League of North American Indian Tribes in 1934; and finally, in 1944, the establishment of the National Congress of American Indians in the United States and the North American Indian Brotherhood in Canada. In the 1960s, as the Black Power movement gained popularity in the United States, pan-Indian alliances exposed the tension between negotiation and militancy that power relations have always engendered for Indians.

In 1961, the National Indian Youth Council focused the disparate voices of young Native American dissidents in assertions of Red Power that produced a "fish-in" in 1964 to support fishing rights in the state of Washington, and the Poverty March on Washington, DC. In 1968, Ojibways in St. Paul, Minnesota, spoke in more militant terms about their experiences in prisons and urban ghettos, initiating a discourse of protest that led to the formation of the American Indian Movement (AIM). Distinct voices of protest arose in Mohawk territory, where Mohawks on both sides of the border became active antagonists in struggles over land claims, border protests, and political resistance. In retrospect, "though opinions may differ as to which gathering or event crystallized the new consciousness, few would doubt the importance of the early 1960s Mohawk blockade of the New York State/Canadian border [in 1968], or the occupation of Alcatraz in 1969" (Moody 1988, 2: 29).

The American Indian Movement led the Red Power movement of the early 1970s, and although Indian issues differed from those of the Civil Rights and Black Power movements that had emerged in the United States, AIM drew upon their rhetoric and tactics to express long-standing demands for recognition of Indian rights and the improvement of living conditions on reservations. For Native Americans, the new movement reached back to the 1950s, when pan-Indianism emerged among urban Indians in the years when returning warriors and displaced workers moved to the cities after the Second World War. But even among those who shared urban Indian experience, the alliances of political protest were contingent and mutable, representing divisions and factions that sometimes coalesced, sometimes conflicted.

Red Power's transformed claims to sovereignty and self-determination arose at a time when, within many reserve communities, "definite political positions had been drawn between the traditionals and the other Indians in the tribe" (Deloria and Lytle 1984: 234). Like Native people in urban areas, tribal members disagreed over strategies to procure land claims, treaty rights, and current obligations to reservation Indians; and they differed in their support for tribal leadership, whose moderate stance was supported by the governments on both sides of the border. In the 1960s, AIM became a player in reservation politics through urban demonstrations, reservation occupations, and caravans to Washington that raised awareness of Indian identity and traditions, land and living conditions. AIM leaders spoke in the appropriated, transformed voices of those whom Indians call "long-hairs," tribal traditionals, who struggled not only with the federal government but also with "short-hair" progressives who had long been associated with support for assimilationist policies. In performances that were "rowdy, irreverent, and sometimes eloquent, they [AIM] took their cause to the headlines and TV news screens across the U.S. bringing international attention to the mistreatment of Native people" (Two Shoes 1998: 28). AIM's tactical appropriation of media for the expression of militant positions moved Gerald Vizenor (1984) to write:

> The poses of tribal radicals seem to mimic the romantic pictorial images in old photographs taken by Edward Curtis for a white audience. The radicals never seem to smile, an incautious throwback to the stoical tribal image of slower camera shutters and film speeds. The new radicals frown, even grimace at cameras, and claim the atrocities endured by all tribal cultures in first person pronouns. (130)

Expressing empowerment in a blend of generic representations of Indianness, transformations of historical rhetoric, and pan-Indian spiritual ceremonies, the new warriors of the American Indian Movement attracted followers from cities and reserves across Indian Country. In the words of Mary Crow Dog (with Erdoes 1990: 73), "The American Indian Movement hit our reservation like a tornado, like a new wind blowing out of nowhere, a drumbeat from far off getting louder and louder." But the drumbeat that symbolized the "Red Road" was dispersed and undisciplined, and it became increasingly aggressive. In 1972, AIM led a caravan across the country on a journey called the "Trail of Broken Treaties." The trek ended in Washington, DC, where protestors occupied the headquarters of the Bureau of Indian Affairs for a week of speeches and press conferences, pep rallies and vandalism. Then, in 1973, AIM occupied Wounded Knee on the Pine Ridge reservation, a move that eventually led to the long and bloody standoff in 1975.

AIM members were called to the Oglala Sioux reservation of Pine Ridge, South Dakota, by a coalition of elders and activists to protest the corruption and protect against the violence of the Pine Ridge tribal government. From the beginning, the conflict among Indians at Pine Ridge was determined by the interests of Others, including the American government's interest in mineral-rich land within Sioux territory. The struggle between factions on the reservation escalated into violent incidents that eventually led to a seventy-one day siege in which AIM members were sealed off by government agents at Wounded Knee. The gun battles that ensued led to deaths on both sides, but in the end, only Indians were prosecuted. In 1975, when two agents of the Federal Bureau of Investigation (FBI) and one AIM member were killed in a shootout at the Jumping Bull Ranch, the battles were finally over. By then, the Oglala Sioux tribal chair had transferred 76,200 acres of Sioux land to the federal government; sixty-nine Indians who were associated with Sioux resistance had been murdered (Hazen-Hammond 1997: 276); Annie Mae Aquash was dead; and Leonard Pelletier was arrested to atone for the death of the FBI agents.

Indians do not agree on the efficacy of AIM warriors or the political effectiveness of the crisis at Wounded Knee, but they recognize the tenacity of AIM's pan-Indian presence. To outsiders, the American Indian Movement seemed to disintegrate in the court trials and prison sentences and deaths that followed the incident at Wounded Knee, but insiders realized that AIM was a force not a framework, a movement not an organization. AIM endures in images of an empowered future built in reconstructions of the past that recall Wounded Knee in 1890, when three hundred Sioux were massacred by the Seventh Cavalry and buried in a mass grave. This call to collective experience is expressed by Leonard Pelletier (in Moody 1988, 1: 57), whose words from Oakalla Prison in 1976 resonate with the ambiguity of Indian tradition, sovereignty, and self-determination in Native communities across North America, both urban and reserve:

> I am the collective Indian voice
> and I cry out from a million graves of unresting souls
> and another million cries that ask the questions:
> Where does my future belong and to whom:
> Does it belong to my people? (57)

When AIM was formally dissolved in 1979 to protect its members, Russell Means (in Hazen-Hammond 1997: 292) said, "AIM never died. It only changed form.... AIM is now in every single Indian community; and it always will be."

In Canada, the formal alliance to the American Indian Movement was always tenuous and tentative. AIM's voice was heard in the Red Power movement of British Columbia, and it echoed across the country with the contentious deaths of Native Canadian activists Richard Oakes after the occupation of Alcatraz Island, Annie Mae Aquash after Wounded Knee, and Nelson Small Legs, Jr. after AIM emerged in Canada. No one knew the details of how Richard Oakes was beaten to death or understood why Annie Mae Aquash was shot, but Indians everywhere recognized the frustration that moved Nelson Small Legs, Jr. (in Wagamese 1996: 65) to write in 1976, before he shot himself in the heart: "I give up my life in protest to the conditions concerning Indian people in southern Alberta.... My suicide should open the eyes of non-Indians into how much we've suffered."

Even before the inception of AIM, the new spirit of Indian nationalism had begun to take hold in Mohawk territory. In 1959—the year that the St. Lawrence Seaway opened, removing Kahnawake Mohawks from the river that centred much of their daily lives—Edmund Wilson (1959: 72) wrote, "To the stranger, the most obvious sign of Iroquois patriotism is the fashion of wearing 'scalplocks' on the part of the boys and young men." Voices of resistance rooted in history and heritage were expressed in the Mohawk occupations that occurred on both sides of the border that cuts across Mohawk territory, including the blockade of the Akwesasne bridge between the United States and Canada in 1968; the Mohawk takeover at Ganienkeh near Altona, New York, in 1974; and the siege of Raquette Point at Akwesasne in 1979. Media attributed these expressions of protest to the pan-Indian movement of Red Power and the organization of AIM. But like the 1990s, when Red Power and AIM were invoked in the rhetoric of Mohawk warriors and the reproaches of their opposition in Kanehsatake, Akwesasne, and Kahnawake, the voices of protest that arose were fundamentally Mohawk and essentially local. The confrontations in Mohawk territory sometimes drew supporters from across the continent, but the issues and actions were distinctive; and although the struggles with outsiders and among Indians on the three reserves were related, the disputes were also separate and specific. Each incident expressed both the common experience of history and culture that Mohawks share and the particular historical inequities and cultural conflicts that separate them. In 1990, Indian leaders emerged in local alliances, in relations of power and politics that sometimes involved Mohawk warriors from other reserves or from the Iroquois Confederacy, but the incidents were not AIM uprisings or warrior revolutions. With the exception of Ganienkeh, the confrontations in Mohawk territory since the 1960s over Indian territory and political policy were led largely by Mohawks who, if they ever identified as warriors, are today Mohawk "traditionals," leaders from Akwesasne, Kanehsatake, and Kahnawake who are implicitly opposed to the Warrior Society, who support the band councils or the Iroquois Confederacy, and who advocate Native sovereignty and land rights with the same voracity today as they did in the 1970s.

Mohawk War Zones

Today, Mohawks associate warriors with the Warrior Society, a term which Louis Karoniaktajeh Hall (n.d.: 35), points out "was supplied by the white man [but] seems to fit nicely." According to Hall—the Kahnawake artist and writer who inscribed much of what the media call the "warrior manifesto"—today's Warrior Society draws its reconstructed form (including women warriors) and its modern mandate from an interpretation of the Great Law of Deganawida that is based on the nature of Indian experience, both historical and current:

There have been some objections by some well meaning Indians against having a Warrior Society. "There is no war," they say. Nothing can be further from the truth. There has been a constant psychological warfare waged against the natives of America right from the start of the European occupation of Red man's land and it's as deadly as the one with guns. It's war against the minds of the people and the casualties are the drug addicts, drunks and suicides which are at the highest among the Indians.... Oppression is an act of war against the people. Legislating the Indians into extinction by way of assimilation is an act of war against the Indians. Legal extermination of the Indians as a distinct people is an act of aggression. Genocide as practiced against the Indians is an act of war and the Indians must act in self-defense. The answer is the Warrior Society whose task is charged with finding ways to protect the people from every form of aggression being waged against them. (37)

Like the discourse of the American Indian Movement, this call to the nationalism of blood and belonging is, as Michael Ignatieff (1994: 10) suggests, a call to violence that is voiced as the protection of the innocent from violence. In Kahnawake during the summer of 1990, the words of the Warrior Society accented the divisions that represent the lived experience of this Mohawk community. The conflict became more complex when, "in Kahnawake, as Red Power traditionalists took over the Longhouse, peaceful traditionalists left it and founded the Mohawk Longhouse of the Mohawk Trail, which remained loyal to the Mohawk Nation Council at Akwesasne and to the condoled chiefs of the Six Nations Confederacy" (Vachon 1993: 80). Kahn-Tineta Horn (1997) explains the Warrior Society's perception of the factionalism that Kahnawake Mohawks experience:

> Today on Kahnawake territory there is a small number of Roman Catholic and Protestant and non-traditional people who support the Canadian government band council system. The political polarization is between the band council system and the Kaienerekowa/Great Law Longhouse on Route 207 who follow the Great Law. In the meantime the Band Council has forged ties with the Handsome Lake Longhouse which, being accomodationist, is able to work with the band council. (15)

Mohawk war zones in Kahnawake have a deep-rooted history. Mohawks there have long been absorbed in divisions between progressives and traditionals—"short-hairs" and "long-hairs"—and fractures between Catholics and Protestants and those who follow different traditions of the Longhouse. But in 1990, the community forged deeper divisions between Mohawks who supported the Warrior Society and the Mohawk Nation Office, which emerged as a parallel government that challenged the authority of the elected band council. The Office also challenged Mohawks whose traditionalism was articulated to the covenant of the Great Peace, which buried the weapons of war and the concepts of war chiefs and Warrior Societies in support of the Handsome Lake tradition of the Longhouse and the traditional government of the Iroquois Confederacy; Mohawks who were Christian; and Mohawks— traditional or Christian—who supported the elected band council.

For many Mohawks, the militant stance of the Warrior Society and the Mohawk Nation Office that was associated with it adopted methods and resources to protect the people that were unsettling and problematic, including casinos in Akwesasne, bingo in Ganienkeh, Kanehsatake, and Kahnawake, and tax-free cigarettes, alcohol, and guns sometimes smuggled over the border between the United States and Canada and sold on Canadian reserves. These enterprises are intertwined with the rhetoric of nationalism which asserts that "as a sovereign Nation, we have every legal, political, constitutional and human right to engage in free trade within our own respective traditional territories" (Goodleaf 1995: 10). But because Mohawk "free trade" is also free enterprise, tax-free cigarettes and alcohol, bingo and casinos benefit individual Indians and the enterprises of the Mohawk Nation Office or the Warrior Society rather than the entire membership of the band. Money from these sources both expands the gap between the rich and the poor on the reserves and provides the guns and butter for the warriors, who sometimes work together under the flag of the Warrior Society and sometimes protect the contraband activities of private individuals.

Some traditional Mohawks are ideologically opposed to the Warrior Society—which is disallowed within the Handsome Lake Code of the Longhouse religion—and the trade in contraband commodities and gambling on the reserves that some members support. Other Mohawks fear the control of the Mohawk Nation Office that is associated with the Warrior Society and the vigilantism of an amorphous group of activists, including young men who, whatever their principles or historical rhetoric, do not exhibit the discipline or control of a parallel police force or a military unit. In May 1991, when warriors surrounded the Kahnawake peacekeepers police station demanding the release of a fellow warrior

arrested for impaired driving, neither War Chief Alan Delaronde nor
Band Council Grand Chief Joe Norton could dissuade them from the
Mohawk-against-Mohawk melee that followed. This incident was reminiscent of the spring of 1990, when Mohawk killed Mohawk across the
barricades at Akwesasne, where the traditional Warrior Society and their
equally traditional opposition engaged in the ultimate cultural struggle. Robert Vachon (1993) writes about the divisions between Kahnawake
traditionals, who have been rooted together in media images:

> Many [traditionalists] did not view Iroquois flirtation with Red Power
> politics and with the American Indian Movement as a positive develop-
> ment. AIM's protests, some of which had led to violence, property destruc-
> tion, trespass and acts of rioting that were seen as antithetical to
> traditional values.... This led to tensions between the Red Power tradi-
> tionalists and the peaceful traditionalists. (77)

Mohawk warriors, like the traditionals and the elected band councillors who sometimes oppose them, are not, of course, unidimensional or
monolithic. The Warrior Society is itself fragmented into intertwined
groups of Mohawks with different ideological and commercial commitments. Warriors include Mohawks like Louis Hall, who believed deeply
that armed self-defence is the only option left for Indians in the struggle
for sovereignty and self-determination. Others are recognized as "money
warriors," who benefit from the lucrative businesses of smuggling and
gambling under the protection of the Warrior Society or warriors-for-
hire. And there are young warriors who identify with the movement
and have become, in the words of Mohawk Mike Myers, "the biggest
thing since Rice Krispies" (in Henton 1990: D5), a position they have
acquired in large part by reappropriating the media's monolithic, military representation of the bandana-masked, khaki-clad, gun-toting warrior and the western Plains warrior from which it has evolved.

The prism of warrior images, ideologies, and actions is built in the
competing narratives of historical struggles over traditional and tribal
governments, over border-crossings and land tenure, over the traditions
of the Longhouse and the Iroquois Confederacy, the Covenant Chain,
the Great Law, and over the rhetoric of Louis Hall and those who have
appropriated his words. In these arenas of cultural persistence, Mohawk
warriors represent those who support peace and those who incite war,
and their contradictory conduct is confusing to both Indians and outsiders. While some Mohawks built barricades in the 1990s, others sup-

ported the approach of the Ogichidaw warriors of the Waswagon Treaty Association in Wisconsin, who stood in the controlled silence of six spring spearing seasons in the 1980s, absorbing the racism and rock-throwing of hundreds of non-Indians who protested their legal right to spear the spawning fish. The Chippewa won this struggle over the exercise of treaty rights through peaceable cultural practice at the boat landings and combat in the courts, where they obtained an injunction against harassment that ended the protest. For Indians, these related, but conflicting, images of warriors blur the distinction between the activism of protecting the sovereignty of Indian land and treaty rights, and the action of initiating paramilitary confrontation. The media dissolved the difference between warriors who were protecting Indian land from an invasion of the police, the army, or businesses, and warriors who were barricading the Mercier Bridge between Kahnawake and Montreal. Both were absorbed into unified images of scuffling, stone-throwing, and gun-toting Mohawks.

In continually headlining one facet of the prism that constitutes the emerging Native social imaginary of the warrior, the media plays a central role in creating a powerful fictive identity that attracts children and the disproportionately large number of Indian youth who are neither in school nor employed. Through media, too, this social imaginary of the monolithic warrior is a force in the nature of the activism adopted by Indians across Canada and the United States, by Native people who are frustrated with the endless battles over land rights, treaty rights, sovereignty, and self-determination. In the failed negotiations of two hundred years of land claims and four constitutional conferences to entrench Aboriginal rights, Mohawk warriors have become figures of Indian popular culture, dominating representations of guns and muscle, who articulate closures of ideology and identity about which Billy Diamond, a chief of the James Bay Cree, says, "The young people of my community think that what the warriors are doing is correct.... They say, 'We believe what the warriors are saying is right and we intend to do the same thing'" (in Henton 1990: D5). More recent and more ominous representations of warriors have emerged in the form of urban street gangs like the Manitoba Warriors or the Indian Posse; and even though AIM seems fractured and brittle today, its voice from the 1970s still resonates, when "the young men tied eagle feathers to their braids, no longer unemployed kids, juvenile delinquents, or winos, but warriors" (Crow Dog with Erdoes 1990: 126).

Philip Deloria (1993: 407) writes, "Defining oneself as an Indian in the twentieth century has meant walking a fine line between the domination and allure of American culture and the resistance and resilience of one's own tradition." This line is blurred and broken in Native communities, where it is expressed in ambivalent cultural and ideological identifications that are articulated to transforming traditionalism. Gerald Alfred (1995: 1–2) tells us that "the turmoil that has been a constant feature of life in Kahnawake ever since I can remember is due in part to different views on the nature and meaning of traditionalism [that] lead to internal factionalism and conflict." In the words of Joe Norton (in Goodleaf 1995), long-standing grand chief of the Kahnawake Mohawks:

> There are some traditional and non-traditional people who want to separate traditional life from the political responsibilities. They are working for the cultural side of tradition, but not actually living and exercising the political side of tradition. In Mohawk tradition, you cannot separate spirituality and politics. (137–38)

In Kahnawake, Indians still struggle over the alliances and ideologies of Mohawks who support the band council and those who endorse the traditional government of the Mohawk Nation Office or the Iroquois Confederacy; over traditionals who support different interpretations of Deganawida's Great Law and the Longhouse religion; over Mohawks who promote the approach of warriors and those who advocate peaceful, legal, or traditional methods to achieve land and treaty rights, sovereignty and self-determination; over Mohawks who support economic development through gambling, cigarette sales, and smuggling and those who reject these enterprises. These expressions of prismal community are etched with monolithic representations of warriors that recall the rhetoric of Wounded Knee, about which Gerald Vizenor (1984) writes:

> Some tribal people will continue to believe in sudden slogans and symbolic forms of protest; and there are people who are convinced that the expressions of internal rage by tribal rage were real revolution. There are also tribal people who will continue to revise the vain advertisements of peripatetic mouth warriors as statements of traditional visions. When the word wars of the putative warriors mumble down to the last exclamation points in the newspaper columns, however, the radical dramas will be best remembered in personal metaphors. (138)

The public texts and specific claims to meaning that media warriors represent play an increasing role in the identities and narratives that

Native North Americans construct and enact today. At the same time, there is a growing political struggle in Native communities over contested ideology and identity and their contingent closures of articulation related to what Vine Deloria, Jr. (1969) calls the "plight" of Native peoples:

> Our foremost plight is our transparency. People can tell just by looking at us what we want, what should be done to help us, how we feel, and what a "real" Indian is really like.... Because people can see right through us, it becomes impossible to tell truth from fiction from mythology. Often we paint ourselves as we wish we were or as we might have been. (9)

If the "transparency" of Mohawks today still revolves around militaristic images of warriors that are contentious, Mohawks share a sense of common pride and purpose in "standing their ground," in a collective perception that "being, and remaining Haudenosaunee is the central issue in contemporary Iroquois-White relations" (Hill in Goodleaf 1995: 12). Former grand chief Joe Norton (in Goodleaf 1995: 37–38) says of Kahnawake's Indian summer, "When the barricades went up, for whatever reasons, the majority of the community supported them." Kahn-Tineta Horn (1997: 15) writes from the perspective of the "Red Power traditionals" of the 207 Longhouse and the Warrior Society, "In spite of this historical adversarial position, the Kaienerekowa Longhouse and the band council worked together during the 1990 Mohawk Crisis to deal with and negotiate an end to the stand-off between the Mohawk and the Canadian army and the Sûreté [police] of Quebec."

In the summer of 2004, a new grand chief in Kahnawake said upon his election, "The first and most important thing for this community is to come together.... We have become an internal, problematic community... we must stand behind one another against outside forces" (King 2004: A7). But even today, as Mohawks speak of unity and take up positions among themselves that can be strongly oppositional and caustically hostile, unlike outsiders, they do not assume that their communities are homogeneous. In Indian Country, the struggles over Indian identities and ideologies that cut between neighbours and cousins, brothers and band members are constant and contentious, but as James Clifton (1968: 206) suggests in writing about Potawatomi factionalism, conflict among Kahnawake Mohawks is neither demoralizing nor disorganizing. Within a kaleidoscope of shifting alliances, Mohawks move through the activities and institutions of community, ignoring some, engaging others as they shift identities and ideological positions themselves. Politicized positions may be contested and contradictory, even capricious, but they are unified in the lived experience of being Mohawk and the diversity and contingency of Mohawk community.

In Kahnawake and other Native communities, the conflicts of different ideologies and identities can only be understood in the unities of common culture and history, experience and political purpose, in collective memory and the continual formation of community. It is the negotiation of relations of power articulated in contested ideology and identity and the continuous unity in diversity that both fractures and binds Native communities in their struggle with an oppressive past and an uncertain future. It is the recognition of this unity in difference, continually reconstructed in collective memory and cultural formation—and articulated to political struggles over land, self-determination, and sovereignty, over representation, appropriation, and materialism—that harbours the meaning and clarifies the importance of media images and Native identities today. Russell Means (with Wolf) (1995: 542) tells us, "We must become independent nations.... When we become as real to other races as they are to themselves, when they get to know us as human beings instead of two-dimensional symbols, they will no longer be able to demonize and dehumanize us."

In 1999, Means and other members of the American Indian Movement were called back to the region of Wounded Knee to protest the long list of unsolved murders and the unresolved conflicts between tribal members and tribal councils. In 2000, AIM founders attended a meeting of the Ogichidaw or Warrior Society in Kenora, Ontario, where today, their voices resonate with younger warriors engaged in the unsettling conflicts over commercial and resource development and unsettled land claims in provinces across Canada. In 2005, the community of Kanehsatake remains embroiled in internal conflict over political power, policing, violence, cigarette sales, and the likelihood of organized crime; and the appropriation and meaning of Mohawk warriors are at the heart of the struggle. Some Mohawks in Kanehsatake "drape themselves in the flag of the Warrior Society, concealing their criminal acts under the cloak of ideology" (Heinrich 2004: 3); others assert that "a true warrior, as we say in Mohawk, is someone who carries the burden of peace.... These people are not Warriors. They are just a bunch of guys who want to exert some kind of power over their community" (Gabriel in Heinrich 2004: 3).

As street gangs like the Manitoba Warriors emerge in urban Indian ghettos and as reserve communities continue to struggle over identity and ideology articulated to the contingent power, and political meaning, media images of Indian warriors will continue to represent conflict and contradiction. In the words of Joe David (1994: 164), a Kanehsatake Mohawk who was behind the barricades in Oka that summer of 1990: "My role in the 'Oka crisis' was inevitable because of my great-grandfather and my grandmother, my parents and the history of the community, but also because of the two governments' disregard of natives' legitimate protests and demands." But as Richard Wagamese (1996) comments:

> The siege continues at Kahnawake. It will for some time and the warriors there will continue to stand up for the protection of their own. But it is not them that native people should attempt to emulate. For the real warriors in Indian country are those who quietly seek to implement growth, change and healing through their efforts as doctors, lawyers, teachers, politicians, mothers and fathers. They seldom make the front page and they don't often attract the focus of the nation but they continue to be the protectors. You don't need a gun to be a warrior. (113)

≪ • ≫

Postcards of My Past:
Indians and Artifacts

Postcards of Indians have always attracted me. As a child growing up on the Lac du Flambeau reservation in Wisconsin, I remember watching cultural tourists search postcard racks for images of Indians, familiar faces overpowered by buckskin and beadwork, horses and headdresses, portraits to supplement the memories mirrored in their photographs:

> And here's one of an Indian
> selling Ralph a trinket—
> I suppose he'll use the money
> to buy some wine and drink it.
> Bacon (in Moody 1988, 1: 346)

Even then I knew that Indian postcards had little to do with Indians. I was drawn to postcards not because they touched some chord of displaced history or identity, but because they didn't. N. Scott Momaday (1976: 22) writes about the experience of being a Kiowa Indian: "Some of my mother's memories have become my own. That is the real burden of the blood." These silent, decorated images masking our struggles of empowerment remain so removed from memory and daily life in Lac du Flambeau. Postcard Indians have to express another heritage. These are the representations of Others, Indian realities transformed into non-Native social imaginaries and frozen in fragments: Indians as living artifacts. Yet I claim these postcards as images of my past.

Reflections

Postcard Indians have long been appropriated in Canadian and American cultural products and processes, where they stand in silent contra-

diction to the lived experiences of Indians. From the romantic representations of Canadian Pacific Railway advertisements of the West and the
vulgar stereotypes of plastic, pot-bellied Indian banks and cross-eyed,
wind-up toys, to the marginalized Indians of historical, artistic, and
political processes, North American images of Indians have worked to
construct a discourse of subordination.

In the Wounded Knee winter of 1973, the Quebec summer of 1990,
and the less-visible confrontations before and since, this discourse has
expanded to absorb multiple images of Indians. These conflicting decla-
rations of sovereignty and self-determination, of land and resources are
filtered through the lenses of Indians and Others in claims and combat,
confrontation and negotiation. Today, Native lawyers, writers, and artists
are ensnared by representations of Indian warriors, the new postcards
of Indians asserting self-determination. Native people themselves struggle in the current battlegrounds of cultural encounter, claiming and disclaiming these conflicting representations of power in the past and
political possibility in the present. Caught in a contest between the threats
and promises of appropriated images and their polarized assertions of
identity, Indians and Others across North America are locked in broader
confrontations of identity and power that are voiced in issues of Aboriginal rights and resources, cultural tourism, and cultural trespassing.

The current range of contested territories is varied and broad. The
litany of conflicts includes logging in Washington, British Columbia,
northern Ontario, and New Brunswick; hydro-electric projects in Alberta
and northern Quebec; low-level military flights in Labrador; mining in
Wisconsin and the west; fishing in Washington and Quebec and on both
Canadian coasts; nuclear dumping in Arizona; disputes over claims to
art, artifacts, and grave articles; Indian stories, photos, and films, gaming and smuggling; and New Age spiritualism. These struggles over
cultural identity and ownership, sovereignty and self-determination are
related to what Michael Ames (1987: 14) calls the "ethnological fate" of
Indians. This claim on the past, written in the shadows of Indian silence,
is finally dissolving in the emerging expressions of Native academics,
writers, artists, and politicians. Their words and images spill into the
wider political arenas, disrupting the discourse of nation-states that
excludes or subordinates Native people. Native North Americans are
voicing a new visibility expressed in land claims and resource contracts,
treaty negotiations and court cases. In the United States, treaties that
have been affirmed by the Supreme Court now force state governments

to recognize the rights of Native Americans. In Canada, Aboriginal rights entrenched in the constitution have been recognized by the federal government and the courts, which press politicians to negotiate the claims of not only Indians in untreatied and treatied territories but the Métis as well. This new political arena emerged in 1990, when Elijah Harper, the only First Nations member of the Manitoba legislature, voiced opposition that was pivotal in blocking the nation's tenuous attempts to construct a new constitution without assuring Aboriginal, multicultural, or women's participation and rights.

The pan-Aboriginal support for Elijah Harper's action was reminiscent of 1988, when Native people across Canada joined the land claims struggle of the Lubicon Cree nation in Alberta by protesting the Glenbow Museum exhibit of the Olympic Arts Festival in Calgary. This exhibit, which gathered together Canadian Indian artifacts now held in museums around the world, was sponsored by Shell Canada, a company that was engaged in a pitched battle with the Lubicon Lake Cree over oil rigs and land claims. The protest over the exhibit, entitled "The Spirit Sings: Artistic Traditions of Canada's First People," revealed the political relationship between museums and Aboriginal rights and the extent to which the ethnographic constructions fundamental to both are reflected in historical, literary, and artistic practice. Bruce Trigger (1988), an anthropologist who resigned from the board of the McCord Museum in Montreal in protest over the exhibit, writes:

> The Spirit Sings has shown that at least one major Canadian museum is still prepared to mount an exhibition in the face of protests from associations representing almost all Native groups across Canada, who in this instance were outraged that a show glorifying the creativity of Native peoples at the time of European discovery should be sponsored by an oil company that is currently engaged in destroying the traditional economy and way of life of the Lubicon Lake Cree. (15)

Tom Hill (1988), director of the Woodland Cultural Centre of the Six Nations reserve in Ontario, has remarked that this exhibit might more accurately have been named "The Tourist Sings," in celebration of the souvenirs collected from "real red Indians" by the earliest European tourists in America. Native artist Joane Cardinal-Shubert (1989: 23) comments, "The exhibition was called 'The Spirit Sings' but it pushed the notion that native culture was dead, wrapped up, over and collected." These are expressions of new voices arising from Indians and anthropologists. Like the voices of Native and non-Native artists, the current concerns of tenuous allies threaten to freeze them in opposition to one another.

Reflexive writing in anthropology continues to propel an increasingly tired and incestuous ethnographic turn. Fabian (1983), Marcus and Fischer (1986), Clifford (1987, 1988), Geertz (1988), and others discuss the extent to which ethnography is caught by the definition of the task, in the conflicting social realities of experiencing, researching, and writing. It is a perspective that, in the process of turning in upon itself, confronts the distance reflecting time, culture, and technique that forms a symbiotic knot between the Aboriginal and the academic Other. Grounded in the axis of encountering and textualizing Otherness, this anthropological discourse struggles with the "rein of worn codes" (Trinh 1989: 47), a range of concepts that constrain Native practice to the past of an "ethnographic present" and the stasis of empirical analysis. But the problem revealed in the politics of difference is even more basic than what Clifford Geertz (1988: 84) suggests represents "the research process in the research product." To the studied, the critique of ethnography is significant, because it probes the framework of the subaltern experience and provokes a discursive opening to expose and to understand the subordinated voice. As Lawrence Grossberg (1988: 381–82) writes, "A reconception of ethnography must begin by recognizing precisely that there is a 'reality,' an Otherness which is not merely its mark of difference within our signifying systems." Without devaluing the conditions of subordination that produce silence, Grossberg (384) challenges ethnography to recognize that "it does matter who is acting and from where; it does matter that the subject is both an articulated site and a site of ongoing articulation within its own history."

This reality embedded in the intertwined, articulating positions of history and heritage is played out in the memories and lived experience of Indians—both among themselves and with outsiders—in the contemporary sites of Native cultural struggle in North America, including the representational practices of museums, art, and literature, and the political processes of land claims, treaty rights, and, in Canada, Aboriginal rights and constitutional change. In these arenas, Indians and Others have been engaged for a decade in pitched battles over issues of appropriation—territorial, cultural, spiritual, commercial, and personal. The struggle to assert control over images, identities, and localities is, at another level, a dispute about representation, power, and identity and the social realities in which these are expressed and lived in political processes and popular culture.

Native reality is grounded in the experience of being inscribed as subaltern in the history of Others and as subjects in one's own heritage. For Indians, these placements are built upon contradictory social imaginaries, upon representations of Otherness that are prescribed by the missionary, the merchant, and the military, which, as Virginia Dominquez (1987: 131–32) suggests, "are inherently appropriative and hierarchical." The images that are entrenched in the relationships between Aboriginal people and newcomers are widely acknowledged in literary criticism as manifestations of "American double-mindedness about the Indian" (Pearce 1967: 76). The ways in which this "double-mindedness" works to construct what Homi Bhabha (1984) calls "the ambivalence of colonial discourse" has been less important to anthropology than reconstructing historical Indian practice and, more recently, the practice of ethnography itself. How the contradictions embedded in discourse are enacted among insiders and are acted upon by outsiders is of interest to writers from Memmi (1965) and Fanon (1967) to Said (1979), Spivak (1988), and Stuart Hall (1981). Their inquiries reveal a bond between academic construction, the domination of discourse, and the formation of "difference." These relationships prod ethnography to move beyond the description and meaning of texts to voice the disordered and discordant realities of the Other, to lay bare the web connecting academic and artistic representations of Indians, and to expose the personal experiences and political processes that these images construct and express.

Encounters

In the resurgent Indianness of the mid-1970s, I remember being among a group of Native people who protested an auction of Indian artifacts at the Ritz Carlton Hotel in Montreal, Quebec. We circled the entrance, then stood silently in the ballroom. Someone carried a sign that said How Many Beaver Pelts For the Mona Lisa? We watched as people bid in the ballroom on a pair of Blackfoot burial moccasins, a child's doll, a ceremonial dress, and a piece of parflesh. Just before the police ushered us out, a Cree from Mistassini slipped off one of his work boots, held it high, and asked, "How much will you pay for this Indian boot, worn by a real Indian?"

Native people have always known that collecting is at the heart of ethnographic practice. This reality is expressed by Tom Hill (1988) who, in the ambiguity of humour, speaks of Indians experiencing the earliest tourists in America through their propensity to collect souvenirs—and those who made the souvenirs—all for European markets. In the words of Frank Conibear (in New 1990: 9), "They collect the artifacts to study the past, out of the bone fragment, chipped stone and delicate cedar, weave a written history long forgotten." It is collecting as conceptualized in James Clifford's (1987: 121) widely recognized "salvage anthropology" with its "desire to rescue 'authenticity' out of destructive historical change," that is the basis of what a Mohawk artist calls "the politics of primitivism" (Jacobs 1986: 3), a discourse that constructs what newcomers—and Natives—know about Native people in representations of Indianness: tribal and traditional, Other and unequal. In the words of Deborah Doxtator (1988: 26), "People growing up in the 1950s and '60s were conditioned to believe that 'Real Indianness' had something to do with not talking very much, never smiling, wearing fringed clothing, being mystical, being poor, riding horses."

As we worked to renew and reconstruct our Indian identity in the 1970s, I remember the wars of heritage we waged at Manitou College, a junior college established and operated by Native people in Quebec. One long night we sat, Mohawk and Micmac, Chippewa and non-Indian, pressed together in the intensity of rising words over a soul-searing question of the times: Is it Indian to watch Rudolf Nureyev dance?

Collecting—customs and clothes; images, memories, and idioms; spoons, songs, and spirits—removes or redefines the lived significations of identity and power that are enacted and acted upon in Indian experience. Museums display glass-cased artifacts and carved canoes, totem poles and berry baskets, all removed from the discursive exchange of daily life and labelled with meanings that are fixed in the culturally coherent narratives of Others. Indian objects for which meanings emerge in the power they invoke or the community they involve are redefined as historical representations and ethnographic artifacts. Native experience is assumed and absorbed in these exhibits of objects and customs, activities and costumes. The significance of cultural confiscation is suggested in a conversation between anthropologist A. Irving Hallowell (1960: 24) and an Ojibway Elder: "Since stones are grammatically animate, I once asked an old man: Are all stones we see about us here alive? He reflected a long while and then replied, "No! But some are." Like drums and masks and medicine bags, stones are alive in the power they mediate between personal and spiritual worlds, and they can be dead in the absence of invocation and action.

For Native people, the objects and subjects of museums are collected by someone else, then absorbed or transformed to disappear or reappear as something else. The past is re-presented in interpretations of history, culture, and national formation that construct Indians as figures defined and confined by difference. Indians are imagined and positioned in the traditional arts and artifacts that characterize Native culture in museums; and the nature of this difference is of political significance. In the words of Audra Simpson (in Alfred 1999):

> To be Native today is to be cultured: to possess culture, to exercise it, to proclaim it, to celebrate it. But we cannot have just any culture; it has to be "traditional" culture—defined, isolated, reflected upon, relearned and then perfected. Our very sovereignty—in the European sense— depends on it, as we must continually prove our difference in order to have our rights respected. (66)

In museums, artifacts are arranged in cases or tableaus and listed, classified, or labeled in exhibits. It is assumed that by looking at and reading about the material items, outsiders can understand the meaning of the cultural practices they represent. But there is a critical difference between the history of Indians displayed in museums and the heritage of Native people as it is remembered, lived, or imagined. For Native people, the meaning of objects is never read off the surface or confined to the texts of the artifacts and images being displayed. The meaning of artifacts and the Indians they portray are continually negotiated within a context of tribalized difference, but it is misleading to assume that "from cigar store Indian, to cowboy and Indian movies, to the 'noble savage,' native people live in a prison of images not of their own making" (Alexander 1986: 45). Native North Americans may claim historical images as postcards of their past, but they also internalize the experience. As artist Norval Morriseau once said, "Whenever you are looking at my pictures, you are looking at my visions"(*Globe and Mail*, March 4, 1989: C13). The meaning of Indian traditional heritage is wrapped in narrative knots that are read or remembered, transformed lived or imagined, and experienced. Revealing Indian realities is never "a matter of peeling away the distortions created by the lamentable history of misrepresentation to reveal a true or historically pure 'reality'" (Townsend-Gault

1998A: 38). Native cultural differences are braided in a web of narratives and practices from the tribalized past that are intertwined with the disordered experiences of the present; and this "'difference' explodes into millions of differences, tiny or huge, that one picks up by living their culture" (R. Hill 1992: 21). As Paula Gunn Allen (1986: 161) writes, "A contemporary American Indian is always faced with a dual perception of the world: that which is particular to American Indian life, and that which exists ignorant of that life."

Native people live in a *prism* of images, experienced in "contradictory symbols of Indianness" (Doxtator 1988) related to history and practices, consumerism and popular culture, which an exhibition at the Woodland Centre in Ontario codified as "Fluffs and Feathers":

> What is Fluff? Fluff is artificial, highly coloured decorative soft stuff ornamenting Indian tourist products. What is Feather? Feather is from a creature that soars between earth and the heavens, symbolizing the spiritual, social, political reality of Indian culture. (Bedard 1989: 2)

There is, of course, no border between feather and fluff. The two are interwoven in Native narratives of culture and identity that are transformed, enacted, contested, and expressed in what Gerald McMaster (1995: 84) calls "borderzones." These are locations of ambiguous meaning and creativity, liminal sites of experience and expression that can dissolve boundaries and confuse categories. There is a growing awareness that Native cultural expression cannot be reduced "to simply the question of modernism or postmodernism, art or anthropology, or whether we are contemporary or traditional" (Todd in R. Hill 1994: 81). Drawing on cultural transformation and creative "injun-uity" (McMaster 1995: 74), Native cultural practices and products emerge within a sense of the past that is not easy to access, understand, or display.

The struggle to inscribe the reality of Indian experience in the memories of Others is a disquieting task, and the early texts that relate the history of North America are not helpful. Virgil Vogel (n.d.: 1) writes, "Perhaps the chief problem in the historical treatment of American Indians and other minorities is not the biased presentation, but the blackout." Native heritage is marked with memories of events that newcomers seldom remember and Indians never forget. Native North Americans remember the Trail of Tears in the 1830s, when President Andrew Jackson ordered that the Cherokees be removed from their lands in the southeastern United States, and thousands died on the march west; they

A postcard photograph of Mrs. Chen-Gu-Os-No-Qua on the Lac du Flambeau reservation, 1910 to 1920. Ben Guthrie Collection, George W. Brown, Jr. Ojibwe Museum and Cultural Center, Lac du Flambeau, Wisconsin.

remember the Massacre at Sand Creek in Colorado in 1864, where Black
Kettle and six hundred Cheyenne were promised protection and peace
before two hundred men, women, and children were murdered by the
United States Army; they remember that, in 1874, gold was discovered
in the Black Hills and the Sioux lost this sacred land to developers; and
they remember that, in Canada, Louis Riel was hanged for his role in the
Métis Rebellion of 1885. If these events seem familiar now, their exposure
owes more to Hollywood films than to early history books. Until recently,
historians told the story of North America from the constrained perspectives of their academic disciplines and cultural experiences. Even
today, the narratives of non-Native history and Native heritage recall
different events and represent distinct memories.

For historians who recognize that "native people have been a determining factor in Canadian [and United States] history" (Fisher and
Coates 1988: 2), Native heritage marks the difference within dominant
signifying systems rather than the historical substance of Indian experience. Bruce Trigger (1988B) writes about the silence of Native history in
North America:

> Even less has been done to integrate what native people write about
> their past with academic studies of native history. It is, however, clearly
> wrong to dismiss such work as only polemical or of ethnological inter-
> est. On the contrary, what native people currently believe about their
> history may provide valuable insights into the significance of that his-
> tory. (35)

This distinction between Native North American heritage and "real"
history situates Indians "outside history," where they can be erased, displaced, reified, and named. The vanquished have been drawn in the
words of the victors, whose assertion that oral tradition is folklore, not
history, constructs Indians as historyless vagrants without an authenti-
cated written past. Like ethnographic constructions, these competing
conceptions of history and folklore are linked to representations that
reinforce the dominant culture's understanding of the Indian as noble or
evil, villainous or victimized. Drawn from the images of the romanticized or savage Indian, neither representation allows newcomers to identify Native peoples as equals, or to recognize Native North Americans
as "real inhabitants of a land" (Atwood 1972: 105). The history that
assigns these images to Indians also constructs the nation-states they
inhabit, creating an imagined coherence and commonness among new-

comers that excludes Native people. Like so many other countries, Canada and the United States illustrate that "the nation has played a critical role in defining what a modern conception of history should be," and, as "history came to mean the deployment of reason in the real world" (Dirks 1990: 25), postcard images of Indians gloss over and reshape the vague realities of Native people and their respective political structures. Louis Karoniaktajeh Hall (n.d.) describes how Europeans understood the Iroquois Confederacy:

> The European immigrants call us tribes. A tribe is primitive man's first attempt at social order.... It's an insulting term.... When the Europeans came to America they made treaties with the Indians and in doing so, recognized them as nations.... Only nations can make treaties. (32)

From the Native perspective, even Canada's Royal Proclamation of 1763, which refers to "the several Nations or Tribes of Indians with whom we are connected" (in Asch 1984: 57–58), is grounded in representations of Indians that express contradictions and misunderstandings. The meaning of treaties differ for Natives and newcomers, and this difference frames the conflicting perceptions of Native rights on ceded and reserved land that treaties express. As a government document acknowledges,

> Indian people view treaties as reaffirmations of their sovereignty and rights and as agreements to allow settlement in certain areas; non-Indians regard treaties as an extinguishment of rights, an acceptance of the supremacy of the Crown, and a generous gift of land to the Indians so they might have land of their own. (Commons, 1983: 12)

In the spreading cultural resurgence and pan-Indianism of the 1970s, I remember being among a group of Indians who travelled across Indian Country to Ottawa for the memorial of Nelson Small Legs, Jr., who committed suicide to protest Canada's disregard for the conditions on Indian reserves. We were absorbed in ambivalence as we listened to the rhetoric and raised fists that echoed from Native uprisings at Alcatraz Island in California, and Wounded Knee and Rosebud in South Dakota. These urban and reservation sites of Native struggles over land and rights, deprivation, and corruption, during the late 1960s and the 1970s, were located deep within the United States. But we recognized something of ourselves in the appropriated red berets and armbands of the tenuous Canadian connection to the American Indian Movement that emerged in those years. We knew the names of Canadian Indians who were sacrificed in struggle: Yvonne Oakes killed during the occupation of Alcatraz; Richard Oakes beaten in a bar room brawl after he left Alcatraz Island and then killed in Mendocino, California; Annie Mae Aquash killed at Wounded Knee; and Nelson Small Legs, Jr. killed by his own hand to protest government neglect. In the sullen darkness of the journey home from Ottawa, someone recalled the issue of the 1969 White Paper, the *Statement of the Government of Canada on Indian Policy* that proposed to remove the Aboriginal status of Indian people entrenched in Canada's Indian Act and disband Indian reserves that are held in the trust of treaties. We spoke of the assertion of land rights that is woven into every Native demand for cultural, political, and spiritual self-determination. In the silence, we could almost hear the drumbeats begin, signalling the Mohawk occupations of Racquette Point, Ganienkeh and Akwesasne in New York and Ontario in the mid-1970s, the confrontations of Kanehsa-take and Kahnawake in Quebec in 1990, and the conflicts over fishing and timber, hunting and gaming that continue to arise across Indian Country.

To non-Natives, treaties are the historical products of benevolent conquest, artifacts of reasonable (if not equitable) surrender. To Native people, treaties have been a process, exercises of ritualized land acquisition, resource exploitation, colonization, and control. For them, treaties were never about surrender but about the prospect of mutual sovereignty, about nations abstracted from nation-states and recognized through agreements in which self-determination is the common ground. What Native people envision is not the self-government of Indian councils grafted onto Canadian municipalities, but self-determination "bound up with sovereignty in all its ramifications—social, cultural, political, economic." Self-determination that in the Mohawk language translates as "carrying ourselves" ("The Mohawk Nation, Kahnawake Territory," in *Tribune Juive* 1989: 5).

In Canada, the distance between Native reality—lived, transformed, and imagined—and the reality of Others is represented in the four constitutional conferences that were held between 1983 and 1987 to define Aboriginal rights, each of which became mired in the questions of identity and power. Who is Aboriginal? Whose values? Whose self-government? Whose land? Whose God? This framework was established at the outset when the first conference opened with Chief Many Bears beginning an Indian prayer and the then prime minister Pierre Trudeau interrupting to ask, "Are you going to pray every morning, in public?" To the answer, "Yes, Sir," Trudeau replied, "Then everybody should pray to his own God, and we'll have a moment of meditation." Everyone did, and the subsequent isolation, ambiguity, and confusion of political prayers in English and French, Indian languages and Arctic Inuktitut echoed the cultural distance between the reality of Aboriginal land, life, and collective rights and the constitutional treaty table. The provincial premiers left the last meeting with no sense of common ground, unaware of the irony in announcing, "We will go home and solve the real problems of Aboriginal peoples" (Bulbulian 1987). But solving the real problems of Native people involves a web of conflicting cultures and histories that connects museums to the political possibilities of Aboriginal nations, cultures and lives. Reviewing the museum exhibit of "The Spirit Sings," the editor of the *Edmonton Journal* wrote (in McLoughlin 1990):

> It has long been clear that we actually prefer our native culture in museums. We certainly do not prefer it running the Department of Indian Affairs. Nor do we prefer it announcing the news on national television or determining its own political destiny. (3)

In the resurging Indianness of the times, Jim Thunder, a Plains Cree from Alberta, remembers a dream about the power of the 150-year-old medicine bundle that once belonged to Chief Big Bear and now rests in the American Museum of Natural History in New York. Jim ran over four thousand kilometres to repatriate the sacred bundle, and he said, "I wouldn't run from Alberta for a historical artifact. This is alive. It has power" (Canadian Broadcasting Corporation 1989). This medicine bundle that can represent and empower Native people is entangled in conflicting accounts of possession, purpose, and meaning. But in the contradictory expressions of an irretrievable or appropriated past, the discourse of both museums and Native people always relates to protecting or protesting the future.

> The bundle, a sack containing sweetgrass, a bear's paw and tobacco was turned over to an anthropologist from the museum in 1934 by Big Bear's son, Jim Pimi ... [who] asked the museum to "keep it well, keep it there.... Is the museum to violate the trust placed in it by persons who deliver things to the museum? (*Montreal Gazette*, 23 March 1989: B5)

Recollections

In the non-Native cultural construct of the museum so far removed from
the treaty table and the experience of sweat lodges and storytelling
Elders, beaded history belts, and mnemonic birchbark scrolls, Native
people remember and reclaim their heritage. This encounter with the
past is not an exercise in remembered identity stripped off then pasted
back on to become the anthropologists' revitalization (Trinh 1989: 59).
Native recovery of collective memory is a transformational process about
which Homi Bhabha (1987: 123) writes, "Remembering is never a quiet
act of introspection. It is a painful re-membering, a putting together of
the dismembered past to make sense of the trauma of the present."
Native re-membering is built through historical reconstruction of the
Indian past and the contemporary recognition of politicized pan-Indian
events. In lived experience that intertwines the reconstructed images of
traditional culture and the contemporary discourse of politicized
processes, Native people entrench the collective memory and identity of
heritage. It is the intertwined experiences and representations and the collapsed time of cultural formation that make the academic tasks of unravelling and interpreting the meaning of traces of cultural evidence so
problematic. Historians and anthropologists are caught in a conceptual
approach that positions them as "their own authority" (Connerton 1989:
13) in the collection of Indian cultural evidence and the interpretation of
its meaning; and Native people are increasingly unwilling or unable to
speak of the meaning of historical experience or cultural practice. Entangled in the vague narratives of Indian "dominance and survivance"
(Vizenor 1994) that Indians tell, and the precise accounts of empirical
or interpretative enterprise that academics generate, the recognition and
understanding of Native social reality remains evasive and rare. These
perspectives of the Indian and the Other that combine and contradict
are intrinsic to the modern construct of the museum.

For Native North Americans, museums like art and literature are
sites of re-membering, re-collecting; living locations of the conflicting
articulations they experience in history and heritage and everyday life.
Here, amid the feathers and fluffs of Indian cultural processes—the con-
dolence cane and the bear claw necklace, the silver cross, the raven mask
and Hudson Bay blanket coat, and the skeletal remains or "grave goods"
and religious artifacts of tribal ancestors—Native people and anthropologists confront each other over issues that are aptly expressed in Bruce

Trigger's (1988A: 13) question Who owns the past? Along with land and treaty rights, Native people are laying claim to Indian objects and images, to museums and to history; in short, to Native heritage that is reconstructed, lived, and imagined. Across Indian Country, this move to transform the present and negotiate the future by recovering the past has contributed to new debates reclaiming memory, experience, and imagination.

As I worked to reconstruct my own identity as an academic and an Indian in the 1970s, I remember reading *Mountain Wolf Woman, Sister of Crashing Thunder: The Autobiography of a Winnebago Indian*, a text that was tape-recorded in Winnebago and English, transcribed, then written and annotated by Nancy Lurie (1966), then curator of anthropology at the Milwaukee Public Museum. I recognized glimpses of my Chippewa great-grandmother in Mountain Wolf Woman's story. My great-grandmother lived across the road and I remember being there as vividly as I remember being home until I was eighteen years old, when I went away to school and she died. I listened in that book to the whispers of my great-grandmother's history and her heritage. But it was years later, reading N. Scott Momaday's books, *The Way to Rainy Mountain* (1969) and *The Names* (1976), when I realized that, beyond all the contradictions that I myself represent, some of my great-grandmother's memories have become my own. In Momaday's (1976) words,

> The journey therein recalled continues to be made anew each time the miracle comes to mind ... it is a whole journey, intricate with motion and meaning; and it is made with the whole memory, that experience of the mind that is legendary as well as historical, personal as well as cultural. (4)

In Lac du Flambeau, where postcards were once the reflection of our Otherness, Native Americans today associate cultural tourism with cultural trespassing. This association expresses an awareness of the political significance of appropriated narratives that is equally evident in the Canadian literary community, where the "Women's Press Debate began with whether white writers should be allowed to publish work in which they adopted the voices of persons of colour" (Begamudre 1989: 11–12). For Native writers and artists, this debate over censorship and access, autonomy and ghettoization, authority and authenticity reveals the boundaries of difference built in the power and privilege of appropriated knowledge and voice. As Rosemary Coombe (1996) expresses it:

Today, many Indian and First Nations peoples find that [North] Americans are far more aware of their presence through the stereotyped images
of them that circulate through sports team mascots, tomahawk chops, and
old cartoons (broadcast ever more frequently now that they are in the
public domain); the conditions of their lives, their poverty and their political struggles are obscured by mythic representations of them that are
owned by others. (217)

As we struggled to build urban Indian services in the 1970s and
1980s, I remember someone at the Native Friendship Centre in Montreal passing me a book written by W.P. Kinsella, a non-Native who has
published six collections of Indian stories about the Ermine-skin family
on the Hobbema reserve in Alberta. The books are a mixture of fact and
fiction drawn from his real experience as a taxi driver in Edmonton and
from his construction of Indian social imaginaries such as Frank Fence-
post, Silas One-wound, and Mad Etta. I remember being among a group
of Native people who travelled the pow wow circuit in the summers of
those years. We moved from the Elder's speeches and buffalo feasts in
the lush foothills of Morley, Alberta, through the dusty back roads, enjoy-
ing Grand Entries and Give-Aways to celebrate the Native struggle on
the Hobbema reserve, sharing Step Dances honouring Louis Riel, the
Northwest Rebellion, and the Métis survival at "Back to Batoche." And
I remember George Brown, Sr., one of the first tribal chairmen from my
own reservation of Lac du Flambeau, elected after the Indian Reorganization Act of 1934 removed the last vestiges of authority from Jim Grey,
our hereditary chief. George Brown seemed to hold that position for all
the years of my childhood. He was a dignified full-blood living out at the
Old Village who spoke in a ponderous voice, trying his best to manoeuvre us through the forced appropriation of foreign political process. No
one ever doubted that he was a real Indian. Yet W.P. Kinsella (1983)
writes of his namesake in Hobbema:

> The family name was originally Two-brown-bears, and both of Lester
> Brown's brothers still carry that name. For as long as I can remember,
> Lester and his family just called themselves the Browns. Then four or
> five years ago, Lester hired himself a lawyer and got his name, and his
> wife and kids' names, changed from Two-brown-bears to Brown. I
> remember seeing the change-of-name notice on the back page of the
> *Wetaskiwin Times* newspaper. "Why carry around a ten pound name
> when a two pound one will do?" Lester joked with everybody. But it be
> kind of a sad joke, and us real Indians look down our noses at the Browns,

take that name change as just another way Lester Brown have of turning himself into a white man. Lester is a friend of our chief, Tom Crow-eye, who, though he ain't changed his name yet, is whiter than most people born with pink skin. (45)

In the years since, Natives and Others have struggled over the stereotyping, appropriation, and the politics of primitivism expressed in Aislin's cartoon criminalizing the Indian as a "Mafia Warrior" (*Montreal Gazette*, 30 April 1990: B2); or Ven Begamudre's (1989: 12) question, Do we really need another rediscovery of Saskatchewan's Native peoples by a white photographer born in Britain?; or the shamanistic adaptation of New Age Indian philosophy with its White Warrior Society; or AIM leader Russell Means voicing the words of Chief Powatan in the Walt Disney film *Pocahontas*. This continuing dispute over ownership, authenticity, and identity is expressed in the spontaneous, pained, often vulgarized voices of Native North Americans asserting control over the instrumentality of indigenous cultural forms. Their struggle reveals that, if "cultural borrowing" sounds benign, "power and power over knowledge are inseparable" (Townsend-Gault 1998B: 43). The concerns of Native people focus on conflicting and floating representations basic to academic argument, political discourse, and commodity culture: public access and profit. Joane Cardinal-Shubert (1989: 20) writes from the Native perspective, "Money, that is what appropriating is all about. Whether the issue is land or art or iconography or ceremonial reliquae, the focus of the deprivation is money. Something to be gained by imitation, copying, stealing."

In the Oka crisis of Quebec's misnamed "Indian summer" of 1990, I remember images of barricades and bulldozers, gunshots in the woods and sudden death. I remember helmeted soldiers pitted against bandana-masked warriors, interceding women, crying children, and struggling reporters. In the silence of all the negotiators' calls for peaceful resolution, I remember two non-Natives from Oka who rushed to the patent office to copyright every marketable aspect of the crisis, over one hundred copyrights for games, toys, dolls, and bicycles, over four hundred names such as "Lasagna" and "Spudwrench," the nick-names of Mohawk warriors who became poster boys for the media and for some Natives themselves (CBC *News*, 19 October 1990). These two non-native men proposed to possess a current catalogue of ambiguous Indian images for profit—the tormentor and the sufferer, the villain and the victim—transformed in the current discourse of appropriated identity and power and used to sell the memories of Kanehsatake and Oka, Kahnawake and Montreal, the recollections of people represented as "whites" or "Indians" everywhere. But today, Indian memories and artifacts are not always for sale. For Native people, heritage is a basis for barter, and cultural knowledge and authority must be negotiated in the industries of museums and movies, academic enterprise or commercial exchange.

Reconstructions

Today, Russell Means (with Wolf 1995: 542) tells us, "if we are to survive as a people, our future must be our past." Native North Americans are asserting their right to take back the Indian images and artifacts that represent the academic past and that position Native artistic, economic, and political futures. Amid the Native voices that protest the production and consumption of appropriated artifacts and images, there is an audible echo of silence, of the secret, surrounding the meaning of Indian art and artifacts. As Charlotte Townsend-Gault (1998A: 37) suggests, the "politics of images today is wrapped in Indian assertions of the inaccessible, the untranslatable, the unknowable." In the borderzones that reclaim, transform, and create heritage, Native people are asserting their cultural ownership of art and artifacts in expressions of transmutable form, undeclared context, and concealed knowledge. This challenge to the power and privilege of outsiders who claim and name Native art and artifacts is unsettling to the institutions that display or sell representations of non-Native history and Indian heritage. The sense of recovered, unattainable, or mystical meaning that Indians transmit to museums and galleries, consumers and students, ethnographers and artists is expressed in the comments of artist Jimmie Durham (in Townsend-Gault 1998A: 37): "Asked about the meaning of a text in Cherokee, which many people would not know, he replies: 'And I don't want them to know.... What I want them to know is that they can't know that.'" In the context of the unknowable Indian, dialogue among artists and curators can be contradictory, distant, or illusive, like the voice of the cunning and mutable coyote of traditional trickster tales that Indians and Others invoke to represent Native creativity and cultural survival. These voices of Indian artists and writers that mystify traditional and artistic practices are joined by Natives who reject the notion of being named and placed, classified and ghettoized as "Indian."

In 1993, after America celebrated Columbus Day and Canada celebrated Dominion Day, I remember listening to Coco Fusco (1993) speaking in Montreal about her personal tribute to the treatment of Indian
cultures. She and a colleague presented a piece of performance art at
museums in the United States, Spain, and Australia. In each city, they
spent three days and nights in a cage dressed as "primitives" who understood neither English nor Spanish. They danced and sang and posed
for photographs for a fee, ate mush and left the cage on a leash. I remember her amazement at the number of spectators who failed to read her
satirical statement on the historicism of Indians as artifacts, her dismay
at the number of people who left the museums believing that she and her
colleague were "real" Indians on display.

In the borderzones where Native artists live, there is a tension
between those who express and exhibit their identity as Indians in the
work they write or paint or produce, and those who may draw upon
sensibilities or symbols of Indianness, but insist on being recognized as
artists or writers who happen to be Native. This debate over autonomy
and identity, categorization and ghettoization, traditional and contemporary culture is fuelled by the dominating discourse of Western art and
literature and sustained through the writing of cultural historians and
critics, who describe Native objects and art as expressions of tribalized
difference. Native writers and artists are absorbed in a discursive struggle over dichotomies that separate, oppose, and circumscribe. Opening
the closures of constricted identity and prescribed practice that this
struggle engages is like unsealing a series of Chinese boxes, each box
opening to reveal another box. As Loretta Todd (in R. Hill 1994: 81)
writes, "When we articulate the dichotomy of the traditional versus the
contemporary, we are referencing the centre, acknowledging the authority of the ethnographer, the anthropologist, the art historian, the cultural critic, the art collector.... And we set up an opposition within our
communities that keeps us in our position as 'other.'" Today, a growing
number of Native artists are disrupting these oppositions in the borderzones of creative and innovative work. Along with the writing of Native
academics and cultural critics, this move to "reclaim the term 'Indian
artist' and use it with pride" (R. Hill 1992: 22), challenges and confuses
old stereotypes through re-presentations of Indianness and traditionalism. The Native movement to reclaim and rename Indian art and objects
has contributed to rethinking the purpose and purview of Indian exhibits
in museums.

The borders between Natives and academics weave though complex issues that double back upon each other in the battlegrounds of museums, where history and heritage are preserved and displayed in exhibits that can educate and inspire, but can also build unities of culture that fortify the politics of difference. The construction of difference through exhibits is widely recognized in contemporary practice, and there is a discernible shift in the authority, autonomy, and approach of both curators and museums. The Native challenge to cultural and processional distances that position exhibits of art and artifacts has been joined by anthropologists themselves. Allied efforts to reassert control and reinsert process have begun to pierce the webs of institutional policies and politics that pronounce upon the heritage of Indians, producing new configurations of historical preservation and ownership, contemporary display and meaning. Museums are moving from the display of decontextualized Indian artifacts to the new contexts of community involvement in public and tribal museums; and Native people are involved in the collection, display, and control of artifacts, including the repatriation of skeletal remains and Indian objects. At the same time, contemporary Native art that seems to float beyond categories is creating and claiming new meanings of Indianness that express Native identity and community. In exhibits that question and confuse, Native North Americans assert that "when we assert our own meanings and philosophies of representation, we render the divisions irrelevant, and maintain our aboriginal right to name ourselves" (Todd in R. Hill 1994: 81).

In 1999, the Glenbow Museum in Calgary exhibited a collection of Native art and artifacts that stands in remarkable contrast to "The Spirit Sings." Stereotypical advertisements and other images of Indians in popular culture were juxtaposed with contemporary artwork produced by Native people themselves. In this exhibit, Indian warriors and princesses who have sold countless motorcycles and apples, corn oil and cars named "Pontiac," were intermingled with images of Native people and expressions of Indianness that invert these familiar icons and subvert their cultural meaning in history and heritage. At the McCord Museum in Montreal, a 1999 exhibit of "Iroquois Beadwork" expressed centuries of heritage—traditional, transformed, and modern—displayed in association with the cultural centres of Mohawk and other Iroquois territories. In the politics of the times of the early twenty-first century, the Glenbow Museum returned 251 sacred objects of the Blackfoot, Blood, and Peigan Nations, and Canada's national museum, the Museum of

Civilization, feasted grave goods and skeletal remains placed in hand-hewn burial boxes and returned to the First Nations of the Pacific Northwest.

In the aftermath of the confrontations at Alcatraz and Wounded Knee, Oka and Ipperwash, Gustafson Lake, Anisinabe Park, and Burnt Church, the memories of Natives and non-Natives that are expressed in personal and communal recollections—ethnographic, artistic, literary, and political—take on new significance. As Loretta Todd (in R. Hill 1994: 81) says, "We are caught in the grasp of neocolonialism, in the gaze of the connoisseur or consumer, forever trapped in a process that divides and conquers." Today, we stand apart, absorbed in a struggle over narratives about Native people—who were not discovered or rescued or redeemed but imagined—in the progression of history and anthropology, literature and museums, art and popular culture. We stand unequal, living increasingly hostile and distrustful social realities in which sovereignty and self-determination are ever more urgent in the lived realities of Native North Americans, ever more present in the current strategies of Native empowerment. But in the inevitable confusion of court cases, treaty tables, protests, and popular culture, the current conflict over art and artifacts has made us all more aware of expressions and practices that name and juxtapose, repress and mystify. In the end, we are all rooted together in the ambiguous postcards of our pasts, in the construction and appropriation of the contradictory Indian social imaginaries and national histories that make Native sovereignty and self-determination so important to understand, so impossible to discuss, and so difficult to achieve.

≪ • ≫

Indian Country:
Claiming Land in Native America

The feathered and blanketed figure of the American
Indian has come to symbolize the American continent.
He is the man who through centuries has been moulded
and sculpted by the same hand that shaped the mountains,
forests, and plains, and marked the course of the rivers.

Luther Standing Bear, 1933
(in Hamilton 1972)

S hawnee tradition proclaims, "No white man knows or ever will know, where we took the body of our beloved Tecumseh and buried him. Tecumseh will come again!" (Eckert 1992: 794). His bones may be buried beneath a simple monument on Walpole Island, Ontario, or his remains might have been washed away by the flood waters of a small creek farther north, near Moraviantown (Eckert 1992). There are rumours, but no records or documents that tell us where he returned to the earth. Native North Americans may not remember the date of 5 October 1813, when Tecumseh removed his British military coat, dressed in buckskin, and faced his predicted death in the Battle of the Thames during the War of 1812. But in the years since, Tecumseh's name has become a battle cry for "Post-Indian Warriors of Survivance" (Vizenor 1994), who recognize that the indisputable markers of Tecumseh's grave are with us all. The inevitability of colonial expansion may begin with Lewis and Clark's expedition to the Pacific Ocean between 1804 and 1806. But in Indian Country, 1813 marks the beginning of western frontierism and the end of Indian independence.

What is known about Tecumseh's experience is a blend of history and heritage drawn from the words and records of Others. Ensnared in the social imaginaries of popular culture, Tecumseh is imagined as an Indian "Paul Revere," rushing through the woods to incite Native tribes against American expansion. As the leader of a "conspiracy," he is cast as an American enemy in the War of 1812, when Americans and British fought over Indian land. For Others, he has become a tragic hero, intriguing in his misguided commitment to a political illusion and the mystical messages of his brother, "The Prophet." But for Native North Americans, Tecumseh represents the pain of the past and the possibility of the future.

The acquisition of Indian lands through the coercion of settlement, conflict, disease, and the politics of treaties began before the nineteenth century. In the years between 1784 and 1871, Indian nations were compelled to relinquish two billion acres of tribal land through 720 different treaties and land cessions (Hazen-Hammond 1997: 89). But in 1800, when Tecumseh began organizing a widespread alliance of Native nations, he knew—and Americans knew—that 80 percent of the land in what became the lower forty-eight states belonged to Native Americans (Hazen-Hammond 1997: 94). Tecumseh's experience is lost to us, but we can piece together parts of his past from the notes and journals, letters and reports of those who encountered him. In the documented fiction of Allan Eckert's (1992) book, *A Sorrow in Our Heart: The Life of Tecumseh*, we recall and reclaim the trails he took, the battles he fought, the negotiations he had, and some of the words he spoke. Natives and historians agree that Tecumseh was a gifted military strategist, a charismatic speaker, and a visionary leader; but they disagree over the efficacy of his vision of a confederacy of Native nations and an independent region of Indian territory. His fight against the American encroachment on Indian land eventually allied him to the British, who betrayed him. In the context of the War of 1812, the alliance between the Indians and the British, which Tecumseh forged and led, played a critical role in affirming the political and geographic borders of Canada and the United States. But during this armed conflict, too, his death signalled the victory of Manifest Destiny and the loss of all hope for Native autonomy—political, economic, and cultural. When the war ended in 1814, settlers streamed into Indian territory. Native people were displaced, herded onto reservations and largely forgotten by those who opened the West to non-Native settlement. Only Indians and outsiders who recalled or recorded the past remembered that this was Indian land.

In 1832, the novelist Washington Irving travelled on horseback to the western frontier. Like the photographers, painters, and anthropologists who followed, he went west to discover and write about "those great Indian tribes which are now about to disappear as independent nations" (Wheeler 1976: 7). In the ensuing years, Irving was joined by Edward Curtis, Horace Greeley, and Franz Boas in the rush to document "disappearing" Indians. None of the many men and women who recorded, reported, and chronicled Indian life in the nineteenth century ever met Tecumseh. But as a Native North American whose interest in land and pan-Indianism drew him beyond the social structures of his tribe to the hybrid cultural experience of his political position, Tecumseh would not have interested early anthropologists.

Indians and Inuit have been at the heart of the anthropological project in North America. The academic work that began with Franz Boas's research on *The Central Eskimo* published in 1888 forged a corpus of empirical research and writing on the patterned thoughts and behaviour of tribal peoples, Indians, and Inuit frozen in the isolation of history and territory, passive or predictable in response to the intrusion of Western culture. The methodological constraints of early ethnography are reflected in Edward Curtis's forty volumes of photographs of Indians posed in tribal regalia against pristine landscapes in the early 1900s, about which Rayna Green (1992: 47) writes, "Just give me one [photograph] in overalls and a cowboy hat. Then we can get serious about what was happening to these people." Like the project that produced "Curtis Indians," studying Native people emerged in an academic context that supported the isolated analyses of tribal world view and land use; social structure, kinship systems, and acculturation patterns; language, lifestyle, and the aftermath of empire.

In the past decade, the post-structuralist wedge that has opened the seams of anthropology has led to a persistent debate over ethnographic practice; and the debate over research, writing, and representation has spread far beyond ethnography. Artists, writers, curators, historians—and Native North Americans themselves—have rediscovered Indians in the politics of interpretation. Today, there is new interest in the range of cultural texts related to Native North Americans, and a new focus on Indians as historical and cultural markers, as appropriated images in the discourse of both cultural industry and commercial enterprise. In recent writing, Indians represent pivotal points of struggle, often over land that is romanticized as landscape for the commodification of culture; or reduced to background for confrontations over land rights; or viewed as location for cultural analysis of Indian lifeworlds in writing about and by Native North Americans in relation to cultural identity and the politics of difference. But land is rarely understood as a discursive place of Indian experience—lived, remembered, and imagined—and an enduring site of Native political possibility.

The full reach of writing on Native North American cultures is now loosely labelled Native studies, an academic and popular umbrella for work in which the object of inquiry is Aboriginal people: Indians, Métis, or Inuit. Native studies reflects the shared desire of the academy and the polity—including Native people—to define the boundaries of difference in being Indian. Native studies is a topic, not a methodological approach; and, although it draws heavily on its anthropological and historical roots, writing about Indians incorporates all the disciplinary boundaries of the fields which are absorbed within it. More recent work reflects a blurring of the disciplinary lines between academic fields, the result in part of writing in cultural studies.

Reconceptualizing culture as everyday action, discourses, and events, cultural studies has unsettled the static analysis of bordered tribes to reveal the experience of individual Indians who live the unity and difference of collectively constructed cultures. In writing that situates historical essentialism and credits the complex, conflicted, and overdetermined nature of discourses, cultural studies can unravel the ambiguous play of power and identity that emerges in Native popular culture. The narratives that Native people enact and act upon today are a kaleidoscopic mixture of intertwined experiences, representations, signifiers, and borders. Native North American cultural struggle is embedded in historical and current relations of power, of domination and subordination including interactions with spiritual power and conflict over the ownership and meaning of land. But even today, in the cultural resurgence of Indianness that North America is experiencing, land and Indians are yoked together in the academic notions and popular narratives that circulate in the discursive images of Native and other North Americans.

Images of Indians and land remain a barometer of the measures of difference attributed to Indians and expressed by Native people themselves. At the same time, Indians are recognized across North America as an ambiguous public marker, in part because Native people have played a small but significant role in contemporary political struggles.

The Native movement that began in the 1960s and 1970s with the occupation of Alcatraz and the standoff at Wounded Knee, propelled an era of Native struggle across the continent. The last decade of the twentieth century began with Canada's so-called "Oka crisis," in which Mohawk "warriors," protesting the expansion of a golf course bordering their ancient cemetery, confronted the Quebec police and the Canadian army. This conflict, grounded in land claims that have never been settled, was reminiscent of the 1970s in Canada, when Cree protested the building of dams in untreatied territory in Northern Quebec; and the 1980s, when spear-fishing Chippewa and angry protesters faced each other on the boat landings of Wisconsin over treaty rights enacted in the practice of Spring spearing; and 2000, when salmon wars continued in the West and conflicts over lobster emerged in the East. Struggles between Natives and newcomers continue to erupt across the continent, over casinos and smuggling, trees and taxes, dams and water and mining, historical representations and literary or artistic appropriations, sovereignty and self-determination. The continuing contests that thread through the meaning of constructed representations and enacted ideologies of Native and other North Americans involve underlying images and issues of land in the United States and Canada: continental terrain—explored, settled, mapped, treatied, reserved, privatized, developed, idealized, contested, and imagined. Roger Moody (1988, 1: 355) writes about the centrality of land in the discord between the Indian and the Other: "Underscoring virtually every contemporary struggle by indigenous peoples—be it against specific damage, or for cultural and political self-determination—is the demand for land rights." The Native demand to recognize rights to the land is a legitimate move to rectify the wrongs of the past; but to Native people, land claims have always represented more than territorial expansion and access to resources. In the words of Sitting Bull (McMaster and Trafzer 2004: 192), spoken in 1882, "This land belongs to us, for the Great Spirit gave it to us when he put us here. We were free to come and go and to live in our own way. But white men, who belong to another land, have come upon us, and are forcing us to live according to their ideas."

The political combat over land is wrapped in a complex of oppositional discourses, contradictory representations and different cultural constructions. As Barri Cohen (1994: 33) suggests in writing about the Cree contest over the expansion of hydroelectric projects in Northern Quebec, the interwoven discourses that reveal Native and non-Native relationships to the land are both fundamental and complicated: "It is a struggle that has unraveled a complex braid of conflict between radically different knowledge systems and representations about the land and territory, progress and survivability, rights and justice—the latter two couplets hitched to differing commitments of nationhood and its attendant cultural and political desires." But the land over which Natives and newcomers struggle is also constructed in what Gerald Vizenor (1994) calls narratives of dominance and survivance, in historical and current accounts of the Indian adopted by Native and other North Americans. These narratives express a continuing dispute over the meaning of land in Native and North America—land linked to contingent history and identity, absorbed in the discourse of spirituality and territory, worked in the power of politics and privilege.

The meaning of land emerges in the historical specificity and cultural practice of Native North American lifeworlds. It is enacted and acted upon every time Native people hunt or fish, plant gardens, visit the graves of ancestors, offer tobacco to spirit rocks, or acknowledge the interrelatedness of these experiences of everyday life. But the meaning of land is also expressed in the stories people tell about heritage and ceremony, people and places, travel, conflict and loss. Not only the ownership of land but also the meaning of land was erased and devalued in the policies that emerged to exterminate or acculturate Indians, about whom Francis Parkman (1908, 2: 101) wrote, "Their intractable, unchanging character leaves no alternative than their gradual extinction, or the abandonment of the western world to eternal barbarism." In the collective heritage of struggle and settlement—of reservations, resource exploitation, and land allotments—the meaning of land that emerges in the lived experience of current practice of Native people is interwoven with images of painful displacement, forced acculturation, and enduring indigence. Land is pivotal in the contemporary culture of Native America; and today, its meaning is negotiated in the discursive construction of contingent history, emerging heritage, and current practice in the stories Native people tell that express empowerment linked in articulation to Native traditional practice and political struggle with non-Natives and with one another. These narratives that deterritorialize place and community, and politicize land and spirituality, are part of the prismal answer to James Clifford's (1988: 275) questions: "What does it mean, at the end of the twentieth century, to speak ... of a "native land"? What processes rather than essences are involved in present experiences of cultural identity?"

Empty Land and Nomadic Indians

The relationship between the "empty land" metaphor and the colonization of "primitive" Indians is well-worked theoretical territory in cultural studies; but this relationship is important to recall because it frames the discourse of Native experience and structures the critique of colonial culture. As Barri Cohen (1994: 48) writes about Northern Quebec, "The territory is a place of Cree and Inuit habitation, history, myth and technology, while for southern power it is 'barren land' and 'wilderness,' passively awaiting further conquest." For Native people, the divergent conceptions that frame the struggle over land have even more ominous implications.

European and North American practice is predicated on the construction of land as a material object which de Certeau (1986: 73) tells us, like the place of Montaigne's Cannibals, "is emptied—it becomes vacant and distant." The texts of the early explorers and anthropologists construct representations as a vehicle for the interests of the dominant culture. In the North American context, Cabot, Frobisher, and Columbus encountered Aboriginal people with whom they interacted and traded, and about whom they and others wrote. As early as 1501, Gaspar Corte Real kidnapped fifty-seven Beotuk Indians for the slave trade in Portugal (Morison 1971: 215), a practice which occurred for a variety of motives throughout the exploration period. The texts that spiralled from encounters with Indians created the basis for the sixteenth-century debate over whether Aboriginal people were mentioned in the Bible, whether they had a soul or a spirit, and whether in their pagan and primitive state they could be considered human beings. The discursive ambiguity of Indians as extensions of the natural or creations of the savage continued to plague Native people long after the Spanish theologian Francisco de Victoria in 1532 and Pope Paul III in 1537 acknowledged that "the Indians are truly men" (Cumming and Mickenburg 1972: 14). The moral argument regarding their treatment continues today.

Joined together, these early texts construct the ambiguous social imaginary of the nomadic Indian in narratives of dominance in which "simulation threatens the difference between 'true' and 'false,' between 'real and 'imaginary'" (Vizenor 1994: 13). The barbarian of an imagined empty land emerges in Abbe Raynal's armchair-travel description of the Inuit cited in Chappell's 1817 journal of his voyage to Hudson Bay:

> Few in number, and scarce any of its individuals above four feet high. Their hands bear the same enormous proportion to their bodies as those of children: the smallness of their feet makes them awkward and tottering in their gait: small hands and and a round mouth, which in Europe are reckoned a beauty, seem almost a deformity in these people ... their men have neither hair nor beard, have the appearance of being old, even in their youth: this is partly occasioned by the formation of their lower lip, which is thick, fleshy and protruding beyond the upper. ([1817] 1970: 83)

In contrast to the people who inhabited the territory, the land itself was represented in early texts as romanticized images of Indians engraved on the cultural landscape of the Americas. While the Spanish were debating the undeclared humanity of Indians, the rugged and wild beauty of the new territory was symbolized by pairs of Indian men and women, Caribbean or Brazilian Natives framed in the exoticism of flora and fauna. By 1575, the bare-breasted Amazonian Indian queen took on the image of the New World. Draped in feathers and furs, carrying arrows and spears, this contradictory figure incorporating the warrior woman and the mother goddess was drawn from European roots to portray the primitive challenge of America: "exotic, powerful, dangerous and beautiful" (Green 1976: 702). When the colonies began to move toward independence, the mother-queen figure of the 1600s was transformed into the more independent princess image of the 1700s. The statue-like figure of liberty in flowing robes was younger and overtly Caucasian; but armed with a spear and a peace pipe or a flag, she was equally ambiguous. This ambiguity incorporating the Native and the noble—which Rayna Green (1976) calls the "Pocahontas Perplex"—circulates with what Berkhofer (1978: 121) calls the "anti-Pocahontas," the drudge or beast-of-burden that accompanies the princess in portrayals of Native women. Images of the princess and the squaw accommodate the colonial experience, the Western expansion of settlement, and—along with the Plains warrior—the development of the land over which Natives and newcomers continue to struggle. Today, Natives and other North Americans are rooted together in the discourse that constructs the land as the mother-queen and the princesses with spears and arrows, and the romanticized Indian representation of Mother Earth, "a misogynous metaphor traced to the long colonial gaze of Christopher Columbus" (Vizenor 1994: 120).

Like Said's (1978: 12) *Orientalism*, the configurations of power represented in these contradictory discourses distribute and elaborate "a whole series of 'interests' which, by such means as scholarly discovery, philological reconstruction, psychological analysis, landscape and sociological description" both create and maintain "a certain *will* or *intention* to understand, in some cases to control, manipulate, even to incorporate, what is a manifestly different (or alternative and novel) world" (italics in original). The discourses that claimed, named, and deeded the land, constructed Native North Americans as nameless, nomadic vagrants who flowed in and out of continental histories. As early as the fifteenth century, John Cabot gave an island in Beotuk territory to a friend and another to his barber (Raimondi 1497 cited in Stefansson 1947: 153). Cabot's actions were legitimized in two judicial opinions written by Chief Justice Marshall in 1823 and 1832, which established both the territorial authority of European nations and colonial land policy in North America by legislating European title acquired by respective discoverers; limiting applications of sovereignty to Native people; and ratifying land surrender by any possible means (Cumming and Mickenburg 1972: 17–18).

These colonial texts, which help empty the land, justify its occupation, and underwrite policies to exterminate or acculturate Indians, also produce the bounty of ethnographic research on Indian cultures, research upon which Native North Americans themselves draw in reconstructing their heritage, history, and culture. But there is an ironic—and strategically important—invisibility related to the lived experience of Indians. As Paul Chaat Smith (1994) writes:

> When we think of the old days, like it or not, we conjure up images that have little to do with real history. We never think of the great city of Tenochtitlan, the capital of the Aztec Empire, five centuries ago bigger than London. We never imagine sullen teenagers in that fabled Aztec metropolis, in some pre-Columbian Zona Rosa dive, badmouthing the wretched war economy and the ridiculous human sacrifices that drove their empire. We don't think of the settled Indian farming towns in North America (far more typical than nomads roaming the Plains)....Yet the amazing variety of human civilization that existed five centuries ago has been replaced in the popular imagination by one image above all: the Plains Indians of the mid-19th century. (38)

The lived experience of Indians has been less important than their presence "as symbolic referents in a discourse about European civilization's virtues and vices, triumphs and failures" (Johnston 1987: 50). This "encoded Indian," imagined by other North Americans, is an enduring representation in the discourse of dominance that collapses Indianness and land. As Philip Deloria (1993: 396) writes, "Symbolic understandings of Indians, whether as savage, noble, vanishing or child-of-nature could not help but effect the development of official Indian policy." But, as he suggests, images of Indians were absorbed in policies of removal, acculturation and land allotment, intended to "dissolve [Indians] into the rest of the population ... and the "Indian problem" would be solved (397). Today, Native people assert rights to land, treaty benefits, and resources appropriated by Others. And in the discourse of struggle, Native experience, endowment, and empowerment related to land emerge in new narratives that recall and reconstruct old traditions as "postindian warriors ensnare the contrivances with their own simulations of survival" (Vizenor 1994: 11).

Approaching Land

The Indian has long been objectified by Others in North America, newcomers who were motivated to colonize the land or to study the nations who owned it. From ethnographic and colonial approaches, the land is part of what Indians and Others are struggling over, whether the arena is territorial expansion, competition for material resources, or New Age ecology. But the physical environment is more significant and dynamic in the discourses of Native North Americans than this struggle over land suggests. Native expressions and practices involve not only space but also time, both of which are fundamental to the spiritual and political construction of Native culture.

In recent writing in cultural studies, geography, and Native studies (Keith and Pile 1993; Boyarin 1994; V. Deloria 1994), there is new interest in the relationship between time and space and the meaning of discourses that temporalize or spatialize. This work recognizes that space is not "dead," barren, or empty, but that it is embodied in relationships that are interwoven with time in collective memory, a perspective that Indians have long understood. Native people know, too, that the articulations linking land and spirituality that they experience and express have been beyond the boundaries of academic analysis. Neither Rosaldo's (1989: 103) "processual" perspective, which emphasizes change more than structure, time more than space in the interaction of everyday life, nor Jameson's (in Keith and Pile 1993: 5) template of "cognitive mapping," which places emphasis on spatial relations, can tell us much about Native conceptions, experiences, or expressions of land. But in the writing of Vine Deloria, Jr. (1994), the Native understanding of space emerges as a dominant construct that not only locates time but also builds Native spirituality, ideology and community in relation to land.

For Vine Deloria, Jr. both tribal cultures and the Native understanding of collective relations are situated in space rather than time. Indian history, religion, and ideology emerge in interaction with a particular land and its life forms, in a lived reality of space that is difficult to discern in non-Native analysis. In Deloria's critique, the reality of place that Indians experience and express in spirituality is almost invisible in Christianity, which expresses religious tenets that are time-centred. This focus on time means that Christian beliefs are directed toward conceptions of history drawn in temporal patterns that occur in cycles or sequences that have beginnings and ends. He argues that "if time becomes our primary consideration ... we never seem to arrive at the reality of our existence in places, but are always directed to experiential interpretations rather than the experiences themselves" (V. Deloria, Jr. in Warrior 1995: 72). For Deloria, the experiential interpretations of Christianity's time-centred perspective attribute Indian religious myths and stories to human imagination, pure or poetic. However, he tells us that it is not the human imagination, but the "experiences themselves" that are the sources of the religious narratives that express tribal spirituality. A Native community's observation or experience of place, land, and environment, gives rise to the Indian spiritual myths and stories that construct the tribal sense of the past; and these narratives move through time in collective memory and oral tradition, building a sense of community that is place-centred. In Vine Deloria Jr.'s (1994: 72) words, "*Something* is observed or experienced by a community, and the symbols and sequences of the mythology are given together in an event that appears so much out of the ordinary experiential sequence as to impress itself upon the collective memories of the community for a sufficiently long duration of time" (italics in original).

This experience or observation of "something" is linked in articulation to the traditional Native understanding of power—both natural and social—as an endowment that is mediated by spirits and represented in the actions that result from this mediation. In this expression of indigenous knowledge, human beings are themselves powerless individuals and collectivities, whose control over their lives comes from interactions with empowered spirits, from a negotiation with non-human and other-than-human forces of nature. The hierarchies of spiritual relations that sustain and empower Indians are located in the range of living beings that are embodied in the natural world, in the environmental, animal, other-than-human persons, which like the land itself, specify the significance of place and extend the presence of time.

But today, when Native North Americans map community onto territory through spatial relations of power, time intermingles with space in expressions that are endowed with an ideological and affective "something more." The "something more" that emerges in narratives of history, heritage, and spiritual experience broadens the ideology and amplifies a sense of cultural continuity among Native North Americans. This sense of cultural continuity, drawn from narratives that endow space and collapse time, is linked to political agency that is conjoined with the land. Ward Churchill (1992) writes:

> Land, as Red Cloud, Hugo Blanco and myriad others have noted, is the absolutely essential issue defining viable conceptions of Native America, whether in the past, present or future. A deeply held sense of unity with particular geographical contexts has provided, and continues to afford, the spiritual cement allowing cultural cohesion across the entire spectrum of indigenous American societies. (131)

Today, the Native "sense of unity" about which Ward Churchill speaks is an expression of collectivity that extends beyond place-centred community to the oneness of pan-Indianism. As new formations of Native community emerge in the urban, academic, professional, and social arenas of Indian Country, Native culture and identity are reconstructed in narratives of past places and practices, transformed and experienced today in pan-Indian rituals and rhetoric. These are not the nostalgic expressions of cultural tourists or the poignant pleas of homeless migrants who are displaced or removed from their cultural or territorial roots. These are the voices of Native North Americans who recognize home in the emergent, reterritorialized constructions of Indian Country. In this reterritorialized reality, the power of place intermingles with time, moving from the experience of local reservations to representational sites, like the Black Hills, Wounded Knee, and Madeleine

Island, or Alcatraz and Oka, or North America itself, known to Native people as "Turtle Island." These representations of sacrifice and spirituality spread and spiral in cultural narratives voiced about and by Native North Americans. The stories that are remembered and retold fill the "significant absences and silences" that emerge in "the anthropologist's will to explain" (Bredin 1993: 304), and the stories that Natives tell that express the will not to explain.

In transforming narratives, representations of oneness move from spiritual and communal experience that is local and place-centred, to experience that transcends personal, cultural and national borders. These stories that reclaim people and place, reconfigure land as territory, terrain that represents not only shared spiritual experience but also common colonial experience. In the words of Paul Chaat Smith (1994: 38), "What makes us one people is the common legacy of colonialism and diaspora. Central to that history is our necessary, political, and in this century, often quite hazardous attempt to reclaim and understand our past—the real one, not the invented one." Jonathan Boyarin (1994: 9) puts it another way: "The emancipatory claims of colonized people were also grounded in narratives of territorial priority ... those whose collective consciousness was articulated in the context of a struggle against European imperialism adopted the notion that collective identity, and hence both loyalty and legitimate deployment of power, was determined by spatial relations." But the nature of these spatial relations, braided with spirituality and heritage and linked in articulation to the land in narratives about and by Native North Americans, is elusive and confusing. Gerald Vizenor (1994: 52) writes, "The literature of dominance, narratives of discoveries, translations, cultural studies, and prescribed names of time, place and person are treacherous in any discourse on tribal consciousness."

The questions of meaning that emerge in discussions of land engage the conceptual borders of both Native studies and cultural studies. Jody Berland and Jennifer Daryl Slack (1994: 2) write about the theoretical challenge of environmental issues, asking How can we understand something as discursive and non-discursive at the same time? nature and not nature? culture and not culture? This perception of the meaning of the land as environmental and difficult to access is joined by Native perceptions of land as spiritual and, therefore, difficult to express. Like the absent background traversed with lines and circles that represent the life force connecting spiritual power and persons in Ojibway artist

Norval Morriseau's modern traditional paintings, or the ancient Indian rock paintings from which he draws inspiration, the land and the environment are represented as spiritualized open space—not empty but unrepresentable—in the emerging discourse of Native North Americans. These images of land as first invisible and now seemingly inaccessible, or inexpressible, reflect points of communality among the representations of commercial and academic enterprise and some Native North Americans themselves. Their different, but equally forceful, investments in land as discursively empty, as silent, support the romanticized narratives that weave through sentimentalized photography, historicized ethnography, appropriations of New Age spirituality, and statements of prophetic Indian traditionalism.

Silence—reflected in the popular and the prophetic words that fill it—rebounds from the discomfort that most academics feel in analyzing the "spiritual cement" that joins Native North Americans to the land and to one another, and the comfort with which Native "warriors of survivance" (Vizenor 1994) mystify the experience of the land in discursive constructions of identity, community, and spirituality. The silent, empty space shared by Natives and non-Natives produces books like T.C. McLuhan's *Touch the Earth* (1972) and *The Way of the Earth* (1994), which add to the accumulation of romanticized Indian words interspersed with static portraits of the landscape and historicized images of Indians. These representations of what Paul Chaat Smith (1995) calls "the coffee-table tribe," conflate land and Indians in new romanticized narratives that dominate the discourse of some Native people themselves. Narratives of historicized, romanticized Indians are a double-edged sword for Native people, encouraging other North Americans to appropriate Indian cultural practice and adapt the meaning of the land that situates Native spiritual and political ideology. But in words that recall, proclaim, and envision, the Indian warriors of survivance both express traditional spiritual experience and generate political possibility. The narratives of the new warriors of words open a space for the discourse of Native empowerment, ideological opposition, and political resistance: for rights to land and resources and the future these rights represent. In stories that are remembered, reconstructed, or experienced, Indians negotiate the meaning of land and territory.

Indian Territory and Sacred Places

Across Native America today, writing about the land reflects the different experiences and practices that are distinctive to Native individuals and communities, even to nations. But these differences are absorbed in an appeal to common experience related to two distinct but intertwined cultural conceptions of the earth. Positioning themselves in the fluidity of space and time, bounded only by stories of creation or migration, Native people tell stories that speak of land as a specific cultural construct articulated to the physical environment, an expanse of territory in which the collective identity and practice of a respective nation or community is rooted. But Native stories also speak of "the land" as a generalized cultural construction linked in articulation to physical landscape, a site as broad as the earth and the sky and as particular as a sacred place upon the earth, that blends into the environment and locates the ideology, identity, and practice of personal spirituality and collective memory.

The meanings of these constructs of territorial and spiritual place are woven together in living traditionalism: the practice of everyday life experienced collectively and individually as heritage, a multivocal past re-enacted daily in the ambiguous play of power and identity. In the language of reconstructed traditionalism, land is both territory and sacred site. These two views of the environment are merged in the discourse and meaning of Indian Country, which is recognized by Indians as a place that gathers Native North Americans together, wherever—on any reservation, at any pow wow or Native conference, in any Indian bar or Native Centre, at any Native ceremony, feast, or communal event. Indian Country signifies both a shared sense of cultural and historical experience and a consciousness of what in Ojibway is called *pimatiziwin*, or "living in a good way"—in physical, social, and spiritual health and harmony; a mixture of meanings that is intertwined with land. In Indian Country, the struggle over land is not only experienced, it is told and retold in the stories of dominance and survival that reconstruct, imagine and, most of all, assert Indian spirituality and empowerment in the memoried past and the politicized future.

Indian Territory

Indian land is a site of enacted meanings that fold in upon one another in the process of being conjoined to cultural nationalism and political agency, and this perception is commonly assumed in the literature of anthropology, Native studies, and even cultural studies. The notion that land is merely territory emerges from the dominant society's belief in "the social fiction that lines on a map and signatures on a deed legitimately divide the earth" (Limerick 1987: 56). This ideological stance represents Native and non-Native struggle over land as conflict over property. Patricia Nelson Limerick (1987: 56) writes, "Of all the persistent qualities in American history, the values attached to property retain the most power." In other words, "The presumption that space is autonomous has enabled the power of typography to conceal successfully the typography of power" (Gupta and Ferguson 1992: 8).

In the long history of popular literature written about Indians, land is understood as material rather than cultural. This representation asserts that tribal peoples have no concept of private property. Joined with the image of the nomadic Indian, Native land is owned by no one and available to everyone. This conception of shared and, therefore, unowned property is reflected in historical treaty negotiations, land allotments, and colonial settlement, and is contested in current Native land claims. Interlaced with the functional relationship to animals on the land, this perception is also a central organizing principle in research on Native social and economic life and the environment.

Research on land and Native people emerged within two distinct trajectories: popular environmentalism and cultural ecology (White 1984: 179). Environmentalist writing is rooted in the early image of the noble savage, the Indian who, as an extension of nature, demonstrates a fundamental "oneness" with the land. In later writing, this essentialist discourse transforms the noble savage into the conservationist, the nostalgic Indian who is capable of living on the earth without disturbing it, without marking the land with destructive human traces. Luther Standing Bear (in Hamilton 1972) speaks in images of nature that seem to ignore the conflicts of culture:

> The American Indian is of the soil, whether it be the region of forests, plains, pueblos, or mesas. He fits into the landscape, for the hand that fashioned the continent also fashioned the man for his surroundings.

He once grew as wild as naturally as the wild sunflowers; he belongs just as the buffalo belonged. (1)

The inherent connection between Indians and the land that circulates in the teachings of Native North Americans is expressed in the Ojibway maxim "All My Relations," an acknowledgment of the connection between humans and all other beings in the environment—animals, rocks, trees, waters. In Stephen Augustine's (2004) words about Mi'kmaq tradition, "All our ancestors—birds, animals, people—have gone back to Mother Earth, and we are all connected though our feet, through the land, to our ancestors." This relationship between Indians and the environment was ignored by early cultural ecologists, who researched the social organization and economic activity of Indians in relation to various products like buffalo, caribou, or corn. Their functional approach focused on the organization and techniques of productivity that Indians developed in hunting and agricultural societies. As early as 1915, Speck (1972) observed that northeastern Algonkian hunting territories represent a system of land ownership; but he focused on the social structure and function of Cree economic enterprise in which, he argued, land was a form of private property through hereditary family tenure. The reconstruction of hereditary hunting territories as land ownership is supported by Adrian Tanner (1987) who, along with Harvey Feit (1973), recognizes the extent to which culture—including spiritual beliefs—mediates social organization. But cultural ecology is drawn from a Marxist analysis that centres on material production as the driving force behind human activities. "The environment itself is viewed as an external entity—a storehouse of raw materials for the ongoing production of material goods" (Nofz 1987: 227). Tanner (1987: 71) describes hunting territory as a "unit of management" in which emphasis is placed "on animals rather than on land, and thus suppresses the question of the clear definition of boundaries." This concern with materialism and boundaries, which is central to anthropological conceptions of culture, has been challenged in the recent work of anthropologists themselves; but in relation to Native people, the theoretical shifts articulated by Clifford (1986), Rosaldo (1989), Geertz (1983), and others have not been widely adopted, and "basic ethnographic research concerning Native American concepts of sacred geography is sparse" (Walker 1996: 1).

In the current era of struggle over Native land claims and land rights, research has focused on land use and occupancy studies, on how Native people use the land. Researchers apply empirical analysis to map the typography of Native North American territory, marking the historical and current placements of Native communities and camps, and their relationship to economic activity. Native land claims have led to ethnographic research that appropriates the demographic methods of geography, which privilege counting—people and fish and beaver and bear—in accessing and defining the meaning of cultural practice. Those who write on Native relationships to the land from a more interpretative ethnographic approach, like Hugh Brody (1981) and Robin Ridington (1992), tend to retreat to the traditional practice, material production, and discourse of tribal people. Both of these insightful books on the meaning of the land focus on indigenous knowledge related to the productivity of the land among the remote Beaver Indians of northern British Columbia.

This disjuncture between academic writing that is based on empirical analysis and historicized culture and Native understanding that is grounded in indigenous knowledge drawn from the affective or spiritual experience of Native material reality is less evident among anthropologists who work from an ethnomethodological, symbolic, or cognitive approach. But until recently, their research has focused on how isolated cultures or individual members of a bordered culture create meaning from the range of experience that defines their reality. In this context, Native conceptions of territory or spirituality are understood as a complex of culturally specific beliefs, rituals, and activities, some of which are expressed or enacted in association with the land. This concentration on decoding the meanings that "real" Indians embody in the discrete environments of respective cultures is redirected in recent writing in feminist theory, cultural geography, cultural studies, and ethnography itself. These new works move toward understanding Native North American land as discursively constructed terrain, which connects the hybrid experience of the reconstructed past to the fragmented politics of the present. But it is not enough to recognize "that memory *has* a politics, and that effective rights depend on shared memories" (Tilly 1994: 244, italics in original). Politicized memory emerges in hybrid culture that incorporates an active sense of place beyond material production, a sense of tentative but material locatedness that works to reconstruct "the relation between identity and the spaces through which identity is both produced and expressed" (Keith and Pile 1993: 9). For Native North Americans, this sense of material locatedness is interwoven with the transforming traditionalism of Native spirituality, identity, and ideology.

Sacred Places

Research and writing about the meaning of Indian culture have long engaged anthropologists more than Native people. Over the years, there have been Indian ethnographers who have studied the culture of their own people; but even today, with more Native anthropologists and new sensitivities and methodologies, the ethnographer's pursuit of cultural knowledge reflects a tension between the Indian and the Other around issues of the sacred or the spiritual. Early anthropologists like Franz Boas ([1888] 1974) and those who followed his focus on describing Aboriginal cultures were interested in recording the songs and stories, collecting the materiality of religious practice, and decoding the organization of action. Most of the early accounts of Indian spirituality were voiced by Christian converts, who spoke about spiritual beliefs they no longer practised. Anthropologists had greater access to bilingual mixed-bloods and Christian converts, like my great-grandmother. She deciphered Rorschach tests for Hallowell ([1955] 1967) and Barnouw (1950), who studied the psychology and world view of the Chippewa. They paid her by the hour to inform or interpret. She spoke at length, but there were clear silences. Even with me, she was evasive in speaking about the traditional Midéwiwin religion of the Chippewa. She sometimes went to the ceremonies, but she wore her cross and sat outside the lodge. She spoke of the drums of the Midéwiwin with undisguised sentiment, expressing an affinity that seemed to contradict her belief in Catholicism; but she knew very little about the teachings or medicines of the Midéwiwin. What she knew was the reality of the multiple identities of her mixed-blood, traditional-Catholic, Indian experience, and this was masked in the silence of questions no one asked.

Ethnography's rejection of ambiguous, affective, or emergent experience and the refusal of Indians to discuss the sacred or spiritual were undoubtedly more common than anthropologists have revealed to us. Hybrid experience was consigned to autobiographies that were omitted from cultural analysis; and other ethnographers must have shared the experience of Boas (in Rothenberg 1972: 3) who, in 1920, was told by an informant, "Long ago her mother, had to sing this song and so, she had to grind along with it, the corn people have to sing too, it is very good, I refuse to tell it."

Yet the search for authenticity that frames anthropological inquiry has never discouraged popular writing on Indians. If, to adapt Said's (1979: 5) quote from Disraeli to the North American context: "Indians are a career, they are also an industry." As Paul Chaat Smith (1994: 33–34) suggests, if anthropologists needed Indians to speak about Indian culture, it didn't much matter to those who wrote—or read—popular books. He reminds us that from *Brother Eagle, Sister Sky* (Seattle 1991) to *The Education of Little Tree* (Carter 1976) to *The Memoirs of Chief Red Fox* (Fox 1971), fictive best sellers on Indian culture often parade as narratives of the "real." According to Castro (1983: 155), "In the late sixties and early seventies, interest in the Indian reached fad-like proportions." The journeys of spiritual experience written by Jamake Highwater (1981), Carlos Castaneda (1968), and Lynn Andrews (1981) affirm that authenticity has little to do with popularity. Even though Native North Americans are now encouraged to speak about themselves, the refusal to reveal remains common; and expressions of restraint are joined by suggestions that spirituality and sacred land are encoded in mystical Indian experience which is elusive, even inexpressible. Joy Harjo (1992) writes about the experience of spirituality that cannot be retold:

> I felt as if I had prepared for the green corn ceremony my whole life. It's nothing I can explain in print, and no explanation would fit in the English language. All I can say is that it is central to the mythic construct of the Muscogee people (otherwise known as "Creek"), a time of resonant renewal, of forgiveness. (89)

And N. Scott Momaday (1995) tells us:

> Those who seek to or understand the sacred in academic terms are misled. The sacred is not a discipline. It is a dimension beyond the ordinary and beyond the mechanics of analysis. For those who come to the sacred, to sacred ground, it is a kind of mystical experience, a deep and singular encounter. Sacred ground is ground that is invested with belief. Belief, at its root, exists independent of meaning. (29)

As dissimilar as their work may seem, it is the Kiowa writer Momaday and the Chippewa author Gerald Vizenor who through their books and poems of the last thirty years reveal much about the meaning of Indian Country. Vizenor (1994: 12, 52) writes, "Nature has no silence. The poses of silence are never natural.... Stories that arise in silence are the sources of a tribal presence." These stories that interlace heritage and spirituality, land and community engage what Vine Deloria, Jr. (1994: 122) calls "sacred geography."

Vine Deloria Jr. (in McLuhan 1994: 419) tells us, "every society needs ... sacred places. They help to instill a sense of social cohesion in the people and remind them of the passage of the generations that have brought them to the present." But sacred places represent more than remembered community. They are sites of the presence of the other world, which provide mandate and meaning to the disturbing reality of Indian history and everyday life.

Sacred places of the land are not fixed locations set by the dictates of religious prescription, nor do they represent Durkheim's opposing conceptions of the sacred and the profane. They are spiritual spots that locate "embedded sacredness in nature" (Walker 1996: 4) which one can access and experience on a personal level. Sacred sites locate points of interaction between individuals, supernatural powers, and the land itself, which if they are indigenous elsewhere, are uncommon constructions in the secular culture of North America. The land may be signed with memorable places, noted for events like Civil War battles or extraordinary features like the Grand Canyon; but their appeal to common experience is historical, not spiritual. The texts of memorable places that circulate in the "storied speech" (Ridington 1990: 192) of Indian traditionalism differ from those of the dominant culture in content, style, and meaning.

Native North American narratives about land as both territory and sacred site are emergent voices that interweave survival stories of history, spirituality, and community. Like Richard Wagamese's (1996: 137) comment "Forget Me Not Ridge—The Land is a feeling," Native voices speak of "the places at which people can anchor themselves into the world, the location of things that matter" (Grossberg 1992: 82). As Lawrence Grossberg (83) suggests, "It is the affective investment ... that explains the power of the articulation which bonds particular representations and realities [and I would add, memories] ... which enables ideological relations to be internalized and, consequently, naturalized." Storied voices act as affective goads to the gathering together of experiences of past generations and current companions of the land—local, national, international, metaphysical. This call to the formation of community—imaginary, symbolic, and real—stakes a claim to a resolute future drawn from the fragments of an unresolved past. Leslie Marmon Silko (1977: 2) writes, "I will tell you something about stories.... They aren't just entertainment. Don't be fooled. They are all we have, you see, all we have to fight off illness and death. You don't have anything if you don't have the stories." Native stories that express the vague "spiritness" of land are articulated in the reality of territory and sacred space through an understanding of heritage that is marked in ambiguous journeys and names.

Journeys and names are referents for a mixture of real, imagined, and symbolic experiences. They signify the prior claims of practices and events, places and people. These claims emerge in the memories of individual Indian experience. In the process of being shared with others, storied referents and reciprocal practices build the collective experience of communities. Communities are always dynamic, and collective experience does not represent a neat process of accessing common histories to form a basis for commonness. Nor do similar memories create a monolithic collective identity within or among Native nations. Like the unities in difference of the communities they negotiate, memoried experiences arise in kaleidoscopic constructions. Memories represent individual, incomplete, contingent images constructed around powerful referents. These referents generate open-ended "strings" of memoried experience that are lived in place and shared over time. Indian journeys and names emerge in the ambiguous recollection of historical and spiritual experience, expressing shared practices and beliefs of culture, identity, and community, both local and pan-Indian.

Journeys

Like other peoples whose language expresses their "relational positioning" in the "entangled tension" (Clifford 1994: 307) linked in articulation to diaspora, the journey is a metaphor of Native territorial claims in the present nation-states, drawn from the fragmented heritage of the past. For Native people, the journeys they recall map representations of relentless and regressive movement, a twisting trail of memoried experience expressed in the stories that emerge in the written silences around Indian origins, spirituality, and nationhood. As Gerald Vizenor (1972: 35) wrote in 1965, "The *Anishinabe* did not have a written history. The past was a visual memory and oratorical gesture of dreams plaiting an endless woodland identity between the consciousness and unconsciousness worlds of *the people*" (italics in original).

In Chippewa heritage, the journey through which the people become a nation begins at the eastern shores of North America, where "'the [Algonkian] people were so many and so powerful that if one was to climb the highest mountain, and look in all directions, they would not be able to see the end of the nation" (Benton-Benai 1988: 94). This migration carried the sacred fire for five hundred years, moving through the waterways of the St. Lawrence River and the Great Lakes, stopping at locations signed in the sacred Megis shell of the ancient Midéwiwin religion and claimed in the Chippewa rock carvings of spirit beings. Eventually they settled throughout what is now Ontario, Minnesota, Michigan, and Wisconsin. Vizenor (1972: 33) writes about this journey, deep in the vague discourse which maps the title to Chippewa territory: "The Anishinabe—the original people of the woodland—believe that they were given wisdom and life color from the sun reflecting on the sacred shell during the long migration" (italics in original). Whaley with Bresette (1994: 8) write, "'We are Anishinabe,' the Elders remind us. We are not Chippewa, not Ojibwe, but the original people, we are spontaneous beings created by the Great Spirit. The Elders tell how Creator used a megis (sea) shell to breathe life into the Original Man" (italics in original). Edward Benton-Banai (1988: 102) tells us, "We descendants of these great people can gather strength from their strength. We can gather courage for our lives today from their courage of yesterday."

The migration stories of the Chippewa and of other Native nations whose narrations of their origins—of "where we all come from" (Augustine 2004)—speak of movement; and movement was common in the Indian lifeways of earlier times. Until Indians were relegated to reservations, "home" was often a territory, not a fixed site, and houses were portable. The places where people lived shifted on the basis of resources and relationships. Chippewa travelled in seasonal cycles to hunt deer, trap beaver, gather maple syrup or wild rice, and trade with other Indians. Plains Indians followed the buffalo herds; coastal Indians moved to different fishing grounds; Iroquois farmers moved their villages to allow the soil to replenish itself; northern hunters rotated their hunting territories. Among all nations, there were travels to ceremonies, sacred sites, and social gatherings.

The consciousness of journeys is expressed in the reconstructed narratives of later travels, forced and voluntary, spiritual and ordinary. The Wisconsin Chippewa were ordered to move to Minnesota to empty the land for loggers, a policy that was enforced by the provision of material goods. In October 1850, Great Lakes Chippewa from nineteen different bands were told to travel to Sandy Lake, Minnesota, to receive promised annuity payments and supplies. When supplies finally arrived in December, 170 Chippewa had died of exposure, disease and starvation. Another 270 died that winter on the arduous journey home (Clifton in Peacock and Wisuri 2002: 54). If history has forgotten, Chippewa have always remembered. In October 2000, stones from the territory of twelve bands were gathered to honour the experience of Chippewa pain at Sandy Lake. Chippewa memories of Sandy Lake bleed into other recollections, like the "Trail of Tears" in the 1830s, when Russell Thornton (in Limerick 1987: 194) estimates four to eight thousand Cherokee were lost to the nation; and the "Longest Walk" of the Wounded Knee Lakota in 1890, remembered through footprints retraced in re-enactments which bear their names; and the walks to Washington, DC, in this era in caravans like the American Indian Movement's "Trail of Broken Treaties" in 1972. Vizenor (1993) rewrites the words of an ancient poem:

> moving forward and back
> from the woodland to the prairie
> Dakota women
> weeping
> as they gather
> their wounded men
> the sound of their weeping
> comes back to us (43)

There are other journeys transformed in time and place in the memoried experience that recall and compose non-linear fragments of collective culture. There are the political journeys calling generations of Indians to treaty tables; the journeys of legendary chiefs and current Native leaders, whose delegations to Washington, DC (like Canadian travels to Ottawa), "have been basic to the administration of Indian affairs in the United States from 1789 to the present" (Viola 1981: 22); the tortured travel to residential or boarding schools since the late 1800s; the moves for military service during two world wars; the trips to cities in the post-war years, when Indian relocation, urbanization, and reservation termination were policies in the United States; the journeys of the pow wow circuit, the "Unity Rides," the Sun Dance, and other spiritual ceremonies; and the imaginative journey that calls upon the collective experience of all these moves away: the journey home.

Momaday (1969) writes in *The Way to Rainy Mountain*:

The journey herein recalled continues to be made anew each time the miracle comes to mind, for that is peculiarly the right and the responsibility of the imagination. It is a whole journey, intricate with motion and meaning; and it is made with the whole memory, that experience of the mind which is legendary as well as historical, personal as well as cultural. And the journey is an evocation of three things in particular: a landscape that is incomparable, a time that is gone forever, and the human spirit, which endures. (4)

The journey about which Momaday speaks represents ragged-edged movement—performed in mythical and real time—*with* the land, not on the land; a pilgrimage home somewhere in Indian Country, which Indians always locate in the recollection, placement, and practice of heritage. As Momaday (1976: 142) writes in his memoir *The Names*, "The events of one's life take place, *take place*.... I existed in that landscape, and then my existence was indivisible with it" (italics in original). The land about which Momaday speaks is an expression of the Indian imagination that is carried from generation to generation in "blood memory," a concept that signifies culture and sacrifice, not biology. He writes (1976: 22), "Some of my mother's memories have become my own. That is the real burden of the blood." For other Native writers, the connection between land and Indian blood is also unequivocal. Mary Brave Bird (with Erdoes 1993: 220), writes in a chapter entitled "The Land Is Our Blood," that "the land is our mother, the rivers our blood." In stories that retell and renew, Indians affirm identity, continuity, and meaning in images that speak of their relationship to the land, no matter where they may be living or travelling.

For some Native people, travel is a perpetual pattern. Their experience of modern mobility seems a nomadic way of life that appears to contradict any attachment to territory. Native people sometimes seem propelled along a trail of lifelong movement between reservations and cities, between houses, jobs, and circumstances. Today there are third-generation urban Native people for whom cities are the territory of choice; and there are Indians who are continually travelling who, in the words of Yellow Bird (in Crow Dog with Erdoes 1990: 55) are "Roaming, Restless, Aimless." Travelling and living in cities involves the movement of personal and cultural boundaries and requires continual negotiation among Indians and Others. But when Indians move away from reservations, wherever they live or work or travel, they leave knowing they will go back for weekends and pow wows and holidays and maybe, eventually, to stay. This consciousness of moving away and coming back, of being elsewhere and attached to home, which represents a dynamic conception of home that emerges in memories of journeys, is a recurring theme in the survival narratives of Native America. William Bevis (1987), writes about the "homing" plots in the Native American novels of McNickle (1978), Momaday (1966), Silko (1977), and Welch (1979):

> American whites keep leaving home: Moby Dick, Portrait of a Lady, Huckleberry Finn, Sister Carrie, The Great Gatsby—a considerable number of American "classics" tell of leaving home to find one's fate farther and farther away.... The home we leave, to Crevecoeur is not only a place; it is a past, a set of values and parents, "ancien regime."... In Native American novels, coming home, staying put, contracting, even what we call "regressing" to a place, a past where one has been before, is not only the primary story, it is a primary mode of knowledge, and a primary good. (581–82)

Gerald McMaster (1995: 80–81) tells us, "Territoriality is important for (Native) Canadians as 'Indian Reserves' are spaces that signify 'home' ... for many (Native) peoples, this does not mean a return to the margins, but rather a return to the centre." The territories that constitute "centres" for Native North Americans are Indian reservations, parcels of land that Indians reserved for themselves in treaties signed with the United States or Canada. However limited in area or resources, these territories—for which the Ojibway word means "leftovers"—are homelands for Native people, for whom identifying other Native people begins with the question Where are you from? This question, which implies Where is your home? and even Who is your family? both identifies Native people and grounds Native identity. The articulation of territory and home that is connected to identity is not a static configuration of place, but a negotiated sense of relatedness built in experience and affect. As Michael Dorris (1994: 348) writes, "Home is an ongoing character in our lives. It serves as elder, as friend, as reference, as point of origin and return, as haven." This signification of home is built in the cultural connectedness of relationships that seem as old as the land with which they are conjoined. For Native people, the relatedness that constructs "home" is always remembered, imagined, and lived with the land. But the articulated perceptions of home and land do not emerge from a sense of nostalgia drawn from memories of an ideal time in the past. As Jonathan Windy Boy says in an advertisement for the United States Census 2000, "My grandfather walked on this land, my father also walked this land, me I like to stroll" (Lac du Flambeau News, Vol. 8, No. 5. May 2000: 28).

On reservation lands, relationships reach across time to affirm a cultural meaning lived and expressed in the habits of constantly changing collectivity. The alliances that emerge from a past in a particular place are rooted in a sense of culture—of Indianness—that stretches the borders of individual reservations. In Indian Country, home is now a territorializing and territorialized space, but this site is connected to elsewhere through family and community. In the gathering places of Native America, Indians speak of work and politics, children and pow wows, all realities of daily life that are threaded together in a sense of Indianness that recognizes other Native people. In the words of Joy Asham Fedorick (1989: 57), "My feet turn home: toward the sights, sounds, smells, tastes— and the hear-touch. Gone. Gone as my grandmother. But I remember her and she is with me." Native stories emerge in "a confusion of loss, a tale of absences, of a culture that was blown apart and changed so radically in such a short time that only the names survive" (Erdrich 1992: 132). The Native journey to the heritage and relatedness of home is remembered and retold in the names of people, places, and the land itself.

Names

If Momaday (1995: 29) suggests that the sacred emerges in belief that cannot be expressed, he also tells us, "Language and the sacred are indivisible. The earth and all its appearances and expressions exist in names and stories and prayers and spells." This seeming contradiction is absorbed in stories and names that locate, recall, and retell the silence of the inexpressible experience. In the stories and memories of Indian Country, names recall the places and people that have been erased by the colonial claims of Others. Nueva Espana, Nouvelle France, New England, Nieuw Netherland, and Nova Scotia are all names that designate new frontiers of territory that were appropriated to expand the Old World (Brotherston 1979: 13).

Like the land, the people who occupied it appeared nameless. Roger Williams (in Berkhofer 1978: 15) wrote in 1645: "I cannot observe that they [Natives] ever had (before the comming [sic] of the English, French or Dutch amongst them) any Names to difference themselves from strangers, for they knew none" (italics in original). In contrast, Vizenor (1993: 10) writes, "The stories of nature were heard in names. Place names and personal nicknames were communal stories. The anishinaabe [Chippewa] were never alone in their names, visions, and stories" (italics in original). This sense of subjectivity and community circulates today in new narratives that locate, construct, and assert the continuities of Native culture.

In the emergent writing of contemporary Native narratives, the nomadic experience of oral tradition is transformed in style and historical content. Rayna Green (1984) speaks of the colloquialism and contingency—and the call to cultural continuity—in writing that reconstructs and renews Indian Country:

> Sometimes she thinks its funny the way the stories change when she tells them. She doesn't know Indian Country the way Grandma knew it, and no matter how much she might wish she looked like the old ladies out in the plaza sometimes, she knows she never will. It's blue jeans and sun-glasses for her after all—save the fringed shawl for powwow. One of her cousins called her a Disco Indian last week. But still, she's not as hip as she looks sometimes. It's not that she could ever get away from the old stories, even if she wanted to. She can't tell them the way Grandma did, but she's hardly ever in situations like the ones Grandma thrived on. Still some of the stories took root so deeply in her that she tells them without thinking, in new forms, especially the ones that have to do with being a woman or being someone with a name. (5)

Today, the details of individual experience or indigenous knowledge are remembered, reconstructed, or imagined in borrowed stories told in English, sometimes interspersed with Indian words. Gerald Vizenor (1994) tells us about the silence and transformation of Indian names:

> Sacred names, those secure ceremonial names, were scarcely heard by missionaries and government agents and seldom translated as surnames; nicknames were assured in tribal stories, but the stories were lost in translation as surnames. Later, most surnames were chosen and dictated at federal and mission schools. Some tribal names endure in stories, and nicknames are identities learned and ascertained in language. Moreover, descriptive names seem to be more esteemed in translation, and certain choices of names are mere simulations with no memories or stories. (33)

Old Native names are uttered in the recovery of memory and practice, and new names are formed in the lived experience of everyday life and the struggles of emerging identity and community. Rayna Green (1984) writes about the emergent narratives of Native community:

> Spending so much time with women from other tribes—in Indian school and now in the city—gives her even more stories and names—so many

she doesn't remember what tribe they came from anymore. She thinks the names belong to her now, and she's right. Clan Mother, White Buffalo Calf Woman, Beloved Woman, Early Morning Woman, Night Wind Woman, Earth Woman, Corn Mother, Iyetiko, Persimmon Woman, Rainwater Woman, Grandmother Turtle, White Shell Woman, Ohlone Woman, Brave-Hearted Woman, Spider Woman, The Woman Hanging from the 13th Floor Window, Suicid/ing (ed) Indian Women, the Pueblo Woman Who Got Down in Brooklyn. She knows her names now, just the way she knows the places and languages she wasn't born to. But every time she starts to tell a story, she remembers more, as though she'd always known. The way she'd always known the laughter and the trouble. Sometimes, she chants them over to herself, the way she'd sing a song. Just for the comfort of it, especially when things get bad or when she feels really out of touch with what Grandma calls "Indian-ness." (5)

The "contrivance of names" (Vizenor 1994: 11) seems to historicize culture as they circulate and situate Indian Country, signifying spiritual experience whose power lies in the practice of the private, even secret, or the words of ceremonies. But these names are public expressions of popular culture that, when they are voiced in the lived experience and memory of the Native struggle with the continually colonizing Other, real or imagined or appropriated, emerge as a call to collective identity. In Momaday's (1976: 61) words, "Memory begins to qualify the imagination, to give it another formation, one that is peculiar to the self." What might be called "storied memory" defines the margins of Indian Country in a mixture of metaphorical and actual experiences, which join with contested attributes like colour, language, bloodline, and tribal enrollment to stake the claim to being Native. It is not historicized oral tradition, but this storied memory, reconstructed in the context of absorbing and opposing non-Native culture, that forges the trajectories of Native North American identity and community about which Robin Ridington (1990: 190) writes, "The oral traditions of people who are native to this land are a form of discourse which connects them to the land and to the generations that have gone before." In the words of Vizenor (1993):

The *anishinaabe* were driven to silence and the fear of space in their dream songs and stories; the names and ceremonies connected humans and animals to the earth and to the communal memories of the tribe; time was heard in the present and not the cause of terminal incertitudes. (12, italics in original).

The names that recur in the storied speech that works to build, reconstruct, and realign identity and community in the always incomplete
process of unity in difference are voiced by Native North Americans in
the mystifying but familiar discourse of persons, places, phenomena,
and objects. Momaday (1976) writes of the names that are drawn from
fragments of the past and redrawn in the vague narratives of the present:

> The names at first are those of animals and of birds, of objects that have
> one definition in the eye, another in the hand, of forms and features on
> the rim of the world, or of sounds that carry on the bright wind and in
> the void. They are old and original in the mind, like the beat of rain on
> the river, and intrinsic in the native tongue, failing even as those who bear
> them turn once in the memory, go on, and are gone forever. (3)

These names signify spiritual power and indigenous knowledge linked
in articulation to the land in interwoven constructions of the ordinary and
the anthropomorphic: human and mythical persons; historical and spiritual places; ordinary and legendary objects; physical and environmental phenomena, all voiced in the transforming speech and storied memory
of current cultural expression. For Chippewa, this discourse with the
land and the other-than-human beings with whom they communicate is
expressed sometimes in fear or desire or hope, sometimes in social connectedness, sometimes in ceremonial practice. But like the names that are
spoken in the hybrid narratives of contemporary re-telling, Chippewa
stories express fragments of lived experience and the "imaginative experience," which Momaday (1976: 4) tells us joins with the historical to
"express equally the traditions of man's reality." Keeshkemun (in Warren 1885: 373), hereditary chief of the Lac du Flambeau Chippewa in the
1880s, responded to the questions of British military officers "with a personal dream song that has become one of the common stories of tribal liberation" (Vizenor 1993):

> Englishmen! You ask me who I am. If you wish to know, you must seek
> me in the clouds. I am a bird who rises from the earth, and flies far into
> the skies, out of sight; but though not visible to the eye, my voice is heard
> from afar and resounds over the earth! (9)

Today, Stephen Augustine (2004) tells us, "All our ancestors—birds,
animals, people—have gone back to Mother Earth ... they hold our
shadow ... we are all connected though our feet, through our blood,
through the land, to our ancestors." And Jo Harjo (in Green 1984) writes,

Look at me
i am not a separate woman
i am a continuance
of blue sky
i am the throat
of the sandia mountains... (133)

Keeshkemun, Augustine, and Harjo speak of a dynamic experience that is not *about* the land but *with* the land and the persons who inhabit it. These are expressions of "All My Relations," of a dialogic, discursive relationship with the material environment that is multi-faceted and includes not only words and sounds but also a range of signs. Like Chatwin's (1988) *Songlines* that identify territorial boundaries in Aboriginal Australia, stories emerge from the shadowed recesses of oral tradition, often translated and written, usually by Others, or inscribed on the land itself in the mnemonic etchings of mounds, effigies, petroglyphs, and particular natural formations. Stories are also invested in natural phenomena like wind and thunder or in mythical persons like the flesh-eating Windigo and the Chippewa trickster Naanabozho, "a cultural folk-hero who disguises himself in many living things to explain and justify through imagination the conflicts of experience in tribal life" (Vizenor 1993: 155). For Chippewa, these signs mediate the obscurity of the spirit world in the reality of experience, both imagined and lived. Hallowell (1960: 22–23) writes of the difference between Ojibway and English-language representations of the animate and inanimate, noting that, for the Ojibway, "trees, sun and moon, thunder, stones and objects of material culture like kettle and pipe—are classified as 'animate.'" It is the recognition of animals, mythical characters and features of the physical environment as *persons*—named and equally involved with people of the past and the present—which, like journeys and sacred places, situates Native North American identity, locality, and ideology in the elusive consciousness of being Native in North America.

Politicizing Stories

The sense of the spiritual as mystical experience framed in a "deep and singular encounter" establishes "the intrinsic power of sacred ground [that] is often ineffable and abstract" (Momaday 1995: 29). This power beyond words seems to transcend definition, comprehension, and analysis, but it signifies ideology and forges identity and alliances of shared experience—remembered, imagined, or real. In vague narratives, sacred power, which is acquired in spiritual interaction with beings of the land, is conjoined with political power, which is articulated to community and to territory. Momaday (29) also tells us, "Sacred ground is in some way earned. It is consecrated, made holy with offerings—song and ceremony, joy and sorrow, the dedication of the mind and heart, offerings of life and death. The words 'sacred' and 'sacrifice' are related. And acts of sacrifice make sacred the earth."

Native heritage is empowered in sacrifice and voiced in stories: the pain of the past endured over time, the silence of ancestors about whom others speak, and the distress of the present lived in struggle. This sense of sacrifice fuses territory and sacred ground in survival narratives that accommodate "the perpetual need to create, conserve and re-create political spaces" (Keith and Pile 1993: 37). Political spaces are formed in the affectivity, ideology, and spirituality of names and journeys—remembered, renamed, and reclaimed—that are linked to the land. A Tewa prayer declares, "Within and around the earth, within and around the hills, within and around the mountains, your authority returns to you" (in McLuhan 1994: 375); and the Chippewa simply say, "For all my relations," confirming the connectedness of all beings. Like sweetgrass—which Stephen Augustine (2004) describes as "the hair of Mother Earth"—and sage and the trickster Coyote, the acknowledgment of "All My Relations" has spread throughout Indian Country, particularly since the 1960s and 1970s.

What Vine Deloria Jr. and Clifford Lytle (1984: 236) call the "consolidated Indian movement" of "ethnic Indians"—as opposed to "tribal Indians" that began in the cities of Indian Country in the 1960s and 1970s—persists today; and the authors contend that "the merging of many tribal identities and histories in the urban setting meant the adoption of a common, albeit artificial heritage":

> The 1868 Sioux treaty became regarded as the common property of all Indians, and when the Indian college students of varying tribal backgrounds invaded Alcatraz Island in San Francisco Bay, and later Fort Lawton near Seattle, they laid claim to these pieces of federal surplus property under that treaty. The claim was mythological and depended primarily upon the memory and oral tradition carried forward by the traditional people among the Sioux. (Deloria and Lytle 1984: 234)

The traditions that have emerged in the pan-Indian protest of urban and academic Indians may seem like artificial expressions of experienced tribal heritage, but they are authentic expressions of transforming traditional practice. Native political agency arises in the expression of traditions that are continually emerging. Heritage—including historical culture and spiritual practice—are adopted and adapted like the religious forms that Vine Deloria, Jr. (in Warrior 1995: 84) tells us, "must, in order to be meaningful, relate to a dramatically changed community in a dramatically changed environment." But as Indian cultures bleed into one another, adaptation and appropriation construct conflicting identities and alliances that challenge cultural practice and political processes. Native people move back and forth across the perforated borders of Indian identities, adopting and enacting different—even opposing—discourses of political possibility. Conflict emerges between those who proclaim trust in the moral possibility of North American institutions to redress Indian inequities and those who assert pragmatic realism in political protests and public strategies (Deloria and Lytle 1984: 242). The friction in Native communities expresses opposing narratives of dominance and survivance that assert the efficacy of casinos and the impact of smuggling; the authority of tribal and traditional governments; the definition of tribal membership; the traditions of religion; the pronouncements of policy. As Vine Deloria, Jr. (1999: 127) writes, "Many younger Indians feel the moral outrage of the government confiscation of tribal lands, although they do not necessarily understand the implications of a tribal religious attachment to them."

Today, land signifies traditionalism and spirituality, identity and community in narratives of political possibility in expressions from treaty tables and court cases, to writers and artists like Rebecca Belmore and John Trudel (Martin 2004: R1). In her performance art called "Speaking to Their Mother," Belmore installed a two-metre wide megaphone to listen to the land. Trudel, a musician who was a spokesman for the American Indian Movement during the Wounded Knee occupation of 1973, spoke to the Survival Gathering organized by the Black Hills Alliance in 1980—a gathering that might have occurred at Lac du Flambeau in 1988, or Oka in 1990, or Ipperwash in 1996, or Burnt Church in 2000. In "At the Gathering," Trudel (in McLuhan 1994) said:

> We are a natural part of the Earth. We are an extension of the Earth; we
> are not separate from it. We are part of it. The Earth is our Mother. The

Earth is a Spirit, and we are an extension of that Spirit. We are Spirit. We
are Power. They (the white power structure) want us to believe that we
have to believe in them, and depend upon them, and we have to assume
these consumer identities, these religious identities, and these racial identities. They want to separate us from our Power. They want to separate
us from who we are.... They can't stop power. We have a spiritual connection to the Earth and collectively, we have the same power as the
Earthquake, the Tornado, the Hurricanes. We have that potential. We
have that connection.... And All Our Ancestors, All Our Relations who
went to the Spirit World, they are here with us. They have power. They
will help us to see if we are willing to look. We are not separated from
them because there is no place to go. This is our place, the Earth. This is
our Mother. (423–24)

Native identity and community—tribal and pan-Indian—are continually adopted, adapted, and negotiated in stories of sacrifice and survival
that claim, name, and assert the meaning of Indian land. Even in the
ambiguous borderlands of urban and reservation experience, Native
people express a primary attachment to the land and not to the nation-
state (Tanner 1983: 27); and like the trickster Coyote, self-determination
conjoined with the land takes many forms. It is the practice of spring
spearfishing and the protection of Native casinos; the rejection of hydro-
electric projects and the growth of "Indian Way" and "Survival" schools;
the rights to resources, treaty benefits and traditional government; and
the protests involving logging, mining, and fishing—all of which are
discursively expressed and contested in the expression of a singular
relationship with the land. This relationship is the basis for the ideological positions voiced by Native North Americans, which both express
cultural continuity and represent the most effective political resource in
negotiations with one another and the nation-states they inhabit.

As Gerald McMaster (1995: 80) writes about Native experience, "The
struggle for land by (Native) Canadians is a struggle to create and expand
space: claiming land, claiming space. A land claim is an attempt to 're-
terriorialize,' to create in law new borders and divisions, and to mark off
rights, privileges and obligations." With their small population and mea-
ger financial means, it is this ideological stance, this "difference" that
distinguishes Native North Americans in the minds of Others and Native
people themselves. The ideology of aboriginality that circulates in the representations of anthropologists and ecologists, New Age spiritualists,
and producers of popular culture continually renews the moral argu-

ment expressed by Native people. Native resistance is cultural persistence; and it is voiced in strategies of difference that recall or romanticize, appropriate or oppose. In the narratives of heritage and spirituality linked in articulation to land, Native people have become, as Paul Chaat Smith (1995) puts it, "shape-shifters for the national consciousness." From this position, Indian stories express not only the power of the past but the empowerment of the future. Land invokes the promise of political autonomy, economic possibility, and cultural survival voiced in "the tribal memories and solace of heard stories" by those Vizenor (1994: 52) calls the "new warriors of words." Momaday (1972: 39) writes, "By means of words can a man deal with the world on equal terms. And the word is sacred. A man's name is his own; he can keep it or give it away as he likes." Chief Austin Bear (2004) tells us, "Land is a gift from the Creator, like our languages, our ceremonies and our right to be here. Without our spiritual connection to the land, I believe we are lost, no longer aware of who we are." And Matthew Coon Come (in Came 1995: 18), former grand chief of the Assembly of First Nations of Canada, says simply, "Our land is our memory. Everything has a story."

Native narratives of memory and spirituality, heritage and experience are not paradigms for Native cultural construction of the land. But the stories of Natives and newcomers engage the meaning of Native environments in the very processes of transforming traditionalism, enacting popular culture, and acting upon political possibility. As Doreen Massey (1995: 189–90) suggests, "In the process of identifying and characterizing places, whatever view comes to dominate and by whatever means its hegemony is assured, the particular characterization of that envelope of space-time, that place, which it proposes is only maintained in the exercise of power relations in some form." For Native people, space and time are cognitively and culturally marked in metaphorical and real expressions of materialism and culture, spirituality and affectivity that transform and renew identity, community, and ideology. In the end, land and Indians are sutured together, and the meaning of land is negotiated in the context of "a politicized consciousness and a radical spatial praxis" (Soja in Keith and Pile 1993: 5). The narratives of heritage and spirituality, community and identity that emerge and mingle with land imagine sovereignty, self-determination, and nationhood in a knot of representations that engages both "the prism through which Indians view their historical experiences" and a move "toward a place and state of being that is our own" (Simpson 1997: 6). The meaning of land is intertwined in the reconstructed representations of the Indian past; the lived experience and emerging traditions of the tribal present; and the political possibility of the pan-Indian future. Woven into this discursive construction are Native voices that speak of North America's entry into the time of the Seventh Fire, a time in which old prophesies tell us Native people will return to Native traditions, and Native spiritual recovery will flourish and extend to non-Natives.

In the narratives of dominance, survivance, and survival that circulate today, Tecumseh remains a contradictory image of American conquest. His experience is impossible to retrieve from the fragmented journals of military men, the narratives of traders, or the memories of Indians. But like Pontiac before him, the meaning of his historical experience lies in the political possibility of a pan-Indian movement linked in articulation to land. This, like his role in a war that nobody won, the British betrayal, and even the burial of his bones, is silent in the discourse that encircles Natives and other North Americans. As Paul Chaat Smith (1992: 99) says, "We are hopelessly fascinated with each other, locked in an endless embrace of love and hate and narcissism. Together we are condemned, forever to disappoint, never to forget even as we can't remember."

≪ • ≫

Sacajawea and Her Sisters:
Images and Native Women

Near Sitting Bull's grave, there is a bullet-ridden obelisk raised in memory of the Indian woman who accompanied Lewis and Clark on their expedition across the American West. A plaque says that her name is "Sakaka-Wea, that she 'guided' the expedition to the Pacific Ocean, and that she died and was buried at Fort Manuel in South Dakota on December 20, 1812" (Duncan 1987: 162). In the years since, Sacajawea has become a figure of popular culture, an Indian maiden with "more statues in her honor than any other woman in American history" (162). While historians agree that her name is Sacajawea, which means in her native Shoshone, "boat launcher," image-makers have labelled her Sakakawea, a Hidatsa word for "bird woman" (163). No one knows for certain whether she died at Fort Manuel in South Dakota at about age twenty-five or lived to be an old woman on the Wind River reservation in Wyoming (Howard 1971: 192). But our image of the Bird Woman is ageless: a shapely Indian princess with perfect Caucasian features, dressed in a tight-fitting red tunic, spearing fish with a bow and arrow from a birchbark canoe gliding across a mountain-rimmed, moonlit lake.

Sacajawea is a recurring representation in the cultural narratives of Native and other North Americans. We imagine her as "blazing the trail" of western exploration, intriguing in the contrast of her actions and our historical images of Indians as passive extensions of the land or obstacles to its development. Her personal experience is lost to us; only pieces of the framework of her life can be drawn from the journals, diaries, and notes of those who were motivated by economic and political purpose to scout the American West between 1804 and 1806. We believe that she was taken from her Shoshone people by the Hidatsas when she was ten or twelve years old. At the time of the Lewis and Clark expedition, she was about sixteen; she was one of two "country wives" purchased by a

Sacajawea, or "Bird Woman," spearing fish with a bow and arrow from a birchbark canoe, 1920s. Print in the private collection of the author.

member of the expedition named Charbonneau; and she was pregnant. Sacajawea travelled with her newborn son, supporting the mission that would expand the prospects of colonial settlement with the panoply of her person and the amity of her languages. At the end of the expedition, she was apparently left in St. Louis when Charbonneau resumed his life as a trapper in the Southwest (Howard 1971: 156). This, like her experience of the land, the people in her life, and even her death, is conjecture drawn from the imagination of those who write popular history.

While Sacajawea's experience with the Lewis and Clark expedition is uncommon, our contradictory mythical memory of her is not. As a child growing up on the Lac du Flambeau reservation in Wisconsin, I remember Sacajawea; and I remember her postcard sisters that are still sold in Lac du Flambeau today, smiling Indian princesses frozen in time and deadpan women identified as "squaws" and covered in baskets or beadwork, or surrounded by children. I was drawn to these postcards not because they touched some chord of displaced history of identity, but because they didn't. What was the connection between these images of princesses and squaws and my great-grandmother who lived across the road? I listened to her narratives of Chippewa struggles for empowerment until I was eighteen when I went away to school and she died. I knew women whom Others called squaws and women whom we teasingly called Indian princesses. But what did these postcard representations mean in the lived experience of my great-grandmother, who was enrolled as a member of the Lac du Flambeau band when this reservation was established and who, at ninety, bought a car and didn't speak to my father for two months because he didn't want her to get a driver's licence?

Imagining Indians

Indians have always been vagrants in the historical, political, and popular impressions of the western frontier. The discourse of the Indian as noble and savage, the villain and the victim—most recently represented in the media coverage of confrontations between Natives and newcomers over issues of land and resources—is threaded through the narratives of the dominant culture and its shifting perceptions of the western frontier as a "land of savagery, or land of promise." (Billington 1981). North Americans have drawn a certain sense of identity from these images of Indians engraved on the cultural landscape; but like the narratives of the western frontier that place and position Native people, these Indians are largely imagined. As Robert Berkhofer (1979: 72) writes, "For most of the past five centuries, the Indian of the imagination and ideology has been as real, perhaps more real, than the Native American of actual existence and contact."

In 1900, Edward S. Curtis, like other photographers and painters of the period, set out for the American West to record images of Indians. He spent thirty years and produced forty volumes of photographs taken between 1900 and 1930, each retouched to remove any traces of acculturation. Curtis's photographs represent a "vanishing race" of Indians seen through the photographer's lens, "dripping dentalia and fur—the sepia kings, shot through spit and petroleum jelly, Lords of the Plains, Potentates of the Potlatch, the Last-Ofs" (Green 1992: 47). His project covered the territory from the Mexican border to the Bering Straits, photographing posed Indians who were now struggling on reservations, fighting the effects of war, disease, poverty, and cultural displacement. All this is forever erased from the fantasies contrived in over forty thousand photographs that are reproduced and advertised today as "a rare glimpse of the nobility, passion and tradition of ... people [who] stare out across the decades and invite you into a world that was tragically destroyed" (Brown 1993). Rayna Green (1992: 47) writes about these fictive constructions suspended in the time and space of essentialist discourse: "Quit taking out your fantasies on us. Just give me one in overalls and a cowboy hat. Then we can get serious about what was happening to these people.... Why are we so grateful for his glorious dreams? Every Indian I know has one of them on the wall. Mine came down a long time ago."

Like the cultural narratives of the western frontier that sustain them, representations of Sacajawea and Curtis's photographs of real Native people reveal stories of conquest and its legacies, historical fantasies of Indians that erase Native histories and trivialize Native cultures. In North America's long imaginary gaze on the Plains Indian in the period of western settlement, Indians are folkloric figures yoked to teepees and war bonnets, buffalo hunts and pow wows. These are images of Native nations frozen in time and history, tribal peoples constructed in silent social imaginaries of print and celluloid. Like the ubiquitous image of the Indian warrior collapsed on his horse above a caption that reads "The End of the Trail," these are Indians without a lived past or a dynamic future.

Today, the cultural chronicles that absorb Indians in stories of colonial heritage are being rewritten by Others and challenged in the writing of Native people themselves. The new narratives and counter-narratives of Natives and newcomers represent contradictory construc-

tions of popular history, different heritages expressed in the 1992 quincentennial program of the American Public Broadcasting Service entitled
Columbus and the Age of Discovery and the Native-made video entitled
Surviving Columbus. In conflicting visions of dominance and survival,
these emerging accounts of colonial and Indian experience reconstruct
the rugged individualism of Frederick Jackson Turner's imaginary American society written in 1893 and the dislocation and desolation experienced by Indians on the frontier at the turn of the twentieth century.
Both narratives reveal that for newcomers, the frontier and the West
have never been precisely defined and have always represented promise more than place, fantasy more than fact. But regardless of how land
or movement is delineated in notions of North American hinterlands or
images of Indian Country, frontiers always mark social borders and margins. Our representations of the western frontier are grounded in a politics of difference that circulates in the cultural formation of both Indians
and Others. Gerald McMaster (1991: 21) writes, "It makes little sense for
Indigenous people to respond to the outrageous historical fictions of the
West. On the contrary, we must focus on our own perspectives." But if
the perspectives of Natives and newcomers interface in the West, they
also intertwine. The West was neither won nor lost, and the social imaginaries that circulate in representations of the West continue to construct
the identities of all North Americans.

Contemporary Native identity and culture are entangled in an ongoing struggle over representation and appropriation, over how Indians are
represented and how these representations are appropriated by Others
in a political process, that confines the Indian past and constructs the
Native future. This struggle over who can represent whom, who can
tell the stories of others—and how they should be told—involves artists,
authors, and academics in a growing debate over the politics of Indianness. Indians are caught with other North Americans in a web of conflicting interests and actions, confrontations over dominant cultural and
political processes, and the Native experience of exclusion or stereotypical inclusion and appropriation. For Native people, this contest over
the politics of difference is deeply rooted in the social imaginaries that
circulate in literary, artistic, academic, and media images. The Indians of
popular culture, which are intrinsic to North American images of the
western frontier, travel and transform in the action and events of our
everyday lives. In the conflicting power relations in which our contem-

porary communities are built, imaginary Indians construct identities with different ideologies and meanings that become central sites of cultural conflict between Natives and newcomers, and among Native people themselves.

Portraits of Pocahontas

Until recently, the narratives and images that represent and construct the experience of Native North Americans have been voiced by Others. For Indian men, there are occasional images of granite-faced chiefs, sometimes named, but the dominant representation—and narrative— of the last century is the warrior of the western plains, the restless Indian protected in war paint or wearing a war bonnet, rallying his horse, ready to shoot. These archetypes of comic-book Indians, which paraded and battled in hundreds of movies and pocketbook westerns, outnumbered the images of Indian women, who emerged as their partners in primitivism. Portrayed as beasts of burden or fetching maidens, Indian women usually fell in love with trappers, traders, or soldiers, the enemies of Indians whose identities and alliances were sometimes reversed in the process of "going Native." But if visual images of Indian women seem less prevalent and more affable in popular culture, the Indian princess is an ambiguous figure that has deeper roots in North America, and her image has transformed and expanded with the development of its nation-states. In their analysis of postcards of Indian women, Patricia Albers and William James (1987: 35, 48) point out that "if a uniform caricature [of Indian women] has existed, it has been the image of the Indian 'princess,'" and this "visual image of Indian women as 'maiden' or 'princess' has increased in popularity over time."

 . The ambiguous representations of Indian women that we associate with the western frontier have been with us since the earliest colonization of North America. As Rayna Green (1976) writes, the rough, earthy beauty of the Americas was initially symbolized by pairs of Indian men and women, Caribbean or Brazilian Natives framed in the exoticism of flora and fauna that depicted the bountiful resources of the continent. But . by 1575, the bare-breasted, Amazonian Indian queen took on the image of the New World. Draped in feathers and furs, carrying arrows and spears, this contradictory figure incorporated the warrior woman and the mother-goddess, drawing from European roots to portray the primitive challenge of America: "exotic, powerful, dangerous and beautiful" (Green 1976: 702). When the colonies began to move toward independence, the mother-queen figure of the 1600s was transformed into the more independent princess image of the 1700s. The statue-like figure of "liberty" or "Columbia" in flowing robes was younger, more classically European, and overtly Caucasian; but armed with a spear and a peace pipe or a flag, this social imaginary wrapped in symbols of peace and power, civilization and acrimony is equally equivocal. And this ambiguous iconography of North America that incorporates the Native and the noble, which Green (1976) calls the "Pocahontas Perplex," persists in the portrayal of Indian princesses constructed to accommodate colonial experience, western expansion, and national formations.

Pocahontas is the paragon Indian princess of North American popular culture that "inspired countless works of art...idealizing the image of the Indian woman" (Berkhofer 1979: 121). Rayna Green (1976: 701) writes, "As a model for the national understanding of Indian women, her significance is undeniable." Susan Donnell's (1991) book entitled *Pocahontas* has on its cover, "She was a princess, a lady and a legend. Her story is the story of America." Like Sacajawea—who did not tramp through the western wilderness to "blaze the trail" for Lewis and Clark's expedition in 1804 but acted as an interpreter and mediator—the romantic myth of Pocahontas is constructed around her alliances with men. In the legendary narrative of North America, fictive history constructs an imaginary Indian princess, a noble savage named Pocahontas, who saves the life of an Englishman for whom she feels a romantic attraction. Her actions bring peace between the Indians and the colonists of Jamestown, Virginia, the first permanent colony in North America. She inevitably marries a non-Indian, becomes civilized and Christian, and assimilates with the settlers.

There is, of course, a counter-narrative, parts of which can be pieced together from documents collected by the Virginia Historical Society. The child who was nicknamed "Pocahontas," which means "playful" or "mischievous," was born in 1595, and her real name was Matoaka. Unlike the Walt Disney animated film, which portrays her as a woman in her early twenties, Pocahontas was a child of twelve when she encountered Captain John Smith, who was then twenty-seven years old. Historians disagree about whether Pocahontas saved John Smith's life, or even met him; but they agree that, in contrast to Disney's golden-haired hero,

Smith was not an innocent bystander to the armed conflict that occurred between the Chickahominy Indians and the Jamestown settlers. He was known more as an Indian fighter than the peacemaker created for the Disney film, and "his conduct may have landed his head on Powhatan's clubbing block, where Pocahontas supposedly intervened and saved his life" (Beam 1995: 17). For their part, the colonists apparently identified her father, Powhatan, who was grand chief of a confederacy of thirty tribes, as an "emperor" or "king," and his daughter Pocahontas therefore became a "princess." But our knowledge of this, like the story of her life, is drawn from historical fragments and individual conjecture. Like Sacajawea, Pocahontas's experience is lost to us.

When fighting broke out in 1612 between Powatan's confederacy and the colonists who settled on Chickahominy Indian territory, Pocahontas was married to an Indian who was an aide to her father. No one knows how she became friendly with the Jamestown settlers and brought food to the starving colonists. But on a visit to Jamestown in 1613, she was lured aboard a ship, kidnapped, and held hostage for over a year as a safeguard against Indian attacks. During her captivity, she learned English, converted to Christianity, and was baptized "Rebecca." In 1614, John Rolfe, a widowed tobacco farmer and her religious instructor, married the eighteen-year-old Pocahontas, about whom he wrote her "education has bin rude, her manners barbarous" (in Woodward 1969: 162). Now hostage to a new persona, her role as an intermediary took her and her young son Thomas to England, where she was presented at court as "Lady Rebecca."

Like the Indian "country wives" of trappers and traders who succeeded her, Pocahontas's mediation between Indians and Others had important political and economic implications. Her presence built a bridge between the Indians and the settlers. Strengthened by eight years of peace and the cultivation of tobacco, the Virginia colony initiated a new empire in North America. But like many Indian women who became economic and political "go-betweens," her own life was very short. She died of smallpox or tuberculosis in England in 1617, when she was twenty-two years old.

Pocahontas's untold story might have been the first of what later became known as "captivity narratives," populist tales that tell the exotic and arduous experiences of woman settlers who were kidnapped by Indians in books like Fanny Wiggins Kelly's nineteenth-century bestseller *Narrative of My Captivity among the Sioux Indians* (Reiter 1978: 64). The encounter of Pocahontas and John Smith that became legend did not appear in Smith's book about his life written in 1608. But in 1624, he wrote a second book entitled *General Historie of Virginia* (Scriba 1995), which built the scaffold for the seventeenth-century cultural narrative of assumed friendship and harmony, co-operation and assimilation at a time of colonial expansion. Smith's storied Pocahontas inspired the play entitled *The Indian Princess; or La Belle Sauvage*, which was performed in Philadelphia in 1808 (Black and Weidman 1976: 149). This narrative of the fantasy princess multiplied and diversified through the ensuing years of conflict between Natives and newcomers. In the modern period, Disney's historical revisionism emerged at a time of new tension between Natives and newcomers, over land and resources, sovereignty and self-determination, artifacts and images. As Coco Fusco (1990) writes:

> For me, the issue of "the other" is one of power, of a dynamic between those who impute otherness to some and those who are designated as other. So the questions I ask about otherness have to do with how others or the other are spoken of, who is speaking about them, and why have they chosen to speak of the other at the given historical moment. (77)

The fairy tale of Pocahontas that absorbs or expresses the Otherness of Indians, ignores not only the presence of sovereign Native nations and occupied Native lands, but also the spread of disease and conflict over settlement that decimated Indians, killing "some ten million at the outside between 1492 and the 1700s" (Green 1988: 31). The narrative of the fantasy princess dismisses the manifestation of Indian death in the illness that killed Pocahontas, along with the intriguing life of Motoaka, who experienced the contradictory cultural realities—and the cultural hybridity—of Pocahontas and Lady Rebecca. Like the Walt Disney film produced in the mid-1990s and the fifty Pocahontas products launched by Mattel toys to exploit it, Pocahontas's social imaginary is monolithic, a representation rooted in ambiguous, sexualized fantasies that appropriate and reconstruct her Indian identity. Rock musician Neil Young's song is explicit:

> I wish I was a trapper
> I would give a thousand pelts
> To sleep with Pocahontas
> And find out how she felt. (In Colt 1995: 69)

For Native people, the counter-narrative to Young's song is expressed in Jimmie Durham's (Mulvey, Snauwet, and Durant, 1996) painting entitled *Pocahontas's Underwear*, an image of blood-red panties decorated with feathers and beads, fabric and fasteners. As Mary Dearborn (1986) writes about the sexualized images of Pocahontas:

> Pocahontas's imaginative power lies in her sexuality, or, more precisely, in the promise she holds out of sexual union between a white male representative of the dominant culture and an exotic, or ethnic, woman. Her story functions as a compelling focus toward what W.E.B. Dubois has called the "stark, ugly, painful, beautiful" fact of American life: miscegenation, or sexual relations between white men and ethnic women. (99)

From the "ministering maiden" (Stedman 1982: 2) image of the princess Pocahontas to her darker twin, the squaw, both the nobility and the savagery of Indian women have been defined in relation to white males— as women who rescued them, served them, married them, and who even gave up their Indian nation for them (Green 1976). While the story of Pocahontas came to represent "the ideal merger of Native and newcomer," the image of the squaw became what Daniel Francis (1979) calls the "anti-Pocahontas," about which he writes,

> Where the princess was beautiful, the squaw was ugly, even deformed. Where the princess was virtuous, the squaw was debased, immoral, a sexual convenience. Where the princess was proud, the squaw lived a squalid life of servile toil, mistreated by her men"—and openly available to non-Native men. (121–22)

Adding to the indignity of this representation that devalued, defiled, and objectified Native women, the label that names the stereotype may derive from the Indian *squa* or *skwa*, a word which, in some Algonkian languages, is a suffix added to build a feminine form of certain words (Herten 1997: 2). But in the prismal meanings that emerge in lived realities, this floating image of the Indian woman as a beast of burden not only moves but also merges.

As the ambiguous imaginary of Pocahontas suggests, it is the conjoined image of the princess and the squaw that is most destructive for Indian women. Dearborn (1986: 99) remarks, "It is precisely because the Pocahontas figure is expected to embody *both* aspects of this image that hers is so convenient, compelling and ultimately intolerable a legend" (italics in original). The progression of these intertwined narratives that are so deeply entrenched in North America's popular culture is summarized in an excerpt from Monique Mojica's (1991) play *Princess Pocahontas and the Blue Spots*:

> Princess, Princess Amazon Queen.
> Show me your royal blood,
> Is it blue? Is it green?
> Dried and brown five centuries old,
> singed and baked and
> covered with mold?
> Princess, priestess Caribe Queen,
> What are you selling today,
> Is it corn, tobacco, beans?
> Snake oil or a beaver hat.
> Horse liniment,
> You just can't beat that!
>
> Princess, Princess, calendar girl,
> Redskin temptress, Indian pearl.
> Waiting by the water
> For a white man to save.
> She's a savage now remember—
> Can't behave. (20–21)

Illusory Sisters

Populist images of Indian princesses emerged in the late 1800s in lithographs of delicate, demure Indian ladies and printed paintings of buckskin-clad maidens. Through the long North American gaze on Indian women, images shifted with the vicissitudes of North American motives for marketing the West and its material and cultural products. The social imaginaries of historicized and romanticized Indian women were appropriated and propagated to accommodate the growth of immigration and industry and the interrelated expansion of railroads, mail service, and advertising.

At the turn of the twentieth century, some images of Indian princesses were seeming transformations of Sacajawea in a birchbark canoe, others depicted wistful princesses looking at handsome warriors, sometimes encaptioned as "Hiawatha's Wedding." There were gold-leaf princesses on cigar boxes and bare-breasted, primitive princesses—and sometimes squaws—promoting apples and corn and natural medicines, like "Swamp-Root" herbal cures. Indians were now relegated to the poverty and pain of reservations, but whimsical and woeful images of women became frontier tropes that "reinforced the belief that the best Indian was the historical Indian" (Francis 1992: 176).

From about 1915 through the 1940s, the dominant representation of the Indian princess was the "lady in red," a maiden draped in a red tunic, wearing the requisite headband and feather, and posed with picturesque mountains, pristine forests, waterfalls, and moonlit lakes. These romanticized princesses that adorned calendars, advertisements, paintings, and postcards—with names like Winona, Minnehaha, Iona, and even Hiawatha—worked in consort with their male counterpart, the Indian warrior, to establish the romanticized Indian as "one of the icons of consumer society" (Francis 1992: 175). Images of Indian women that "garnered good will but bore no referential relationship to the goods they advertised" (Coombe 1996: 213), proclaimed products that were now mass-produced, including corn, peas, apples, Mazola oil, Land o' Lakes butter, Kraft foods, beer, and beverages. Advertising expanded through "branding," which created an image to fix the idea of a particular product in the mind of the consumer. As promotional products evolved from inviting territorial expansion to enticing commercial enterprise, imaginary Indian women became the first North American "pin-up girls."

Calendar-girl princesses gazing wistfully or looking longingly appeared in a remarkable range of poses and settings. There were paddling princesses, fishing maidens, sewing princesses, and maidens of the feathers or the flowers. But the most common were maidens—sometimes almost twinned—merely posed as fanciful Indian princesses amid chaste, romanticized scenery. These statue-like figures of the imagination marketed the North American West as alluring, unoccupied, available, and now open to railroad travel. Daniel Francis (1992: 176) writes, "More than any other single aspect of White civilization, the railway transformed the world of the Indian." A paper parade of Indian princesses promoted settlement and tourism on Indian land, which had been captured, claimed, treatied, or just taken and then advertised as "1001 Switzerland's rolled into one" (177). With the onslaught of settlement and tourism between 1880 and 1910, princesses urged audiences to come to

Buffalo Bill's Wild West Show and the rodeos and pow wows it spawned. As the West mined the imaginations of easterners, these posed princesses spread throughout the continent and the decades. After the First World War, some images of Indian women took on the "flapper" fashion of the 1920s. Indian maidens appeared in the wilderness wearing long strands of corn or beads, feathered headbands and fringed shawls, which were sometimes tied around their hips. They were joined by calendar-girl princesses, who were more enticing, in their sexually explicit outfits of low necklines, net stockings, and slit skirts. But years earlier, regular mail service had created a new market for both calendar-girl princesses and historicized images of Indian women.

Photography was brought to North America from France in 1839 and, after 1873, when picture postcards were introduced into the United States, mailed images of faraway places became the common means of popular communication (Smith 1989: 9). Scenic views of "unoccupied" and rugged nature were transformed into reproductions of fantasies carrying greetings for every occasion. By the 1920s, travel postcards carried images of sad-looking squaws lined up all-in-a-row, of brow-beaten Indian matrons surrounded by children, or of ancient Indian women heavy with beadwork. Contradicting this sense of the uncivilized, there were endless variations of picture-postcards with fantasy princesses, some as single-feathered ladies, others wearing full war bonnets.

At the same time, Indian maidens, princesses, and "chieftain's daughters" began to appear on the wide range of cultural products that reflected the imaginary landscape of the West. Indian princesses decorated wood-burned plaques and mirrors, puzzles and playing cards, thermometers and ink blotters. Like the Indians in Buffalo Bill's Wild West Show at the turn of the twentieth century, these two-dimensional maidens became the props of popular culture. In addition to bookends and paperweights, cups and salt-and-pepper shakers, princesses emerged as romanticized subjects in popular songs entitled *Red Wing, Falling Star, Laughing Water,* and *Pretty Little Rainbow*; and as objects of history in textbooks, children's stories, and ethnographic studies. Princesses abounded in the popular literature that was published by the mid-1800s, when Lydia Huntley Sigourney (in Black and Weidman 1976: 205) described Pocahontas as "a forest-child amid the flowers at play!... Her spirit-glance bespoke the daughter of a King," and Henry Wadsworth Longfellow wrote about the imaginary Minnehaha in his famous poem *The Song of*

Hiawatha. When "dime novels" appeared, "in the tradition of Pocahontas, some of the heroines were brave Indian maidens. *Malaeska, The Indian Wife of the White Hunter* sold briskly" (Reiter 1978: 22). Publishing circulated the imaginary Indian women through generations of comic books and pulp magazines like *Western Story, Wild West Weekly*, and *Ranch Romances* (Pronzini 1994). Princesses and squaws sold books like Zane Grey's (n.d.) *Spirit of the Border* or Paul Joseph Lederer's (1982) *Manitou's Daughters* which, as part of Signet's Indian Heritage Series, proclaims on its cover, that this is a story of "proud women of a proud people—facing the white invaders of their land and their hearts." The invented social imaginaries of Sacajawea and her sisters became a staple commodity in the flood of movies, plays, paintings, and photographs that celebrated frontierism in the West.

In contrast to the representations of Indian squaws, the images of Indian princesses share one thing in common: they all look like replicas of fashion magazine models. As Virginia Driving Hawk Sneve (1987: 72) writes, "The models for the original paintings were not American Indian women but attractive Caucasian women who frequently besieged the artists to be allowed to pose as an Indian princess." These models, like children re-enacting a pow wow or impersonating cowboys and Indians, were engaged in what Rayna Green (1988: 30) calls "playing Indian." In her article entitled "The Tribe Called Wannabe," she writes that the performance of "playing Indian" is "one of the oldest and most pervasive forms of American cultural expression, indeed one of the oldest forms of affinity with American culture at the national level." "Playing Indian" situates Indian princesses in the politicized construction of North American and Native identity.

Encountering Princesses

Vine Deloria, Jr. (1969) writes in *Custer Died for Your Sins*:

> All but one person I met who claimed Indian blood claimed it on his grandmother's side. I once did a projection backwards and discovered that evidently most tribes were entirely female for the first three hundred years of white occupation.... Somehow the white was linked with a noble house of gentility and culture if his grandmother was an Indian princess who ran away with an intrepid pioneer. (11)

1920s print of an Indian princess wearing a war bonnet. Print in the private collection of the author.

In Mary Dearborn's (1986: 100) words, "Intermarriage seems to yoke in a rather neat fashion the concepts of ethnicity and American identity." If, as Deloria and Dearborn suggest, non-Natives overcome a sense of North American alienation by being distantly related to Indians, the great-grandmothers and grandmothers who married fur traders, trappers, and settlers were caught in a maelstrom of cultural misunderstanding and conflict that produced both personal acceptance and rejection.

In the formative histories of the nation-states in North America, "there is an important Indian woman in virtually every encounter between Europeans and Indians" (Kidwell 1992: 97). The importance of Indian women grew in the early days of the fur trade, which began in 1671, when France declared possession of Indian land in what is now eastern Canada and the Great Lakes region of the United States. Traders sought "country wives" for not only companionship and convenience but also for the strategic alliances that supported peace, trade, and the supply of furs. The relationship between European traders and Indian women was more problematic after 1760, when Britain took over the territory that supported the fur trade. The roles of wife, interpreter, mediator, and even trader that engaged Indian "country wives" as the fur trade moved west ultimately reverted to mixed-bloods, who were in turn replaced by non-Native women. As British women struggled with the hardships of bringing "civilized ways" to new settlements of the fur trade frontier, Indian women were abandoned or ignored. The exclusion of Indian women from "civilized society" was built upon the images of Indian women as workers and drudges, and as competing sexual and marriage partners. Positioned as sexual objects and valued for their physical features and family connections, Indian women became commodities whose desirability and destiny were linked to the declining market for furs and the increasing availability of European women. In the context of colonial erasure, displacement, and competition, "despite her important contributions and influence in certain areas, the Indian woman in fur-trade society was at the mercy of a social structure devised primarily to meet the needs of European males" (Van Kirk 1980: 88). The long shadows of the Indian princess and her sister, the squaw, wind through Indian experience of this tenacious social structure and its cultural constructs. Braided together, these images of the primitive and the princess framed the voice of Indian women who later performed or spoke publicly about their Indian culture and living conditions.

The autobiography entitled *Life among the Paiutes: Their Wrongs and Claims*, by Tocmetone or Sarah Winnemucca and published in 1883, was one of the first books written by a Native person. She was born in Nevada in 1844, the daughter of a medicine man and a mother who starved to death during the desperate circumstances experienced by the Paiute. She spoke about the plight of her people in New York, Boston, and Washington, DC. But when she lectured in California, she was identified as "Princess Sarah," and the report in the *San Francisco Chronicle* referred to her "extensive and diversified matrimonial experience, the number of her white husbands being variously estimated at from three to seven" (Canfield 1983: 163).

Years later, Emily Pauline Johnson Tekahionwake reappropriated her imaginary sister, the princess, in performances that established her as "the voice of the Indian" (Francis 1992: 114). She was born on the Six Nations reserve in Ontario in 1861, the daughter of a Mohawk chief and an English mother. She was an accomplished student of English literature, a published poet, and an author who spoke about her Native experience in theatres across Canada. But to be heard, Pauline Johnson replaced the formal gown she wore to recite her poetry with a buckskin dress and "toured the world as the 'Indian Princess' regaling crowds with romantic tales of Native American Life" ("An Altitude Super Card" n.d.). For most of her career and long after her death, "Johnson's literary work was almost always received and assessed in relation to her performance" (Strong-Boag and Gerson 2000: 117).

The experiences of Indian women gained greater visibility in ethnographic studies that broke the male-focused mould of anthropology in documenting women's roles and lives, like Ruth Landes's (1971) *The Ojibway Woman* and Nancy Oestreich Lurie's (1961) *Mountain Wolf Woman*. These ethnographic studies of Indian women neither analyzed nor promoted the images of the princess and the squaw, but they reflected assumptions of time-distanced, tribalized, traditional culture that were misleading. Women anthropologists may have been more interested in the roles of Indian women, but like their male counterparts, they studied the structure and function of Indian culture and neglected the social meaning of hybrid identity and power relations built into the conflicting representations, interactions, and alliances Indian women experienced.

Today, feminist writers recognize the fragmented and contradictory representations of Native women in the ambiguous, male-oriented

Minnie Cloud, Lac du Flambeau reservation, 1910 to 1920. Ben Guthrie Collection, George W. Brown, Jr. Ojibwe Museum and Cultural Center, Lac du Flambeau, Wisconsin.

images of all women. But the meaning of conflicting cultural narratives is negotiated in the context of a specific culture and a specific experience and political process, whether historical or current. From the unpredictable and perplexing experience of being "country wives" that Sylvia Van Kirk (1980) documents in her book *"Many Tender Ties,"* to the "Bush Lady" of Alanis Obamsawin's poignant song of a reserve woman's painful experiences in the city, Native women have lived a legacy of images that devalue and defile them. Fragments of the persistent, historicized fantasy of fetching maidens have been reappropriated in the counter-narratives of Indian popular culture. Like Pauline Johnson's performance, the pow wow princess is a transformation of the enduring representations of the Indian princess, appropriated and redefined in hybrid expressions of contemporary Native culture. Related to these images that continually transform and emerge, Native women experience daily struggles with identity—and with men, both Indian and Other—that are neither simple nor straightforward.

Native women have always been clan mothers, care-givers, educators, and energizers in Native communities, and their economic visibility and political presence has grown significantly since the 1960s. But battles over blood and belonging, exclusion and reinstatement, position and power are entrenched in the political landscape of Native communities. In Canada, Native women still sometimes encounter issues of exclusion, membership, power, and politics related to the Indian Act which, until 1985, declared Native women legally non-Indian if they married a non-Indian; and women on both sides of the border challenge the governance and policies of male-dominated band councils. Across both countries, Native men and women struggle with a legacy of poverty, domination, and history in which, "whether princess or squaw, Native femininity is sexualized" (Anderson 2000: 107). There are open wounds of abuse, prostitution and murder perpetrated by Others, for whom Indian women are disposable; and there are painful memories of Native people mistreating one another, which leave Native women vulnerable. Today, the Native struggles over appropriations of the Indian chief or the western warrior, and the contemporary transformations of the princess or the drudge, are perforated with voices of resistance and reclamation. But if Native women and other women are allied in narratives of identity, emancipation and empowerment, there is a sense of disconnection linked to different histories, realities, and ideologies, even among Native women who draw upon the words of women of colour and non-Native women who speak of Native sisters.

Native Sister Stories

Amid yesterday's Curtis-like historical photographs and today's "Leanin' Tree" greeting card's teepee-posing princesses with longing looks and unruly hair, Monique Mojica (1989: 40) is moved to write, "I am not your princess—I am only willing to tell you how to make fry bread." The imaginary Indian princess is deeply interwoven in the lives of Native women and their enduring struggles over its ambivalence and significance, but as Mojica's comment suggests, neither the princess nor the squaw has led to the "loss" of Indian identity or alienated Native women from their cultures and communities. The identity of Native North American women is constructed in the intertwined discourses of grandmothers and mothers, daughters and Others. In narratives that situate, reclaim, and transform the past, Native women express the identity, community, and empowerment of the present. Native women speak of themselves or people they know—real, memoried, or imagined—in stories that construct individual and collective identities. Louise Erdrich (1992: 132) reminds us, "There once were women named *Standing Strong, Fish Bones, Different Thunder*. There once was a girl named *Yellow Straps*. Imagine what it was like to pick berries with *Sky Coming Down*, to walk through a storm with *Lightning Proof*." Rayna Green (1984: 7) writes that "the taking of new names and the reshaping of old names is the essential process for becoming." These voices, which sound nostalgic or sentimental, appropriate the past in emerging representations of cultural continuance and contemporary empowerment. In their book *Walleye Warriors*, Rick Whaley and Walter Bresette (1994) write about Bea Swanson's experience during the protest over spring spearing, a traditional treaty right of Wisconsin Chippewa:

> "When I was young," she reminisced, "I always wanted to win the beauty pageant and ride in the parade waving to the crowd. I didn't realize then that Indian girls couldn't win [those contests]. But when I was asked to lead the Was-Wa-Gon group [of Chippewa spearfishers] in the Minocqua Fourth of July parade, it didn't matter all the harassment we got there. I was so proud. I finally got to lead the parade." (233)

Ojibway elder Arthur Solomon (1990: 132) says of his narratives, "I have borrowed this story from someone who had borrowed it from someone else who had borrowed it from someone else." Passed on through kinship and gossip, ceremony and social drinking, books and lectures and paintings, Indian stories are stitched to a polyvocal past as "acts encapsulated in time, 'enacted' every time they are spoken aloud or read silently" (Anzaldúa 1987: 67). Tales told in books like Leslie Marmon Silko's (1977) *Ceremony* and Louise Erdrich's (1984) *Love Medicine* intertwine with the lived experience of history and heritage and everyday life. The traditional knowledge that proclaims women as "the heart of the nation" and the "centre of everything" is conjoined with the seemingly contradictory images of Annie Mae Aquash, warrior of the American Indian Movement who was murdered in 1975, during the modern battle of Wounded Knee, or Shelley Niro's (1991) playful photographs of her own sisters, posed with captions like "Mohawks in Beehives" and "The Rebel." Spliced within the kaleidoscopic representations of contemporary Native realities that interweave the mundane, the humorous, and the prophetic, there have always been Elders who represent Native empowerment in stories of Mother Earth and Grandmother Moon.

Natural Sisters

Paula Gunn Allen (1988: 21) writes, "The Native American roots of white feminism reach back beyond Sacajawea. The earliest white women on this continent were well acquainted with tribal women. They were neighbors to a number of tribes and often shared food, information, child care and health care." If women were sometimes casual companions in the everyday life of different colonial realities, their experiences are erased in populist images of Indian women. Posed, paper-doll princesses are homeless vagrants of the imagination. These illusory women are alone, alienated from one another and Others in the scenic backdrops of the land and nature that they entice Others to occupy, first as settlers, then as tourists. In the parallel representations of tribalized "real" Indians, women are equally isolated or grouped with other women, among children or the material objects of Indian culture that are valued by Others: jewelry and art, baskets and beadwork. In the historicized or exoticized world of the posed princess or tribalized drudge, there are no families, no clans, no communities, no kinship networks, no nations. In fact, there is no recognition of the formative social relationships that not only place Native North Americans in relation to the land and to one another, but that also construct the colonial polices of Native exclusion, assimilation, or containment they experienced. As Sarah Carter (1997: 161) suggests, "The contrasting representations of white and Aboriginal femininity articulated racist images that confirmed cultural difference and the need for repressive policies. Powerfully negative images of Native women served to symbolize the shortcomings of that society."

But laced through the heritage of repressive policies and devalued practices that Native women live, there is an enduring sense of cultural continuity and Indian community, however transformed and conflictual. Even in the current contests over power and placement, Native women know that the narratives of the princess and the squaw have not been experienced by women alone. Beyond the difference of their gendered experience, Native men and women are yoked together in the cultural heritage and lived reality of subalterns, Indians whose roles and responsibilities, culture and customs were eclipsed. And in the stories of Indian heritage they tell, women hold a special place.

In the narratives of traditional knowledge that express Indian identity and community, women have always represented empowerment. A poster that is common in Indian Country carries the warning of the Cheyenne Tsistsistas: "A nation is not conquered until the hearts of its women are on the ground. Then it is finished, no matter how brave its warriors or how strong their weapons." In the words of Arthur Solomon (1990: 34–35), "The [woman] is the foundations on which nations are built. She is the heart of her nation. If that heart is weak, the people are weak … the woman is the centre of everything"; and he tells us why: "The women 'were of the earth,' they were connected to the earth mother and to the grandmother moon whose work was to govern when all things were to be born, plants, animals, humans."

From a feminist perspective, this traditional image of Indian women as close to nature is essentialized and problematic. The feminist critique is an ideological knot tied to Western culture's project of conquering the natural world, an undertaking linked in articulation to frontierism, which constructs culture and nature as oppositional. The assumption underlying this critique is that nature is more basic than culture, and because the project of Western culture is to transform nature, culture is conceived as not only different from, but superior to, nature. Historically, women have been characterized by natural qualities in opposition to men, and since men, not women, are identified with the institutional and symbolic forms of Western civilization and cultural change, this distinction between culture and nature supports the suppression of women. From this perspective, the physiological and social roles that constitute women as "the heart of the nation," support the ideology that constructs both the romanicized image of nature's pristine beauty, the Indian princess, and her earthy beast-of-burden sister, the squaw.

But from a Native perspective, culture and nature blend and intertwine in traditional teachings that express the discourse of unbroken connectedness. This position prompts Mohawk lawyer Patricia Montour-Angus (1992) to tell us, "I used to shrivel when people called me a feminist. The issues that feminism has tried to focus on are not the issues that occupy First Nation lives." She adds, "We have to remember to respect Mother Earth. A lot of ways women are treated on this earth are reflective of the ways Mother Earth gets treated." Paula Gunn Allen (1988: 18) warns, "We as feminists must be aware of our history on this continent."

Native women, of course, enact and act upon the contradictory and essentializing images related to the nature/culture paradigm of Western society. But their identities are also constructed in the circling discourse of Native knowledge and experience, including women's relationship to the land, to nature and to each other. The narratives that move and multiply in transforming traditionalism and the practice of everyday life, express the multivocal play of power and identity linked in articulation to the earth and the Creator. The spiritual and the natural encode the power and practice of Mohawk clan mothers, Ojibway Odgichidawque, urban drum groups and contemporary healing circles. In the cultural and political struggle of contested identities, the unity of culture and nature is expressed in transforming stories of Indian experience and the spiritualized land that position the meaning and purpose of practice.

It is the land—real and imagined, lived in heritage and in current political processes, and expressed in discourse—that constitutes the connection between nature and culture for Indians. As Kim Anderson (2000:35) writes, "As traditionally land-based peoples, we can uncover many common values about how we relate to the earth and all of creation, including how we define our human relationships." The struggle over appropriation of the discourse related to land and to nature is a struggle over land rights and treaty rights, Aboriginal rights and women's rights, New Age spiritualism and ethnographic accounts, and the words and representations of history, culture, and power.

Today, Native and non-Native women recognize a connection between domination of the land and domination of people on the basis of race, class, and gender. In asserting the link between ecology and feminism, eco-feminism both supports historicized images of Indians who lived on the land without disturbing it and recognizes a point of social and political connectedness between Native and non-Native women, and men. The struggle over clear-cutting forests, diverting rivers, and building nuclear waste dumps sometimes expands to include Native land rights and treaty rights, a prospect that speaks to the political possibility of plural narratives, representations, and perspectives that are different but allied.

First Nations Frontiers

Native people are entangled in the interests of Others, and these interests are always linked to the politics of difference in which Indians themselves are absorbed. Native North American communities struggle over issues of membership, money, and cultural meaning. The expression of these battles over economic strategy and political power can be blunt and blistering. But the Native contests over different ideologies and adopted or appropriated Indian identities can only be understood in the context of shared culture, history, experience, and political purpose, in shifting unities built from transforming memory and from the continual formation of community. It is the negotiation of relations of power—hierarchical, conflictual, and communal—expressed in contested ideology and identity that both cuts through and knits together Native communities in their struggle with domination and resistance. This political process, which is rooted in the western frontier, frames today's debates over traditionalism and treaty rights, representation and appropriation, and constructs the strained connectedness between Native North Americans and Others.

Rayna Green (on CBC *Ideas* 1992) expresses the inevitable predicament that the image of the ministering maiden poses for discursive interaction in saying, "Once you put on the princess costume … you can't ever take off the princess outfit." Speaking on the same CBC program, Kathy Mallet tells us, "Squaw? I remember being called that word and

I just kind of froze. You know, it's like somebody shot you. That's how I felt: like a bullet went right through me." These contradictory images of Indian women continue to objectify and degrade in transformations of the villain or the victim, the torturer or the sufferer; and neither the romanticized Indian princess nor the primitive squaw allows newcomers to identify Indians as equals, as owners of this land, as Native North Americans with homes, families, jobs, and indigenous governments. The cultural distance of elevation or debasement that these conceptions reflect is contrary to the actual process of "one set of people in overalls displacing another set of people in overalls" (Green 1992: 53), which removed Indians from their homelands and their resources as the frontier moved westward. The voices of Native women now shatter the silence of the past, expressing real experiences and imaginary tales that challenge and recast the old narratives of dominance. But new narratives of difference continue to emerge in the contemporary cultural and political struggles over literature and art, land and resources, reservation and Aboriginal rights. As newcomers and Natives transpose the representation of the primitive Plains warrior into the media warrior, and women press tribal governments for recognition and reform, Native communities struggle with the factionalism of power relations entrenched in the threats and promises of appropriated and continually emerging identities.

Filmmaker Loretta Todd (1992) tells a story "of how [like Curtis] a European painter in the nineteenth century journeyed into the great plains of this continent to 'record' Native people, a common occurrence of the time, born of the ethnographic":

> While he was painting a Native man on a horse, another Native man observed the artist's work and remarked how his painting was wrong. The artist, painting the horse from the side, had shown only two legs of the horse and one leg of the rider. The Native man reminded the artist that the horse had four legs and the rider two, which should all be shown. (72)

The difference in perspective between the artist's horse and the Indian's horse is compounded, of course, through appropriation. Whether one is appropriating New Age Native spiritualism through the books of Lynn Andrews (1981), Native culture through the film *If Only I Were an Indian...* (Paskievich 1995), warriors and Indians through team mascots and militants, or representations of Indian princesses and squaws through media images, the horse has only two legs. In privileging the perspective of a two-legged horse, dominant cultural narratives continue to detach, essentialize, entice, and deceive, constructing a progression of social imaginaries that not only limit Native North Americans' access to voice but efface the understanding of Native power and knowledge, and blur the pluralistic experience that Indians and Others share.

In the recreated image that circulates today on the golden dollar that the United States issued in 2000 to commemorate the new millennium, Sacajawea remains romanticized as the "guide" of the Lewis and Clark expedition. The face on the coin is actually that of a native woman named Randy'L Teton, who posed for the mould. She represents Sacajawea, who, in an advertisement for the coin, is "looking back over her shoulder, leading us on another journey.... It is a fitting reminder of her personal accomplishment and an inspiration for all of us to explore the challenges of the new millennium" (*Native Peoples Magazine* 2000: 3). Sacajawea's actual image and her experience are impossible to retrieve. The meaning of her presence is silent in the discourse that surrounds her, but Sacajawea must have signified to Indians that this group of men, travelling with a woman and child, was not a war party. Like the bullet holes in the obelisk that bears her name, "the monument stands, the plaque calls her the expedition's guide, and the public [including Indians] considers anything that says otherwise vandalism" (Duncan 1987: 165). Like Sacajawea's contradictory social imaginaries, we are all yoked together in the construction and appropriation of images of Indians that build different identities and enact intertwined ideologies in an ageless western frontier.

≪ • ≫

Dance Me Inside:
Pow Wow and Being Indian

Round Dance

Don't break this circle
Before the song is over
Because all of our people
Even the ones long gone
Are holding hands.
　　　　Sarain Stump (1974:9)

My memories of growing up as an Indian on the Lac du Flambeau reservation in Wisconsin and your memories of Indians growing up wherever you did are rooted together in images of pow wow. Some of you may have experienced pow wow through one of a complex of activities, which Rayna Green (1988: 30) calls "playing Indian"— a symphony of tom-toms, stomping feet, and war whoops; or flashes of Hollywood's brightly painted warriors building up to battle; or performances of "real" Indians in a blur of feathers and fantasy moving to the beat of a time-distanced drum. For me, like others from Indian Country, pow wow recalls a kaleidoscope of deeply felt, ambiguous images of power and identity. As a child, I remember walking the rutted road to the gathering grounds of our summer pow wows at Bear River. There, the Lac du Flambeau drum sat beside visiting nations and Chippewa cousins surrounded by moving images of the identifiable: dancers in familiar outfits of beaded buckskin, appliquéd ribbon, or silver bullet cones. At the Bear River pow wow grounds, I was drawn by the beat of the drum into a circle of socialization, a mixture of forceful, fragmented feelings of community and spirituality framed by the closeness of my great-grandmother, and the distance of Bert Skye, who might, without warning, transform himself into a bird or a dog.

Today, my memories of the Bear River pow wow are interwoven with years of going to other pow wows elsewhere: urban and reserve, western and eastern, competitive and traditional, local and commercial. For Native Americans and Canadians themselves, each pow wow reflects the cultural specificity of a tribal nation, a unique community, a particular ceremony. But for the different Native people who experience them, pow wows express certain cultural similarities and a deeply felt and shared sense of "being Indian" that threads through the dichotomies used to analyze power and identity—belonging and exclusion, knowledge and ignorance, control and resistance—all signified in the rhythm of the drum and the collective singing of seemingly wordless songs. In this site of cultural struggle over conflicting identities and competing ideologies, Natives, newcomers, performers, and spectators negotiate the meaning of Indianness.

Pow Wow Country

Pow wow has become an important site of Native North American popular culture. Over fifty thousand dancers circle the drums in Albuquerque, New Mexico, each spring. Pow wow is smaller but equally important in the east. In the summer of 1991, over three thousand people gathered in Kahnawake, Quebec, to witness the first pow wow held in recent history on this Mohawk territory. In the summer of 1992, as Canadians recognized the nation's 150th birthday and Americans celebrated the Columbus Quincentennial, Indians in Ontario hosted the first annual Toronto International Pow Wow. More recently, twenty thousand people attended the Mashantucket Pequot Nation Pow Wow in Connecticut, a celebration of culture that included a rock concert with rap artists, country and western singers, comedy acts, and performances by American Indian Movement (AIM) leaders Russell Means and John Trudel (Gonzalez 1998: 227). The summer pow wow circuit is now a Native institution, and the pow wow trail winds through reservations, college towns, and cities across Canada and the United States all year long. This uniquely Native cultural activity, which is rooted in traditional heritage, historical representation, and commercial venture, has gained new popularity at a time of increasing struggle over the politics of difference linked to Native treaty rights, land claims, and self-determination. Amid the tensions over non-Native appropriation of Native land and culture, pow wow is unusual in Indian Country because of its openness to outsiders and its potential for understanding Indians as "active agents in the representation [and production] of their culture rather than static objects of scholarly contemplation" (Simpson 1997: 4).

Pow wows are as different as Native North Americans themselves. These gatherings can be flashy spectacles offering thousands of dollars in prize money for competitive dancing, small celebrations of sobriety, traditional tribal socials, or even a combination of all three. Pow wows are not Native religious rites and, as Michael Greyeyes (1997: 32) points out "the two are not to be confused." But pow wows are an important public expression of Indian culture and a form of Native social practice. The contemporary meaning of this practice cannot be explained in writing that adopts the functional focus of structuralist analysis or that dissects pow wow as being "magical," having shamanistic rites, or being historically situated ceremonies.

As Victor Turner (1969) suggests, rituals and ceremonies are not just passive cultural repositories, they are active agents of cultural creation in which symbols not only transform and maintain cultural forms but also express meaning in social action. For Turner, rituals and ceremonies are qualities of action, not specific events or types of action, and ritualized practices occur in a wide range of social activities as well as religious rites. Because culture is not only the web of meaning we spin for ourselves but also the struggle over meaning that we continually negotiate, the way we make sense of particular events and practices in ceremonies or social rituals is not inscribed in these events themselves. The meaning of symbols, signs, and actions is negotiated in the discursive exchange that occurs in and around the performance of ritualized customs and ceremonies. For Native people, pow wow is part of the "imbroglio of heritages" that characterize Indian culture and express "an enduring belief in the efficacy of ceremony or ritual as a vehicle for personal and social negotiation" (Townsend-Gault 1992: 51). The social ritual of pow wow expresses cultural continuity and the creative liminality of "inventing our lives collectively as we go on, playing games, performing our own being" (Turner in Ashley 1990: xix).

Understood from the perspective of social agency, "being Native" is linked in articulation not only to particular historical conditions but to the contradictory and conflicting representations that define and claim the meaning of cultural forms and their relationship to social reality. Our webs of cultural meaning are always spun in a discursive process, in an ongoing conversation with one another. Among Native people, pow wow is part of a conversation which, like other cultural forms, expresses "the ways that Indians render their own experience into being, how they represent themselves and their people *to each other*" (Simpson 1997: 7, italics in original). The music and movement of pow wow is like Geertz's Balinese cockfight, which "offers the Balinese a text that represents Balinese society to itself and so provides the opportunity and the occasion for the Balinese to think and rethink, to feel and feel again what being Balinese means" (Mukerji and Schudson 1991: 21). But the practice and performance of pow wow are not simply an affirmation of personal identification. In these contemporary social gatherings, the sights and sounds that lure the senses draw participants and observers alike into an arena of ambivalent relationships that merge the past and the present. Pow wows express contradictory memories that are rooted in Indian tradition and ethnographic testimony. In the cultural struggle over the meaning of Native popular culture—over what Indians know, experience, and express, and over who Native North Americans are— pow wow is linked in articulation to ideology, identity, and political possibility.

Pow wows are relaxed, improvisational, and playfully creative, an occasion for the spontaneous interaction among people that Turner (in Raybin 1990: 30) associates with "communitas." There is an organic flow to pow wow activities, a pattern of movement built in the process of seeing old friends, camping, preparing food and outfits, which are all part of the event itself. The form and the pace of this social gathering, which can last an evening or a week, mean that pow wow can seem loosely organized, arbitrary, or even haphazard to outsiders. But the competitive and traditional pow wows that dot the map of North America are structured, and they share common signifying practices of traditional music and stylized dance genres, each identified by a particular outfit and style of movement. There are men's and women's traditional dances with their controlled movements, for which men wear buckskin outfits or ribbon shirts and "roaches" (headgear made of porcupine hair); and women wear buckskin, appliquéd, or jingle dresses. And there are the "fancy dances"—named for the fancy footwork—including the high-flying steps and the brightly coloured outfits of the men's Grass Dance and the twirling, butterfly-like movements of the women's Shawl Dance.

Pow wow takes place around a dance arbour built for the occasion. The sequence of the dances is proclaimed by an announcer and begun by lead dancers, who escort the participants into the circle. Pow wow opens with prayers before Grand Entries of the dancers in the afternoon and evening, each followed by the Flag Song—the Indian National Anthem sung without movement—and the Veteran's Song that honours warriors. Throughout the event, the open participation of inter-tribal dancing—often open to Natives and non-Natives alike—is mixed with traditional sets or competitions and performances that showcase different dance styles. The sequence of different dances blends with dances to retrieve a fallen eagle feather, and with Honour Songs and Give Aways that celebrate the first dances of children, recognize Elders or remember individuals who have walked on. In the evening, there is a communal feast for dancers and their families; but all day long, there is a celebration of consumption at the craft tables and food stands selling ageless arts and endless curios, or fry bread and Indian tacos. In the words of one pow wow dancer, "We laugh, we visit, we eat—and then we follow the sounds [of the drum] into the circle" (Venza 1989).

Within the fluidity of this social celebration, the ceremony of pow wow is framed by the presence of the sacred fire and centred in the essence of the drum. Outsiders may not see the sacred fire or notice those who offer tobacco before they dance or sit in lawn chairs placed around the circle of the dance ground. In the modern celebration of pow wow, the sacred fire and the drum may seem to express "ritualized markers of recovered power, exercised in a new way" (Townsend-Gault 1992: 51), but the meaning of these markers emerges in practices that are shared with distant grandfathers and grandmothers. Today, like pow wows of the past, "the drum is the main thing" (Conklin 1994: 19); and the meaning of the drum is layered in the ambiguity and continuity of tribal memories, both personal and collective. The program for the Toronto International Pow Wow, *Pow Wow Time* (1992) notes:

> All the activities of pow wow dancing stem from the beat of the drum and encircle the drum. The term drum, which encompasses the singers as well, is a more symbolic representation than simply being regarded as a musical instrument. Drums are blessed and given names by most singing groups. The drum is sacred to natives and … is the heartbeat of the Anishnabek nations. (18)

The drum, which is the unifying force of pow wows, is actually many drums, which are animated by a series of drum groups that alternate drumming and singing in turn, each recognized for a region or repertoire,

Marcus Guthrie dancing at a winter pow wow, Lac du Flambeau, 1975. Photograph by Gregg Guthrie. Reproduced with permission.

each setting the pace and the style for the dancers. Dancers move in and out of the circle, taking breaks to talk with family and friends. This is a social occasion, but dancers like James Watt (in Roberts 1992: 120) tell us, "When we are dancing, we have a relationship with the Creator. We have a relationship with the drum." Some traditional dancers say that when they move to the drumbeat, each small step that touches the earth is a prayer to the Creator. Others remind us that Indians embody the memories of their ancestors and through the beat of the drum, those memories arise. Even performers in the American Indian Dance Theater, pow wow's most commercial venue, recognize the power of the drum. As one dancer says, "We hear the songs of all those who have gone before. The drum calls us" (Venza 1989). The pow wow drum of which these dancers speak is a mnemonic device that recalls not words but sentiment. However, the expressions of Indian sensibility that encircle the drum and that express personal, cultural, and political possibilities have not always been evident.

Positioning Pow Wow

The textual reconstruction and analysis of Indian social and religious behaviour such as traditional songs, dances, and regalia have been the work of anthropologists and musicologists since the late 1800s. Their writing reflects the descriptive analysis of Indian costumes, music, and dancing with—and sometimes without—details of the specific ceremonies or occasions of which they are a part. But pow wow was not a topic of research until the 1950s, when anthropologists extended functionalist analysis to the study of pow wows as institutionalized events, locating them in Plains Indian culture, which formed the basis of the modern pan-Indian practices that spread eastward (Howard 1955; Lurie 1971; Corrigan 1970). More recently, Powers (1990) has analyzed the Plains War Dance in relation to tribalism and inter-tribalism; Noel Dyck (1979: 78) has argued that pow wow "serves as a means for achieving symbolic resolution of some of the long-standing problems which confront Indians"; and Valda Blundell (1993: 17) has undertaken semiotic analysis of pow wow as performed texts that can be read as "sites where aboriginal cultural producers engage in an oppositional politics of meaning production." The analysis of these academics discusses the hybridity, popularity, and significance of contemporary pow wow, but something is missing.

The practice of pow wow is rooted in the historical and cultural realities woven together in external representations of Indianness and the internal experience of "being Indian." It is the affective and ideological qualities of being Indian that are articulated to Native cultural beliefs and practices, that establish pow wow as critically different from "playing Indian." If this is suggested in the writing of Geertz (1973), Turner (1969), Baktin (1981), Williams (1981), Hall (Morley and Chen 1996), and others, the significance of pow wow—with all its discursive inconsistencies, individual innovations and cultural tensions—has been largely ignored in academic analysis because of borders that reflect anthropological method, academic approach, non-Native appropriation, and Native reappropriation. These borders that separate subjectivity and objectivity, historical and modern, authentic and popular are compounded by the long-standing imbalance between access, legitimation, and authority related to ethnographic and Indian testimony.

Read off the surface, the practice of pow wow is understood as little more than a specific—or a generic—contemporary Indian carnival. An article on new Native music in the Toronto *Globe and Mail* (20 March 1993) was headlined "Pow Wow Rock"; and in the 1990s, too, a popular film among Indians was entitled *Pow Wow Highway*; and an art gallery in Montreal sponsored a "Cyber Powwow." This mixture of the traditional and the transformed can cause confusion among outsiders and conflict among Native people themselves. Native activist Russell Means (with Wolf 1995) writes, "Since the powwows began, the Indian nations have become ... caricatures of their own traditions, unrecognizable as communities, as nations, almost as Indians." In August 1997, Mark Abley reported in the *Montreal Gazette*:

> I remember attending a pow-wow on a sultry July day in Kahnawake. The host drum was beaten by a couple of Assiniboines from southern Manitoba; the master of ceremonies had moved from Pennsylvania to Navajo territory in Arizona; the head male dancer was a Michigan Ojibwa. According to my souvenir program, one of the sponsoring businesses was East of Texas Westernwear in Kahnawake. The program described the Grand Entry song as "probably an imitation of rodeos and Wild West shows." A melange, a hotchpotch, a bit of this and a bit of that. The pow-wow bore the name Echoes of a Proud Nation. But what exactly was the nation? Mohawk, Iroquois or pan-Indian? ... if the hybrid future of a newly-public, inclusive aboriginal culture can be symbolized by ersatz rodeo songs and East of Texas Westernwear, it won't be only white writers who feel a huge sense of loss. (D3)

To Means, Abley, and others, pow wow expresses a mixture of transformed and appropriated practices, an Indian popular culture devoid of the "authentic" cultural content they have read or remembered and, therefore, bereft of meaning. In the struggle over traditionalism, this view is supported by some Native North Americans who say that pow wows "have transpired into nothing more than trendy social gatherings

where Native people armed with buckskin, feathers and enthusiasm try
to revive a once-dominant lifestyle" (Wetelainen 1982: 50). Some Indians
object to the individualism and exhibitionism of competitive fancy dance,
which they regard as a move away from the collective quality of traditional dance. Other Indians recognize the Grass Dance and Shawl Dance
as innovations in the dynamic cultures of Native North America. But
Indians agree with the Native testimony that tells us "a pow wow celebration is a way of life and one of the most forceful manifestations of
Indian cultural beliefs" (Stump 1970: 9).

The performance of pow wow and the development of its contemporary forms cannot be fully explained as appropriation, revitalization, or
a statement of Native resistance; and the meaning of pow wow cannot
be understood in the isolated analysis of a historicized practice or a local
event, as an expression of recent political conflicts, or as the enactment
of long-standing representation, deprivation, marginalization, or culture spread. For Indians, pow wow involves more than artistic or ethnic
performance. Catherine Whipple (1995) writes about experiencing pow
wow and the sensibilities of ceremony that academic approaches to
Native social analysis erase or ignore:

> Drums vibrate through the dirt and grass to my feet. The sun dips into
> the earth and the wind swirls in different directions mimicking the grass
> dancers. Jingling sounds from dresses mix with grasshoppers.... I focus
> on feathers, beads, and braids all shifting in and out of focus as dancers
> twirl by, sometimes dipping and disappearing from my view. High
> pitched voices sing with the rhythm of the drums, sing with the shaking
> of the earth as dancers move together in one circle. (1)

Indians sometimes disagree about the origins of pow wow or the
integrity of more recent pan-Indian innovations. But for most Native
people, pow wow constitutes what Lawrence Grossberg (1992: 82–84)
calls a "mattering map," a site of popular culture in which Indians "can
attempt to organize a stable identity which finds them 'at home' with
what they care about, and which in the process of that alliance, produces an empowerment legitimated in ideology." The affective sensibility of pow wow operates as "a crucial ground where people give others,
whether cultural practices or social groups, the authority to shape their
identity and locate them within various circuits of power." Pow wow
expresses different representations of tribal and Native identities that
are linked in articulation to tradition, defined by Jan Vansina (1985: 160)

as "memories of memories." These are fragmented memories of history, heritage, spirituality, and popular culture that move through oral exchange; they are memories that float in time and shift in place. As T.S. Eliot (1932: 14) reminds us, tradition is "not only a perception of the past, but of its presence." For Indians, the presence of the past is built in shared stories of dominance and resistance, connection and purpose that construct a sense of a common Native heritage—remembered, transformed, and imagined. In communities unified in difference, Native North Americans identify with the reconstructed commonality of pan-Indian cultural formation and struggle. The collective meanings that emerge in pan-Indianism are ambiguous and contested, but they neither dissolve tribal identities nor erase tribal differences.

Native people do not forget the individual and tribal experiences that express who they are as they remember and reconstruct the collective traditions of who they were. Like the representations in which they are built, Native identities and alliances are constantly shifting. The distinct tribal experiences of some nations are transformed and appropriated by Native people from other nations in continually emerging cultural formations that express not only tribal identities but also a sense of collective culture and shared political purpose. The shared sense of the affective empowerment of being and becoming Indian is what Robert Allen Warrior (1991/1992: 35) calls "the sweetgrass meaning of solidarity." In the sweetgrass solidarity of pow wow, "the *feeling* of heritage, traditions and beginnings is always there for the exploring" (Wagamese 1996: 59, italics in original).

The sensibility of pow wow—differently felt and expressed, contested but remembered, imagined and constructed in contemporary ceremony—is articulated to collective culture and the political possibility of Native empowerment. This feeling of collective identity and shared community is not an expression of nativistic revitalization but an awareness of cultural persistence, which is built in pan-Indian images of oneness. In the commonness of ceremony, Native people not only remember the past but also imagine the future. The narratives of culture and history that emerge and mingle, imagine sovereignty, self-determination, and nationhood intertwined in a knot of representations that engages both "the prism through which Indians view their historical experiences" and the movement "toward a place and state of being that is [their] own" (Simpson 1997: 6). As Grossberg (1992: 83) suggests, "It is the affective investment ... that explains the power of the articulation which bonds particular representations and realities [and I would add, memories] ... which enables ideological relations to be internalized and, consequently, naturalized."

Academic enterprise has never been comfortable with the analysis of the phenomenological or affective experience of Indian testimony or ceremony. But it is the discursive articulation of affectivity, ideology, and cultural identity—which is lost in academic literature—that links the social imaginaries and memoried histories rooted together in the outsider's representations of Indianness and the insider's experience of being Indian. As one pow wow dancer expresses it, "The drum talks to us to tell us who we are. In our circle, we are in touch with our world" (Venza 1989). Yet, like Native identities, the cultural formation of pow wow is continually changing. Evelyn Nelson-Kennedy (1990) says,

> Little things at powwows bother me—the MC's blaring voice over the speakers while the songs are in progress, the selling of everything from bannock to T-shirts emblazoned with the sad faces of old Indians. At times, I know it isn't these petty happenings that irk me but rather the reflections of myself that I see in them. I am a mixture of the old and the new. Like the powwows, I have changed. (227)

In Indian Country, the memoried past and the self-determined future are articulated to ceremony. In the presence of ceremony, "the imaginative experience and the historical express equally the traditions of man's reality" (Momaday 1969: 4). Paula Gunn Allen (1987: 577) explains: "The ceremonial is the means of achieving wholeness of being; it is the vehicle of the imagination which allows the human being to imagine himself fully ... that part or function of consciousness where the Spirit and the Human meet and merge and become one, and it is beyond history or time as it is far from the narrow conflicts of pure reason." As Stephen Augustine (2004) tells us, "The first thing we ever hear is our mother's heartbeat, like the sound of the drumbeat of ceremonies or pow wows." In the words of Bren Kolson (in Perreault and Vance 1990), "Stick of life, drum of hide, beating out ancestral songs. Memories of life's defeats and life's enduring will to go on and on and on" (134).

Removed from the "mattering map" of transforming traditional ceremony, pow wow signifies the social imaginaries of the noble and the savage Indian. These familiar stereotypes displace tribal identities with the monolithic Indians of North America's political heritage. From the beginning, pow wow played a part in the politics of difference and domination. The program for the Toronto pow wow notes:

The term pow wow is a European term that has since been borrowed back by natives…. "Pau wau" which means medicine man or conjurer, was misconstrued by European settlers who witnessed the healing practices of the village shaman…. The word was taken to mean "the gathering of natives" that surrounded the medicine man during healing practices, rather than the individual himself (*Pow Wow Time* 1992: 7).

In the *Handbook of American Indians North of Mexico*, Hodge (1910: 303) defines pow wow as "a medicine-man; the conjuring of a medicine-man over a patient; a dance, feast or noisy celebration preceding a council, expedition, or hunt; a council; or a conference." Today, this sweeping definition of pow wow that has emerged from the history of observing Indians can also refer to a meeting or a dance, but it always invokes images of Indians.

Pow Wow's Past

Whatever the definition of pow wow, non-Native testimony has long essentialized the carnival image of Indians dancing, an activity which has materialized into a way of seeing and understanding Native people since the earliest reports of encounter. As early as 1534, the French explorer Jacques Cartier wrote of the Indians he met at the mouth of the St. Lawrence River that they "approached neere unto our boate, dancing and making many signs of joy and mirth…. Some of the women who came not over, we might see stand up to their knees in water, singing and dancing" (in Laubin and Laubin 1977: 3). Throughout the 1700s and 1800s, missionaries, merchants, and military men marched west, leaving a legacy of encounter rich with observations of Indians dancing. Basil Johnson (1976: 146) writes, "It is said that 'song is the utterance of the soul.' If such is the case, then dance is the enactment of the beat of the mood of the soul." But early testimony recalls ceremonial dance as "'a crude jumping about,' 'a mere hopping up and down,' 'a leaping about in the most comical manner imaginable,' 'a frenzied expression of uncontrolled passion'" (Mason 1944: 3). Among the more memorable records are the Jesuit Relations written between 1610 and 1791, which remark upon dancing (along with sorcery and incantations) among the religious practices of the Indians whom they worked to Christianize (Mason 1944: 3, 20); and the sketches and paintings by artist George Catlin from the 1830s that "first taught Americans to look at their West" (Pearce

1953: 111) and have remained the referent for a century of representations of Indians primed for pow wow. Catlin painted Indians from fifty-five different tribes, an accomplishment which Hassrick (1988: 31) notes as "an inestimable contribution to the nation's understanding of the Native American's heritage." When he visited the Mandan in 1832, Catlin wrote:

> The Mandans, like all other tribes ... devote a great deal of their time to sports and amusements, of which ... dancing is one of the principle.... These exercises are exceedingly grotesque in their appearance, and to the eye of the traveler who knows not their meaning or importance, they are an uncouth and frightful display of starts and jumps, and yelps, and jarring gutterals, which are sometimes truly terrifying. (In Laubin and Laubin 1977: 41)

But Catlin (in Laubin and Laubin 1977: 42) also noted the ritualized quality of Indian dance, which "enters into their form of worship, and is often in their mode of appealing to the Great Spirit." Others also recognized the importance of Native ceremonial performance. George Nelson (Brown and Brightman 1988: 143) wrote about the Cree and Ojibway in 1823, noting that "dancing, drumming and singing were intended to communicate with and show respect for the spirits." Henry Schoolcraft visited the Chippewa in 1848 and wrote that, "singing and dancing are applied to political and to religious purposes by the Indians." Furthermore:

> Dancing is both an amusement and a religious observance among the American Indians.... Tribes the most diverse in language, and situated at the greatest distance apart, concur in this. It is believed to be the ordinary mode of expressing intense passion, of feeling, on any subject, and it is a custom which has been persevered in, with the least variation, through all the phases of their history. (In Laubin and Laubin 1977: 44–45)

Schoolcraft (45) concludes that "dancing is thus interwoven throughout the whole texture of Indian society, so that there is scarcely an event important or trivial, private or public, which is not connected, more or less intimately, with this rite."

Early anthropologists may have recognized the uniqueness of Indian dance forms, but the significance of these cultural practices are not always evident in their writing. As the first ethnographers researched the lifestyle of Native North Americans, songs and music became items of study that were removed from the collective cultural practice and spiritual expression of dance; and drums became valued as artifacts, interesting because of their design, construction, or use more than their endowment and purpose. One of the most remarkable of the early ethnographers was Frances Densmore, who began to document Chippewa music and customs in the region of Lac du Flambeau in 1893. She collected songs from my great-grandmother and from Bert Skye's father, Anawabe, for her reports on *Chippewa Music*, published by the Bureau of American Ethnology in 1910 and 1913. She all but ignored the ceremonial context of Indian dance; but long before anthropologists spoke of pow wow and pan-Indianism, Densmore (1913) wrote of the cultural transformation remembered by Anawabe, Lac du Flambeau's medicine man:

> The first of the following songs used in the begging dance is said to have come from the Assinniboin, or Rock Sioux, many years ago. The dance also was derived from the same tribe but has been practiced among the Chippewa for so many generations that it may be regarded as one of their tribal dances. (228)

If anthropologists were slow to recognize the power and practice of Indians drumming and dancing, missionaries and Indian agents were not. Working in consort, they mounted a forceful spiritual and legal attack on Indian religious and cultural practice that is entrenched in the memories of Native North Americans. In Canada, the battle against Native religions began in the 1850s, when William Duncan, a missionary whose contention that Tsimshian potlatches were barbaric, led a movement that strongly influenced the government's passage of an anti-potlatch law in 1884. In that year, an amendment to the Indian Act which governed tribal life, dictated that participating in the potlatch or tawanawa dance rituals practised by the Native nations of the West Coast was a criminal offence punishable with prison sentences. When Franz Boas began his fieldwork among the Kwagiulth in 1886, he was met with the words, "We want to know whether you have come to stop our dances and feasts, as the missionaries and agents who live among our neighbors try to do. We do not want anyone here who will interfere with our custom." A Blackfoot spokesman remarked, "I do not understand why the white men desire to put an end to our religious ceremonials.... If they deprive us of our religion, we will have nothing left, for we know of no other that can take its place" (in Nabokov 1991: 225–26). The potlatch, songs, and dances—objects and practices that sustained these and other religious ceremonies—were illegal in Canada until 1951 when the Indian

Pow wow at Bear River, in the Old Village on the Lac du Flambeau reservation, 1938. Photograph courtesy of the author.

Act was revised and the law was repealed, granting Native people religious and cultural freedom. But as Gerald McMaster (1993: 102) writes, "By that time, many generations had passed. The government's cultural genocide had taken its toll."

In the United States, Indian religious ceremonies, such as the Ghost Dance and the Sun Dance, and the Native American Church with its peyote rituals, all met the same fate in 1890. In that year, federal troops, fearing an Indian uprising related to the nativistic ideology and nationalism of the Ghost Dance Movement, killed over three hundred unarmed Sioux at the Massacre of Wounded Knee, in South Dakota. The Ghost Dance was a ritualized ceremony, a simple healing ceremony in which participants joined hands and danced in a leftward movement that linked them together with those in the next world. To Indians, the Ghost Dance expressed a prophesy spread through the teachings of the Paiute spiritual leader Wovoka. In 1889, he recounted that "the time will come when the whole Indian race, living and dead, will be reunited upon a regenerated earth, to live a life of aboriginal happiness, forever free from death, disease and misery" (Mooney [1896] 1996: 139). Similar nativistic prophesies that combined traditional and Christian beliefs emerged among other Native nations, mediated by medicine men who prescribed healing dances that projected a future in which Indians would regain control of their lives. Among the Sioux, some medicine men encouraged Indians to fulfill the prophesy by stemming the continual encroachment of non-Natives, who were now moving west in greater numbers to settle in Indian Country. But according to Indians and the anthropologist James Mooney, whose seminal study on the Ghost Dance was written in 1896, the Ghost Dance pressed Indians to discard their weapons of war in preparation for a time when "all race distinctions [were] to be obliterated," including the divisions between Indians and Others (Mooney [1896] 1996: 139).

To non-Natives, the religious revivalism seemed ominous, especially in Sioux territory, where for some Indians, long-standing grievances conjoined prophesy and empowerment in an expression of religious ceremony that ultimately cost many Sioux lives. When the army attacked under the guise of an uprising, the ghost shirts and dresses painted with stars and eagles that Sioux believed made them impervious to bullets, were shattered by gunshots. Today, the anguish of Sitting Bull and Big Foot, of brothers, mothers, grandmothers, and others, still echoes across Indian Country, in voices that remember the battle of Wounded Knee fought in 1890 and fought again in 1973, when the occupation of the American Indian Movement brought the Ghost Dance back to this place consecrated in Indian blood.

The religious laws in the United States were enacted to attack the Ghost Dance and the Sun Dance, but the impact extended to all Indian religious activities. Native religious practice was caught in a maelstrom of fifty years of spiritual and cultural oppression. The ban on Indian spiritual activity eventually eased, but it was not fully lifted until 1978, when the American Indian Religious Freedom Act affirmed that Indian religions were protected by the constitution's First Amendment. Native ceremonies, including pow wow, survived in secret, spread in silence, or openly expressed contestations of government control. Henrietta Mann Morton (in Roberts 1992) says:

Following non-Indian contact, the pow wow, like many of our dances, was misunderstood and subject to repression by the United States Federal Government. Pow wows, however, have endured; so have the people, as have many other aspects of their culture. Just as important, so has the Indian spirit. (20)

There may not be a connection between the emergence of the Ghost Dance, the tragedy at Wounded Knee, and the spread of Native cultural traditions, but the pan-Indian ceremonials and social practices that began to advance across Indian Country in the 1900s are, to a significant extent, Sioux traditions.

With the growth of anthropology after the turn of the twentieth century, ethnographers moved with new zeal to describe and document Indian religious ceremonies and spiritual practices before their assumed disappearance. These early anthropologists were uncomfortable with Indian experience that was ambiguous, hybrid, or processional. Some ethnographers recorded testimonies that express Christian influences or emerging practices, but autobiographies were marginal to ethnographic analysis; and because anthropologists were interested in documenting traditional culture, testimonies were often silent about the experience, practice, and meaning of cultural transformations. Fieldworkers reported on specific ceremonies, noting chronologies of action, details of regalia, and interpretations of custom. Ethnographers collected songs, dances, outfits, and artifacts—testimonials to personal dreams, individual industry, and communal practice—most often removed from the affective and ideological performance of respective ceremonies and set into the conceptual frameworks that emerged to explain the transformative nature of Indian dance: relative deprivation, nativistic religion, acculturation, assimilation, revitalization. As Bernard Mason (1944: 5) writes, "After all is said and done, the scientists, regardless of type, have done little better for the dance than the early travelers, explorers and missionaries." In the their haste to report on old traditions, anthropologists neglected the contemporary popular culture that emerged among Indians, including pow wow.

Michael Greyeyes (1997) tells us that the roots of pow wow go back to the early 1800s when the dances, regalia, and stories of the Sun Dance of the Mandan and the Hidatsa, the Hethuska Dance of the Ponca, and the Grass Dance of the Omaha, the Pawnee, and the Dakota were given as gifts to other Native nations. He speaks of the styles of dance and dress that emerged through tribal adaptation and individual innovation when pow wow spread to the east. This mixture of social and spiritual practice moved in silence and secrecy to conceal religious performance from Indian agents and missionaries. But in the 1940s, pow wow emerged from the shadows to celebrate the return of the several thousand Indian warriors who fought with Americans and Canadians in the Second World War. Even then, few anthropologists were interested in pow wow, and no one recognized a connection between the social expression of pow wow and the spiritual significance of ceremony.

Ethnographers did not associate Indian ceremonial dance with pow wow until the early 1950s, nor did they recognize its phenomenological meaning. Writing in 1970, Samuel Corrigan (254) cites three articles on pow wow written in the 1950s and 1960s, noting that "the topic has been otherwise neglected." In the anthropological silence, pow wow assumed the position of a purely touristic performance associated with the Wild West Shows of the late 1800s and the development of western rodeo, a commercial, folkloric expression of culture sometimes co-present with, but always removed from, the processes of personal, collective, or spiritual ceremony. Corrigan (253) writes, "Powwow … is merely a gathering of Indian people for singing and dancing, and has no religious or magical significance in itself."

For three decades after the 1880s, "probably the most important force for Indians and whites alike in casting the image of the Indian in the lineaments of the Plains dancer and warrior was Buffalo Bill's Wild West Show" (Hertzberg 1971: 25). Buffalo Bill Cody toured the country with a cast of characters that were reminiscent of dime novels, including Wild Bill Hickock, Annie Oakley, Calamity Jane, and a troupe of Indians, the most famous of whom was Sitting Bull, known for his leadership in 1876 in the incident Natives call the Battle of Greasy Grass and non-Natives know as the Battle of Little Big Horn or "Custer's Last Stand." The dance named the Hethuska by the Ponca Warrior Society had become a trope of the performing Plains Indian in the years before the First World War, and with the advent of the Wild West Shows, this representation merged with the image of the war-dancing rodeo Indian (Greyeyes 1997: 29–30). The Hethuska was highlighted as a performance of "wild Indians" when rodeos began in Canada with the Calgary Stampedes of 1912 and 1917 and in the early 1900s, too, the touristic celebration known as "Banff Indian Days." These local fairs and festivals, complete with parades, pageants, pow wows, and riding competitions—variations of which still occur today—"have done much to paint the character of the imagined communities they address" (Burgess 1993: 2). But even as these performative expressions of western social imaginaries placed and appropriated Indians in secular ceremonies, pow wow continued to embody a sense of Native spirituality. Abe Conklin (1994) writes about the double meaning of pow wow:

> After the turn of the century, with the Wild West Shows, they started calling this dance a powwow. It didn't sound too exciting if you called it a Man Dance or He-thus-ka. It didn't sound exciting enough because all these people were coming from the east by the trainloads to see the cowboys and the Indians. So, they said, War Dance, and that excited the people. They would get out there and dance. And it was just a show then. But the Poncas still had their own. They called it He-thus-ka Society, and that dance they would do in a sacred way. (17)

In Lac du Flambeau in the 1920s, as the Hethuska and other dance forms spread to this reservation from the west, the medicine man Anawabe, my great-grandmother, and other Indians sang personal, social, or ceremonial songs for Indians and for anthropologists. The pow wow grounds at the Bear River remained a site of summer celebrations, complete with dances and feasts that continued in the winter at the Round House in the Old Village, where socials and ceremonials were held. The invisibility of this ceremonial life in Lac du Flambeau diminished as waves of tourists discovered the lakes of this reservation land. Following the trails of the missionaries, traders, and loggers who entered here before them, men came to the fishing camps and families came to summer resorts to frolic in the sun. Tourists, who were fascinated by exotic Indians but frightened by the foreignness of Native daily life, were drawn to the safe arenas of summer pow wows. As pow wow became part of the touristic pleasures of this place, visitors found their way to the tall pines on the banks of the Bear River to watch this "ceremony of the aborigines with rhythmic tum-tum of drum and pounding of moccasined feet" (*September Outer's Book* 1917: 178).

Thirty years later, as Hollywood moviemakers were rediscovering the war-dancing Plains Indians of dime novels, the eastern expansion of the western pow wow circuit spawned a new notion of cultural dynamics to describe the cultural emergence of Indian dance. In 1955, James Howard wrote a seminal article on Oklahoma pow wows that established the concept of "pan-Indianism" to describe what he understood as the dynamics of Native cultural exchange (Powers 1990: 51). Howard (1955:

215–16) argued that, rather than assimilating to the dominant culture upon the collapse of traditional tribal lifestyles, many Indians have "become members of a supertribal culture." For Howard—like Russell Means and Mark Abley—tribal distinctiveness had been replaced through the uneven diffusion of a non-tribal or inter-tribal Indian culture, incorporating modifications of old tribal customs and innovations peculiar to pan-Indianism. Howard's analysis, which described the evolution and spread of Plains Indian dance, reconstructed pow wow as a new cultural form, which "has only been taken up by the Indians in Western Canada since the 1950s" (Dyck 1979: 85). Understood as an expression of "playing Indian" more than "being Indian," the concept of pan-Indianism was widely adapted to describe urban Indian culture and emerging political movements (Hertzberg 1971). Some scholars argued that pan-Indianism would dilute Indian culture and disband tribal groups, and Indians would be absorbed into the pluralistic societies of North American nation-states. Others suggested that pan-Indian innovations would enrich rather than replace the cultural traditions of individual tribes. In the discussions of pan-Indianism that ensued, the portent of pow wow articulated to Native cultural and political transformations was largely disregarded. Reservation pow wows were understood as expressions of inauthentic culture and economic enterprise in the years when performances of Indian dancing and drumming were organized by Others for vacationers in Lac du Flambeau.

In 1951, the Indian Bowl was built in Lac du Flambeau to attract summer tourists for ambiguous exhibitions of pow wow for profit. Chippewa cousins and neighbours no longer gathered on the banks of the Bear River to dance in celebration of the summer, to acknowledge children entering this circle of Indian socialization, or to mark the passing of an elder. The old pow wow drums seemed suspended in silence, along with the Midéwiwin drums of Chippewa religious ceremonies. Jim Bell, the keeper-of-the-drums in Lac du Flambeau, had died; in his absence, the drums that he protected had passed to practising Midé or had been acquired by anthropologists. Reminiscent of Wild Bill Hickock and his troupe, Indians danced three nights a week at the new Indian Bowl, the destination for city tourists who flocked to Lac du Flambeau. Audiences applauded Grand Entries of exhibition dancers enacting elaborate narratives, complete with torch-lit canoes landing from the lake, inter-tribal battles, Chippewa socials, and stories that were sometimes ageless legends, sometimes just imagined. Indians from other tribes began to mix and mingle in the spectacle of Chippewa heritage and dances at the Indian Bowl, all coordinated by our respected tribal chairman, who announced the sequence of events. And in those years when pow wow for profit became a strategy for Indian economic development in Lac du Flambeau, the outfits worn by Chippewa men and women spread to other nations in Indian Country. Traditional male dancers in pow wows everywhere wore buckskin, floral beaded vests and dance diapers, beaded armbands and legbands, and the "roach" headpiece; traditional women dancers wore buckskin dresses characteristic of the Chippewa.

For anthropologists, the advent of pow wow for profit was understood as an outcome of cultural adaptation among Indians who were experiencing the structural strains and psychological uncertainties of cultural change. In the 1950s, the anthropologists Hallowell (1955, 1967), Barnouw (1950), and Ritzenthaler (1953) came to Lac du Flambeau to study the psychological stresses of Indians who seemed caught between conflicting cultures, entangled in disparate realities, and suspended between tradition and acculturation. These visiting scholars recorded selected life histories, probing and testing individual Indians, whom they paid to take Rorschach tests and tell stories, hoping to unravel the personality of our last medicine man, the disposition of our hereditary chief, and the psychological state of elders like my great-grandmother. In an effort to understand patterns of individual change and personal conflict, anthropologists classified Indians in categories that designated degrees of cultural accommodation—traditional, transitional, or modern; assimilated, acculturated, or marginal—typologies of personal characteristics that harmonized with the anthropological approaches of the times. But the Indians on this reservation were impossible to classify. In his analysis, Hallowell (351) concluded:

> Thus even the highly acculturated Indians at Flambeau are still Ojibway in a psychological sense, whatever their clothes, their houses, or their occupations, whether they speak English or not, or regardless of race mixture. While culturally speaking they appear like "whites" in many respects, there is no evidence at all of a fundamental psychological transformation. (351)

The daily lives that Indians lived and the emerging meaning of Indian identity and power were concealed in questions that early anthropologists never asked about negotiating contradictory narratives and conflicting alliances, mediating diverging life worlds and lifestyles, and living the cultural struggles of a community built in unities of difference.

In the end, "neither the structural nor the psychological approach, or any combination of the two, has satisfactorily treated a problem of increasing significance: the persistence of what has been called 'ethnic identity'" (Braroe 1975: 9). Linked in articulation to Indian identity and power, pow wow has persisted despite succeeding waves of colonial policies and anthropological practices. As Thomas Vennum, Jr. (1982) recognizes in his book entitled *The Ojibwa Dance Drum*, Indians dancing have always been more than a scaffold of social form devoid of "authentic" cultural content; and in the pan-Indianism of the 1970s, pow wow and spiritual ceremony became absorbed in the new arenas of Indian politics.

Pow Wow Politics

In the 1970s, when modern warriors formed the American Indian Movement, their expressions of resistance involved more than walks to Washington, protest rallies, and armed occupations. AIM appropriated tactics from the Black Power movement to promote Indian causes, customs, and rights; but the movement also urged Indians to return to traditional beliefs and practices. In mobilizing urban, academic, and reservation Indians, AIM reconstructed earlier expressions of pan-Indianism, building ideologies and alliances of activism through spiritual ceremonies and pow wows. In the midst of violence among Indians and between Indians and Others, AIM revived the Ghost Dance at Wounded Knee and the Sun Dance at the Rosebud reservation in South Dakota, ceremonies that were suspended or concealed after the progression of prohibitions that forbade Indian religious practice (Crow Dog with Erdoes 1990). In those years of Native political protest, AIM's radical rhetoric, armed barricades, and media eruptions drew supporters from across Indian Country. Led by AIM spiritual advisors, the Sun Dance was introduced to Indians whose tribal traditions were different, fragmented, or absent. Mi'kmaq and Mohawk, Chippewa and Sioux, urban and reserve were allied through emerging ideology, political purpose, and collective performance. As Anita Gonzalez (1998: 227), writes, "Ceremonial dances like the Sundance galvanized the disparate cultural beliefs of the organization's members around a common set of practices." Within and around the spiritual ceremonies affirmed by the American Indian Movement, there was always the ambivalent practice of pow wow, which was now widely recognized as a common expression of Indian popular culture.

Since 1971, when the state of Nebraska decided to re-enact Buffalo Bill's Wild West Show, playing cowboys and Indians has been reclaimed and performed across the United States and in twenty-six other countries. In this period of renewed interest in the performance of pow wow in exhibitions, competitions and spiritual ceremonies, Abe Conklin (1994) tells us about the meaning and the evolution of pow wow,

> Like Grandpa Fool's Crow said, "It don't mean nothing." And that's true. It doesn't mean anything because we keep the sacred part of this He-thus-ka, but we give the social part of it to the Lakotas. We gave the social part to other organizations. But they treat it in a spiritual way, which I think is good. And they can do it this way if they feel like it. (21)

Russell Means (1995: 69) writes, "It is our songs, not our languages that have always been the most important part of our cultural heritage … because of 'powwows,' many Indian nations have all but lost the songs and dances that were unique to their nations."

But the Chippewa remember that sometime between 1860 and 1880, a Sioux named Tailfeather Woman testified about a vision in which she was instructed by the Great Spirit to make a large dance drum as an instrument of peace and to pass this "Dream Drum" and its songs on to other tribes (Vennum 1982: 45). The religious complex that Indians in Minnesota and Wisconsin called "pow wow" was also known as the "Dream Dance" or the "Drum Dance" (Ritzenthaler and Ritzenthaler 1983: 88–90). Today in Lac du Flambeau, we call this ceremony, once known as pow wow, the "Big Drum." The practice of the Dream Drum or the Big Drum may be an adaptation of the Plains Grass Dance that spread to Lac du Flambeau from the west; but whatever its origins and however it was transformed, the ritualized performance of the Big Drum is Chippewa. Along with the Chippewa themselves, the Big Drum has endured in the struggle over culture that intertwines the past and the present, the secular and the sacred, the experienced and imagined in continuous articulations of Indian identity, power, and community. Like the Big Drum, the traditional religious ceremonies of the Midéwiwin are practised today by some, ignored or opposed by others. But everyone welcomes the pow wow drums at Bear River, which began to beat again in 1983. Each July, Indians arrive in reservation trucks and shiny city cars, wearing buckskin or bermuda shorts, eating fry bread or hot dogs, buying trinkets and treasures. Amid the struggle over what pow wow represents, expresses, and means in these days of dance contests, pow wow princesses, rock shows, and renewed religious rituals, the drum discloses that "the modern day Pow Wow is a descendent of summer tribal gatherings, where political decisions were made and ceremonies performed by the medicine societies" (Wetelainen 1982: 50). In the contemporary performance of pow wow "an inherent code of the dance drum is its function as an identity indicator" (Haefer in Vennum, Jr. 1982: 12).

Pow wow is part of the social imaginaries and historical narratives that spiral through popular culture, political policy, and academic analysis to construct representations of Indianness that can marginalize memory, fragment testimony, and eclipse the transformative nature of Native experience. But pow wow is also part of the process through which, "after centuries of suppression, the cultural past is being recovered, the present reclaimed and the future renegotiated" (Townsend-Gault 1992: 51). Indian culture is being shared and reshaped in performances of pow wow that transcend tribal boundaries and challenge tribal identities. As Michael Greyeyes (1997: 33) says, "When we hear the drum and see the dancers, each step reminds us that at this moment, the past and present are linked." In the collective memory and political possibility of emerging tradition, ritual, and practice, pow wow situates the affective and ideological investments in what matters. Through all the layers of Indianness embedded in the discursive construction of history and anthropology, heritage and tradition, sovereignty and self-determination, what matters for Native North Americans is the silenced sensibility—and political possibility—of being Indian. In the words of Dana Runs Above (in Roberts 1992: 124): "I love powwows. I can sit and listen to the songs, bells and drumming for the rest of my life…. The feeling of being part of it, the whole scene, singing and dancing, being Indian, is an extraordinary feeling."

≪ • ≫

Drumming the Past:
Researching Indian Objects

A hundred thousand years have passed
Yet, I hear the distant beat of my father's drums
I hear his drums throughout the land
His beat I hear within my heart.

Shirley Daniels
(in Gooderham 1969: 196)

Some experiences burst upon our everyday reality with an intensity so profound and relentless that the future is forever seared to the past. The death of my father was such an experience, and the disposition of a drum in his possession became part of the pain of his passing. The compelling object is a water drum, a source of communication with the Great Spirit, known to us as Gitchee Manitou. The water drum is associated with the Midéwiwin or Grand Medicine Society, which Indians also call the Midé or Medicine Dance. This secret society is the traditional religious rite of the Anishinabe, who were renamed the Ojibway by the traders and are known in northern Wisconsin, where I was raised, as the Chippewa. The Chippewa water drum my father had is a small, hand-hollowed piece of wood, fully painted on the bottom with bright circles of yellow, red, green, and black. Five red and green bars painted around the outside are barely visible. The drum skin is detached and faded, but the half-green surface bordered by a red line is still evident. Two wooden rings are intact, one around the bottom of the drum and one around the top, which holds the drum skin in place. There are four wooden drumsticks, each rounded at the end, the shanks trimmed with strips of fur.

How my father got the water drum, we will never know. He left detailed notes on the history and experience of the Chippewa, which he compiled through half a century of reading books and talking to people. But my father left no records of the objects that he collected on the Lac du Flambeau reservation where he lived. He was an enrolled member of the Lac du Flambeau Band of Lake Superior Chippewa, and his extensive collection of photographs and nameless artifacts has long since been placed in the tribal museum that he worked to establish. The objects were placed on loan to protect them against sale or neglect, but the permanence of the arrangement was never in doubt. He had a large collection of stonepipe bowls which he loved to discuss, pointing to seven that were from Lac du Flambeau, including one with a crack that belonged to Anawabe, our last Medicine Man who walked on long ago. But none of these details were written down. Maybe he didn't keep documents on the objects given or sold to him because they became communal in his mind, or maybe he didn't want to record the claims to personal ownership these objects could engender. The issue never arose during his lifetime.

Years ago, the water drum was placed in the tribal museum, but it was never a comfortable fit. It was relegated to the remove of the storage room when, in the fall of 1995, it appeared in the dream of two young Chippewa women, one of whom worked at the museum. They had attended Midéwiwin ceremonies and they spoke about their dreams to a respected Midé Elder, who came from his home reservation in late September to ask the museum board of directors for the release of the drum, which he would restore and empower. My brother is on the museum board. He, too, is an enrolled tribal member; he is also a born-again Christian and an ordained minister.

I did not witness this meeting of the Elder, the dreamers, and the museum board. But I know from the retelling that testimony about the drum was distinctly emotional and unequivocally spiritual: an appeal to the past woven in the words of the heart and the heritage that claim objects in mystical meanings. If this was once a personal drum, it now seemed conjoined to a sense of Chippewa identity and Midéwiwin community forever, and the expressed connection was affective, harboured in the soul, where it signified the power and pain of being and becoming Indian.

The endowment of the old wooden drum was a revelation for my brother. This small object placed in trust at the tribal museum had moved in memory from the realm of a historical artifact to the reality of a spiritual mentor. For my brother, the drum took on the power of the unpredictable and the pagan with which he had struggled for two decades. The meeting to decide the destiny of the drum was both revealing and unsettling. In his words:

> This meeting was about the drum. It was a hard meeting for me. People either opposed me or were silent. There were none who spoke to support me. [Two young people] had a dream about the drum. [One] was very emotional. I was told that I was holding the culture of the people captive—things like that. I don't remember the non-Indians saying anything. Some people felt that, "You can't own a drum," others knew nothing or said nothing about it. [The Elder who spoke for the drum] was not threatening, [one person] was threatening. After about one and a half hours, I left. Before leaving, I said that I knew who the King of Kings was, I knew who was the Lord of Lords and that it was the Lord Jesus Christ. I also said that I would seek counsel on the issue, which I did later—talking with [several traditional elders] and members of the Lac du Flambeau Bible Church. (G. Guthrie, 1996: 2)

My brother remained troubled about the destiny of this drum. For two weeks, he reflected upon its ambiguity and discussed its meaning and morality with other Indians, both traditional and Christian. In an October meeting with eight tribal members of the Bible Church, my brother spoke about how he might lay the drum to rest:

> I thought that I would take it by canoe from Dad's house, past Strawberry Island, past Medicine Rock and the Old Village, and take it by canoe down the Bear River, where I would find a place somewhere in the woods and leave it there. [One church member] then told me that I was "worshipping that drum" and after reflecting a bit I couldn't help but agree with him. (G. Guthrie, 1996: 3)

The discussion that followed was about the destiny of the drum, but everyone knew that removing the drum involved an act of spiritual belief that could have repercussions. The drum signified ideological differences in this community that would not be dispelled in its absence.

> Some of the people felt that the drum ought to be burned. We talked also about burying the drum. Finally, after considerable discussion, we took a vote. It was decided unanimously that the drum should be buried off the reservation. The people did not want the drum buried on the reservation. When I asked if the people would stand behind this decision publicly and stand with me publicly if it came to that, they all said very clearly that they would. The people wanted nothing to do with the drum,

nor did they want any of their children or others to have anything to do with it. A few days later, I asked permission of the Museum Board of Directors to remove the drum from the Museum (following our policy on the removal of objects on loan to the Museum at that time). (G. Guthrie, 1996: 4)

Confirmed in his conviction by Christian Indians in Lac du Flambeau, my brother walked into the woods alone and buried the drum. A traditional Elder expressed his support for any decision my brother made and said about a drum he owned that "when he got it fixed up, his drum would be on exhibition in the museum and would stay there—it would not leave the museum. He said it's too bad that it had to come to that (i.e., the drum being buried)" (G. Guthrie, 1996: 5, 8).

In Montreal, a thousand miles away, I received a frantic phone call from the director of the tribal museum who recounted the dilemma of the drum. The telephone discussions with my brother that followed were prolonged and prophetic. We struggled over distance, siblings pitted against each other in a battle over traditional and Christian culture, identity and ideology, meaning and morality, public and private property; each voice reflecting the historical experience and the contemporary reality of this Indian community's fragmented, contradictory, entangled cultural journey from the Ojibway settlement of Waswagoning to the Chippewa reservation of Lac du Flambeau. In the end, confirmed in his respect for our shared ownership and our unresolved differences, my brother walked into the woods alone and dug up the drum. Later, he wrote:

> Dug the drum up
> In October
> Before the Snow
> Hid the grave
> In the morning
> Shovel in hand
> And paper
> Bag...
> Gail's now...
> (G. Guthrie, 1996: 6)

Today, the drum is wrapped in white cloth and stored in a safe place. Like the reservation and its tribal members, this Midé drum is suspended in an interwoven maze of conflicting spiritual and ideological visions,

caught in the cultural web of displacement, transformation, and acculturation that is remembered in contradictory testimonials to Chippewa
tradition and practice. Some Elders in Lac du Flambeau say that as a
medium of personal communication with the Great Spirit, Gitchee Manitou, the drum should be properly laid to rest in the earth, buried like bear
claws and medicine bundles, a position shared by some traditional
Chippewa and many stalwart Christians in the community. Others say
that, with its detached drum skin and distinct age, this drum is forever
powerless, dead, an artifact that can be displayed in the tribal museum.
Still others speak of the drum's potency and potential for the revived
memory and practice of the Midéwiwin that is now evident in Indian
Country. The water drum rests in an uneasy state of improbable compro-
mise, caught between re-empowerment and final removal, awaiting a
decision that will never resolve the ideological issues that divide this
community. But I want to know about this drum.

Locating Research on the Drum

The testimonies—Indian, ethnographic, and archival—that reveal and
record the memory and meaning of drums form a jumbled trail of criss-
crossing, overgrown paths. How am I to research the past of this nameless Midéwiwin drum? How am I to understand its descent, legacy, and
endowment—and the significance of the dreams—in the contradictory,
conflicting, and ambiguous testimonies and ideologies of Indians in Lac
du Flambeau today? And how do I deal with my personal involvement
with this drum, with the ethical issues of research and the cultural issues
of ownership, display, and disposal?

These kinds of questions are not new, but they are now urgent. At this
historical moment of revived traditionalism and contentious ethnography, Indian experience, and cultural objects or artifacts are increasingly
important to Native North Americans themselves. But researching the
heritage of Native culture means following a trajectory that is continually reconstructed. The process of searching and sorting out traces of
interwoven testimony, ethnography, and archival evidence involves
negotiating the vagueness of traditional Indian cultural narratives and
the specificity of early anthropological fieldwork. The trail is woven into
the lived experience that defies the "complex fusions that *we* like to call
modernity and magicality, rationality and ritual, history and the here

and now" (Comaroff 1992: 5, italics in original). For me, researching Indian culture is always, in the end a personal migration filled with the fascination of discovery, the frustration of dead ends, the recognition of my own ideological and interpretative biases, and the realization of my tenuous but tenacious connections to a past that constructs who I am.

Researching the drum begins with recognizing again what is common sense to academics: methodology and meaning are conjoined. The questions that drive this research and the conceptions that render evidence and ascribe significance frame the process of uncovering and sifting through the academic and idiosyncratic information that provides the answers. In other words, what I am searching for is related intrinsically to the questions that I ask, the information I access and value, and what I know, or at least can recognize and understand. In this project, the questions arise from the meaning and practice of Indian spiritual experience, and the search for evidence and answers emerges in the interwoven traces of the past—ethnographic and Chippewa—and the culturally transformed Chippewa present. This all seems obvious at a time when interpretative anthropology and cultural studies recognize the importance of contingency, transformation, and subjectivity in social analysis, and when academics write about issues of interpretation and cultural encounter related to research. But for Indians, researching the drum—and Indian culture—involves particular problems related to the availability and nature of archival and personal evidence, and the ambiguous and contingent meaning of material objects and discursive texts.

Indians, ethnographers, and ethnohistorians tend to ask different questions and value different evidence. Even when the methods of gathering information are similar, the significance of objects, events, texts, and practices often differs for Indians and academics in ways that are either not easy for most social scientists to analyze or are not relevant to their analysis. The writing of Geertz (1973), Clifford and Marcus (1986), Rosaldo (1989), and others has expanded the critique of ethnographic practice and the range of anthropological inquiry and interpretation. But ethnography has been slow to move from analyzing cultural transcriptions of what Indians do and say to understanding the messiness of Native experience, practice, and meaning; and ethnohistory is usually interested in documenting time-bound issues of practice or studying the historical implications of social and cultural change. These differences of purpose and position extend to the analysis of Indian material culture as well. Even recent anthropological and ethnohistorical research neglect the subjective and transformative significance of objects themselves. In Indian Country, the ambiguous meaning of artifacts that empower, enable, and embody personal and collective experiences is often wrapped in a discourse of almost inaccessible vagueness; and the vagueness that permeates the personal, ceremonial, or spiritual experiences of Indians and objects is ignored or amplified in the ethnographic analysis written by outsiders.

For ethnographers, drums are important as material objects; they are instruments that participants use to produce sounds of symbolic, spiritual value that frame, punctuate, and engage ceremonial and personal performance. But for Indians, drums are not representations of power but agents of power, or they can be; and both their phenomenological presentation as persons and its situational variability are complex. The transformative nature of drums relates to what A. Irving Hallowell (1960: 31) calls the "other-than-human-persons" that inhabit the Chippewa ontological and social worlds. The belief in the transformation of physical forms draws upon a personification of natural phenomena and a mythical past that, for many Native people, shapes their spiritual experience in the present. Even today, Native people hold a belief or a suspicion that the natural world is inhabited by powerful other persons, beings who can shape-shift, taking different forms and taking on different spirits. Like bears, birds, and spirit rocks, drums can be animate beings and potent participants in personal, spiritual, and ceremonial interaction, an identification that is related to the observable power they manifest, not to their outward appearance. If drums are themselves powerful persons, they also empower the drummer in a reciprocal process that enjoins communication with a superior force. The power of drums lies in the relationships that drums enact and the strength of the spiritual force drums exhibit in the exchange of social relations. But because this embodied power is not innately inscribed, predictable or constant, its presence or absence constitutes the status of drums as unstable and ambiguous.

The power of drums is particular to their possession, use, and endowment in the interchange of communication with other Indians and the forces of the spiritual world. In other words, drums are discursive, and their power is constructed in relation to those who invoke the information they express, which relationships they enact, and the personal experience they engender. Drums can voice doctoring and divining, sorcery and "bad medicine" or even pretense, depending upon who establishes communication with the spirit world through the drum, the relationships that person establishes, and the consequences of the spiritual experience. Because the meaning of material objects is embedded in discourse and cultural context, their signification is never stable; and the reflexive empowerment of Indian drums, drummers, and spiritual forces involves a triple embodiment of the signified in a "chain of sliding signifiers" (Grossberg 1997: 65). This relationship between people and power is complicated by the transformative nature of some drummers, who can assume the form of other-than-human persons, and the transformation of drums, which can lose, gain, or change their demonstrated force through spiritual circumstances or neglect. For drums, signifiers are not only "inserted within the signified" (65); signifiers can also become the signified, a status which they can gain or lose. This cultural context suggests the importance of analyzing material objects as discursively engaged subjects. But for most ethnographers, drums are incidental to action, accessories that cannot speak. The difference in Indian and ethnographic perceptions of drums contributes to the contingency of their emergent meaning, and this ambiguity also frames the nature and extent of the anthropological documentation that is available to research and to understand the past of a particular drum.

For Chippewa, the memory and meaning of a drum is linked in articulation to a person or a ceremony, to its presence in a community, and, related to the people of that place, its discursive power can generate spiritual relationships of personal and communal recognition, reparation, or retribution. For some Indians, the legacy of an empowered drum is threatening, even harmful; for others, it can reorder reality, transform the turmoil of the cultural and personal past, transfix identity in the present, and locate the political possibility of blood and belonging in the future. But almost everyone in Indian Country would agree that this drum once expressed actual spiritual power. It is this sense of power intertwined with meaning—ambiguous and transmutable—and articulated to persons that prompts the contestation of ideological views surrounding the fate of the water drum in Lac du Flambeau and propels research related to the conflict over its placement.

Unlike most ethnographic writing on artifacts, this is not an inquiry into the function of the drum or an analysis of its tone, construction, or role. Because the drum's discursive nature, power, and meaning frame the research, the tasks are to establish that this drum *is* a Midé drum, to locate it in Lac du Flambeau, and, finally, to understand its personal or ceremonial endowment and ownership, or at least heritage and kinship, and the implications for our family and the tribal museum. But the archival documents and personal texts that can inform this project are perforated by the meaning that drums have acquired in ethnographic research, Indian memory, and contemporary culture. Researching what Indians call objects and what Others call artifacts is complicated by issues related to the nature and analysis of Native texts and material culture.

Native Cultural Evidence

When my midéwiwin drum
sounds for me
the sky
clears
the sky is blue
he hi hi hi

when my midéwiwin drum
sounds for me
the waters are smooth
ho ho ho ho
                    Vizenor 1965: 37

The meaning of Indian cultural evidence—both material and textual—is effervescent, obscure, even tainted. From Edmund Leach's (1989: 34) claim that "all ethnography is fiction" to Lola Lemire Tostevin's (in Brydon 1996: 136) conception of "contamination as literary device," concerns have been raised about the project of rendering and reconstructing "traditional" discourse and interpreting its meaning. Michael Ames (1992: 59) writes, "Anthropologists help to create through their own work the societies they purport to be discovering." About the tracts of tradition that anthropologists preserve, Gerald Vizenor (1994: 68–69) tells us that "social science narratives, those unsure reins of final vocabularies and incoherent paracolonialism, overscore the tribal heard as cultural representations."

But even if the conceptual borders of tradition are increasingly unstable for academics and imprecise for Indians, current knowledge and practice emerge from interpretations of past practice and experience.

For Indians today, the meaning of drums is articulated to the "memories of memories" that Jan Vansina (1985: 160) defines as tradition, or Edwin Ardener (1989: 25) understands as "an infinite sequence or rememorizations, of bricolage and debricolage." The personification of a drum weaves through "the tribal memories and solace of heard stories" to emerge in the ambiguous, reconstructed knowledge and practice of "new simulations of survivance" (Vizenor 1993: 52).

The process of finding fragments of the Indian past and understanding their emergent meaning in the messiness of the culturally transformed present involves more than piecing together empirical evidence or historical and current traces of Indian experience. Ethnographers, photographers, and writers—Indian and Other—engage in social agency, and the power and authority they exert in the research process draws upon cultural practices and institutional relationships produced in their respective communities. The interpretation of artifacts and events, like all ethnographic research, exposes intersections of different ideological, affective, and instrumental realities; and writing, like photography, works to reify the conceptions, insights, and representations of both insiders and outsiders. The critique of ethnographic enterprise is well-worked territory, given the work of Clifford and Marcus (1986), Van Maanen (1988), Marcus and Fischer (1986), and others. But there has always been an enormous imbalance between writing about Indians and writing by Indians. The abundance of ethnographic documentation by outsiders has contributed to constructions of "anthropology's Indians" that have unrelenting and painfully pragmatic implications.

For Native people, there are blind spots that resonate with the academic approaches and personal perceptions that characterize and define aspects of Indian culture, and these disjunctions produce misconceptions and omissions of information that cannot be retrieved. Indian experience is framed forever by backdrops of the ancient and the aberrant that bleed into anthropological images. Early ethnographies are enormously valuable, but they are constructed as islands of practice that are often removed from the dynamics of cultural interaction, from the cultural change or social chaos that underwrites the contemporary meaning of Native experience. What is missing or misunderstood is compounded today not only by functionalism and structuralism but also by linguistic erosion, cultural diffusion, literary illusion, and personal interpretation. For this research, both what anthropologists know about Indian

practices and what Indians know of the traditional are equally perforated. Like ethnographic analysis, the few Indian counter-narratives
written in the eighteenth and nineteenth centuries—when Indian spiritual practices were suppressed by colonial governments—and the growing number of contemporary Indian accounts are personal and partial.
The absent voices and missing meanings in field notes and books and
museum collections are silenced or reconstructed in ethnographic interpretations or in Indian memory and imagination.

However objectified, cultural analysis is a personal memoir, a chronicle of action and interpretation that always involves more than reading
through and around ethnographic material and blending the perceptions and ideologies of outsiders with the words and practices of insiders. Researching Indians means interpreting practice, decoding silence,
and reconstructing absence, a project that is open to the "contamination … of differences … brought together so they make contact" (Tostevin
in Brydon 1995: 136). Like the coffee-table books and mega-movies that
reconstruct and collapse ethnography and history into North American
popular culture, abstract images and practices of Indians float and inter-
mix in imaginary time and space. Today, being Indian embodies a blend
of culturally specific and pan-Indian experiences; and researching Native
North Americans involves filtering the narrations of ethnographers,
travellers, historians, and Indians, a process that however informed, can
be neither objective nor conclusive. Indians and Others ask different
questions and they access and value different sources of information.
Their interpretations of cultural meaning are often situated differently
in relation to research, writing, and readers. But ethnographers, historians and Indians share a common legacy of "partial truths" (Clifford and
Marcus 1986: 7), and these "truths" are culturally encoded, changeable,
and ambiguous.

What Indians remember about objects—and the individuals who are
associated with them—is episodic, situational, instrumental, and personal. The past of Indian tradition is remembered in narratives in which
knowledge and experience are expressed in entangled beliefs and practices that are linked in articulation to language and myth, ritual and stories. This connection between knowledge and narrative has always
informed anthropology; and today, the interpretive turn in ethnography has forged links to literary production and criticism, and fostered a
new interest in oral tradition that is reflected in the work of Krupat

(1992), Ridington (1990), and others. But the deeper roots of Indian discursive construction are revealed in the distinct approaches of Native writers such as Momaday (1976), Erdrich (1993), Silko (1977), Allen (1986), and Vizenor (1994). The bridge between signification and ethnographic research relates to characteristics of oral discourse that, however remembered, imagined or transformed, emerge in Indian texts as "postindian simulations ... [that] create a new tribal presence in stories" (Vizenor 1994: 12).

N. Scott Momaday (1975) suggests that Indian oral tradition involves a deep belief in language that relates not only to a conception of the sacredness of words but also to the singular role words play in constructing personal and social reality and in preserving the culture itself. For the researcher of Indian tradition, the endowment of words can be baffling. Researching the drum, or other spiritual objects, involves negotiating both the anthropologist's "linguistic cages" of "hypothetical constructs and theoretical frameworks" (King 1997: 116) used to describe Indian experience, and the ambiguous silences, mystical revelations, and linguistic concealments of Indians themselves. These are narratives told in unexplained words, fragmented images, and shape-shifting myths that evade interpretation. Indian explanations call for "a certain attitude of belief that 'recognizes that these are not stories but story like,' mythic, never evolved but evolving ever" (Momaday 1976: 61). For Chippewa, the mythological beliefs that circulate in social interaction—like the metamorphosis of the drum—are real, not metaphorical. However, the meaning of their reality can be deeply entangled in transformation, contradiction, or imagination; submerged in secret, silent, or unseen relationships; or expressed in "the free, allegorical style of Ojibway thought and feeling" (Dewdney 1975: 10). This is the case for the emerging meaning of Midéwiwin visions and dreams.

For Midé members, dreams and visions are sources of inspiration, information, and influence. Some Indians join the Midéwiwin during illness, but even then, as Ruth Underhill (1965: 92) suggests, "to join it [the Midéwiwin], a man must have a vision and one or more helping spirits who recommended such a career." Events and knowledge that occur in dreams break down the barriers between realities—physical and spiritual, past and present—and the information they provide is integrated into the lived experience of everyday life. Dreams can be provoked by fasting or attending a "sweat lodge," which "purifies the body and the mind and makes a person receptive for messages coming from the spirit world" (Benton-Banai 1988: 83). But these rituals are individual and particular, and even for visions that are legitimized and interpreted in the religious beliefs of the Midéwiwin, the meaning of dreams is personal and subjective. Gerald Vizenor (1965: 9) tells us that visions and dreams that can provide inspiration and knowledge "were natural sources of intuition and identities, and some tribal visions were spiritual transmigrations that inspired the lost and lonesome souls of the woodland to be healed." However experienced, imagined, or transformed, visions and dreams mediate power and negotiate the meaning of ambiguous spirits that can be affable and accommodating or unpredictable and even ominous. Hoffman (1891: 163) writes, "The Ojibway believe in a multiplicity of spirits, or man'idos, which inhabit all space and every conspicuous object in nature." And Ruth Landes (1968) tells us:

> In the world-view provided by Ojibway religion and magic, there is neither stick nor stone that is not animate and charged with potential hostility to men, no circumstance that is accidental or free of personalized intent, not one human creature to be taken for granted. At the same time, all difficulties may be appeasable through governing spirits. (21)

If Hoffman's and Landes's perceptions of the Indian interactive environment seem exaggerated today, the myth-like figures of the trickster Naanabozho or the flesh-eating Windigo still roam the Chippewa imagination. Their ambivalence is expressed in a lingering sense of "bad medicine" that can issue from persons, both human and other-than-human. "Bad medicine"—like "good medicine"—is as real as it is shape-shifting and silent. Dreams access and claim the unpredictable spiritual world, but drums are its voice.

Approaching the Drum

The Midéwiwin is a complex, secret society that is widely known among the Ojibway, Menomini, and Winnebago in the region of the Great Lakes. Most ethnographers consider the Midéwiwin a religious "organization of wonder-workers" (Underhill 1965: 92), but Frances Densmore ([1929] 1979: 86) tells us that "The Midéwiwin is not so much to worship anything as to preserve the knowledge of herbs for use in prolonging life." The Midéwiwin ceremonies focus on healing and understanding that "rectitude of conduct produces length of life" (87). This secret society may draw its name from the water drum that is central to its ceremonies. Basil Johnston (1982: 95) points out that *Midéwe* means "the sound" or "resonance," referring to ceremonial drums and chants; and Densmore (96) notes, "It is said that a Midé drum stick is more valuable than the drum, and frequently is older."

The Midéwiwin is based on the life of the Ojibway folk hero and trickster Naanabozho who, in the formative days of the world, received secret knowledge from Great Dawn and the spirits of the Upper World and the Underworld about prolonging life through proper personal conduct, using herbs and medicines to cure illness, and making a safe journey to the home of the dead. Membership is always sought, and it can include at least four degrees of secret knowledge. Information and status are acquired through visions, purification, conjuring, and lengthy traditional teachings, which are purchased. Each degree is conferred in a four-day initiation ceremony usually held in late spring. These ceremonies enact ritual death and rebirth through the process of being "shot" with the sacred Mégis shell from a medicine bag. Individual medicine bags made from different animal skins are both the insignias of membership and office and the sanctuaries of secret Midéwiwin medicines. Initiation and curing ceremonies, and the knowledge and preparation associated with them, are the responsibility of Midé leaders or priests, who conduct ceremonies that involve songs and speeches, drumming, dancing, and feasts.

I am an "outsider" to the Midéwiwin, but it is not new to me. I wrote my master's thesis on the Grand Medicine Society and, later, I wrote a long ethnographic analysis of the origins of the Midéwiwin. I have never been to an initiation ceremony, but in the spring of 1991, I attended an all-day Midéwiwin funeral ceremony. Some of the Ojibway rituals were explained in English, but even without the translations they seemed familiar. I have been surrounded by the silenced power of the Midéwiwin and its cultural milieu of drumming, dancing, and speeches all my life. I remember as a child going with my father to visit Jim Bell's small house in the Old Village. He lived on the banks of the Bear River, near the dam, and he was the keeper-of-the-drums. My memory of four drums of various sizes wrapped in white cloth is vague, but I recall clearly sensing the power and the presence of these drums, even the sound of their rhythm echoing across the lake in the Lac du Flambeau spring, or wailing the pain of someone's passing into the next world, or pounding the proximity of unseen and unpredictable forces. But what drums were these? And whose? And what happened to them?

Lac du Flambeau was once a centre of Midéwiwin activities, but the ceremonies at the Old Village seemed to cease in the 1950s, and, in the 1960s, I went away to school. Who were the Midé members in the Lac du Flambeau, and what happened to the ceremonies? Did the Midéwiwin continue here, or has it been revived and reconstructed? And even though the testimony and markings claim this drum, is this a Midé drum? There are many drums in my memory, including peyote drums, clan drums, and the personal drums of the medicine man Anawabe, his son Bert Skye, and others. I remember the Dream Drum or what we call the Big Drum, other ceremonial drums like the Woman's Drum, and the many pow wow drums that sang for circles of dancers. I also remember Midé drums; but I recall an image of a drum much smaller than this one, a water drum with stones worked into the lacing that holds the drum skin. My father had a small drum like this, which he called a Midé drum. But I do not remember if that small drum with the stones—or this larger one with wooden rings—is a particular ceremonial drum, whether these drums are specific or unique objects of Midéwiwin ceremonies; whether these are personal, or communal, or ceremonial drums, or even if a distinction can be made between the personal and ceremonial meaning of spiritualized drums, historically or currently. I have traced the trail of drums before, but the project of this research is more complicated.

My search always begins with personal testimony, in part because the questions that drive the research arise in discourse, in the exchange circulating around contested practice or policy or objects; and in part because testimony is the most fragile, illusive, and uniquely informative evidence, particularly if it emerges in direct dialogue as it did with Benaise and the other people I visited to search the past of another drum.

The water drums were not the only drums that my father had, nor was this small drum the first to raise questions about meaning, display and disposition. In the spring after my father died, there was concern about a Woman's Drum. This large drum, identified by two blue circles painted on the drum skin nested in an elaborately beaded stand, was at one time on display at the tribal museum but is now relegated to storage. I went to see two men from the Old Village about the drum, friends of my father whom I'd known since my childhood. When my separate conversations with them turned to drums, they were each clearly uncomfortable. They spoke softly, haltingly, saying they knew very little. But each assured me that the Woman's Drum was a social drum, not a religious drum like the ones at Jim Bell's house; that Jim Bell's set of four "Flambeau drums" passed to Benaise when he died; and that none of these drums were now here. Two were just "gone" and two were down at Neopit, a Menominee reservation south of Lac du Flambeau. These separate affirmations of the primarily social, not spiritual, purpose of the Woman's Drum seemed reassuring, but the disposition of the drum remained unsettling for the tribal museum and our family.

My brother wrote to Nancy Lurie, then curator of anthropology at the Milwaukee Public Museum, to ask about the protocol that emerged when the museum was involved in a dispute over a Dream Drum that was placed on display. Her response detailed the controversy and spoke of a meeting with Tom Kitchume, a respected Potawatomi Elder and member of the Dream Drum Society, who came to the museum with five young men. "The Elder sat there quietly listening to the young men's complaints about my discussion and finally said, 'Doesn't matter. Drum's dead.' Then he went on to explain that the Drum had passed through so many hands it no longer had ceremonial value." He spoke for some time, then "concluded that he thought maybe this particular Drum was supposed to end up here to educate non-Indians. The Iowa [tribes] had not kept up the ceremonies nor passed it on to another tribe which is how Drums should be treated" (Lurie 1991: 2). The story of this Dream Drum's disposition is important, but it does not provide an uncontested course of action for the Woman's Drum in Lac du Flambeau. Each drum is particular, each struggle is local, each determination is personal. The meaning—and the placement—of this drum is entangled in the realities and relationships that Chippewa remember and enact here, in this place.

I took tobacco to Benaise, a respected Lac du Flambeau Elder who was now old, blind, and ill. We began a series of conversations about ceremonies and sacred items that continued on an occasional basis until he died two years later. In our first talk, I asked him about the disposal of amulets and medicine that my father had, items whose power I knew to be both personal and unpredictable. He told me how to bury them and I followed his instructions.

From Benaise, I learned that this Woman's Drum had belonged to Cobasheen, a woman we knew as Mudhen, who had inherited it along with her position as head of the Woman's Drum Society, about which he could tell me little. It passed from Mudhen to her daughter, Laura, before the cultural disruption of alcohol blurred its purpose and dissent. Laura had died, but I followed the trail to her son. He was fifty-four years old when he told me that as a child, he went with his mother to see my father, and she sold the drum to him for one hundred dollars. When I told Benaise, he said only that she had a daughter, but the drum could not be kept in a house where there was drinking and my father had kept it all these years. I left with unresolved questions about the Women's Drum Society about which Thomas Vennum, Jr. (1982: 86) writes, "the dance and its drum were considered to be owned by the women." The individual or tribal disposition of this drum was uncertain, but its heredity and dissent over three generations were clear.

This personal and specific information about the drum is an important part of what Native people want to know, what they value about research on material objects. This information may be buried somewhere in the archives of museums or the notes of anthropologists, but details about the personal, historical, and cultural placement and legacy of Indian objects cannot be retrieved from archival documents or ethnographic analysis. In fact, ethnographers often view with suspicion informal fieldwork drawn from personal and sporadic visits. Even now, in this new era of research and museum ethics, ethnography places value on impersonal, abstracted, distanced analysis, written for career and academy with little regard for what Indians might want to know, to record, or to restrict to their communities. The distinct interests of Native North Americans and anthropologists are overlaid with difficulties related to fieldwork itself, for which research and writing is complex for both Indians and Others. Like ethnographies, life histories, accounts of personal experiences, and kinship studies, research on spiritual items can embarrass or upset people in Native communities. At the same time, anonymity ignores the relational meaning of material objects and the contributions that ethnography can make to Indian interests in cultural legacy, ownership, and disposition.

My own approach has been to inform, ask permissions, and change or remove names when information might be troublesome to people who are living in Lac du Flambeau or elsewhere. But I know that these strategies are ineffective for several reasons. My father, my brother, and I are implicated in this research, and our family's relationship to this drum is as uncomfortable as it is irrepressible. Moreover, people in Lac du Flambeau who remember the relationships and objects at issue are not

fooled by the nicknames or changed names that respect the confidential-
ity of community members; and for those who are younger and may
not recognize the personal histories of different drums, whatever I learn
about the ancestries of these artifacts will be buried in code or absent from
our written records, remaining inaccessible. But regardless of the pitfalls, I will pursue the past of this drum.

In my research on the Midé drum, dialogue is increasingly beyond
my reach. Many of the old people who know about the practice, purpose,
and possession of traditional drums have walked on. Like the Indians
who lived in Lac du Flambeau in the first half of this century, the anthropologists who studied them are all gone now. There can be no revised or
reinterpreted "thick description" (Geertz 1973) of earlier ceremonial
action or objects, no interviews with Jim Bell or old Lac du Flambeau
Midé priests, no questions for the anthropologists Hallowell and Ritzenthaler, no discussions with Benaise or my father or a long list of others.
Even the Elder who asked to repower the drum has since died. Already,
it is impossible to connect this drum to a specific owner or a family. But
drums have always been part of the practice and purpose of ethnographers and Indians. My search must take up whatever traces of evidence
surface in Indian memory and early anthropology.

Since the late 1800s, anthropologists have collected drums and other
material expressions of Indian culture in the region of Lac du Flambeau.
The earliest was probably Frances Densmore (1910, [1913] 1972; [1929]
1979), who began to document Chippewa ceremonies and music in the
region in 1893. She was followed by Hallowell ([1955] 1967), Barnouw
(1950), and Ritzenthaler (1953), all of whom wrote about some aspect of
the traditional spirituality and religious practices of the Chippewa, and
all of whom probably bought drums, some for the museums or univer-
sities that sponsored their fieldwork. I will reread their work, go over my
notes on the Midéwiwin and my father's notes on the Chippewa, and
look again at Barrett's (1911) work on the Dream Dance, the 1851 account
of the geologist Henry Schoolcraft, and William Warren's *History of the
Ojibways*, published in 1885 by a half-Chippewa "insider" whose writing is recognized by Indians in Lac du Flambeau as the critical source of
Lake Superior Chippewa experience in the nineteenth century. I will
reread Edward Benton-Banai's *Mishomis Book* (1988), a narrative of Ojibway history and practice drawn from his knowledge of Midéwiwin oral
tradition that has become a primary cultural reference for Lac du Flambeau Chippewa, and revisit Hoffman's seminal writing on the Midéwi-

win published in 1891, which has become the standard text against which ethnographers judge the authenticity of the Grand Medicine Society. But I know my search for information will be discouraging. Warren's 1885 history does not detail the Midéwiwin; most ethnographic research contains little about drums; and only Benton-Banai speaks about the Midéwiwin beliefs and practices of today. For this research, which requires the local specificity of Lac du Flambeau, my father's notes and his four books of local photographs are indispensable. On the basis of these photographs, I can distinguish various types of drums and perhaps I will find a photo of a Midé drum, which is called the "grandfather" by Indians who participate in ceremonials.

Photographs and Researching Indians

I have copies of all my father's photographs and an illustrated history of Lac du Flambeau (Guthrie and Goc 1995) that my brother and I published after his death. I have thumbed through these photographs many times in the past, sometimes to search for a particular image, sometimes just to reclaim who I am and where I come from, or to reconfirm the privilege and possibility of doing research on Lac du Flambeau at all. This time, I am acutely aware that photographs are both critical and questionable documents for historical research on Indian culture. As Michael Dorris (1994: 70) writes, "The thing about a photograph is that a present is fixed, mute and preserved, and so it becomes in retrospect a doorway from the past to the future—a doorway passed through, open once, one way."

It is difficult to convey the significance—and the ambivalence—with which Indians view historical photographs. Several years ago, I was at a feast where I was introduced to a man who was about sixty years old. I knew his name from my childhood, but I had never met him because he was raised in the city. I remember telling him that I had been looking through some old Lac du Flambeau photographs that my father collected and that I had seen two photographs of his father. He looked startled, and then he said, "We don't have any photographs of my father. He died when I was very young. I don't know what my father looked like." The next weekend, he brought his eighty-three-year-old mother and his sister to Lac du Flambeau for the Bear River Pow Wow, and I gave them all enlarged copies of the two named photographs I had found in my father's albums. His mother looked at the photographs for a long time. When she finally looked up, she said, "He looks kind of mean in this picture." Then she looked at me and, in a voice that was almost inaudible, she said, "But he wasn't mean."

My father's collection of photographs includes several photos related to the Midéwiwin. Most are images of an empty Midéwiwin lodge or Midéwigan, a long wigwam constructed of saplings and birchbark with a blanket door. In one photo, three women are sitting inside the lodge during a ceremony, but there is no drum. In the next photograph, I find what I have been searching for: a picture of a Lac du Flambeau Midé drum. Here, there is an image of an open Midéwiwin lodge, fully lined with Indians during an initiation ceremony, and centred in the doorway is a man wearing a black suit and a large black hat, with a drum in front of him. The drum is identical to the one dreamed and discussed in the Lac du Flambeau museum. But what about my memory of a small Midé drum, distinctive because of the stones laced around the rim? As relieved as I am to find a photograph of a similar Midé drum, I feel a sense of unease about this picture. Is this a Lac du Flambeau photo? I refer to the Guthrie and Goc (1995) book and it is there on page 119, with the photo of the three women, with the caption "Inside the medicine lodge at the Old Village." But it is also in my master's thesis and the source is Densmore's first volume of *Chippewa Music*, originally published by the Bureau of American Ethnology in 1910, and I have not mentioned Lac du Flambeau. This photograph might be a snapshot my father gave me that was among the papers and pictures he brought home from my great-grandmother's house when she died in 1958. My great-grandmother was an interpreter for Densmore ([1913] 1972: 121–22) and her full-page photograph and a song she sang for the ethnographer appear in the second volume of Densmore's *Chippewa Music*, published in 1913, along with a photograph of Lac du Flambeau's old medicine man Anawabe. But this image of a Midé ceremony may also be a photograph that I gave my father years ago, when I researched the Midéwiwin. Finding the photograph is a twist in the path that will take me back to the library to check Densmore. But I know that the ceremony in this photograph is Chippewa, and that the drum in question is definitely a Midé drum.

In the library, paging through Densmore, I remember again how remarkably valuable and utterly frustrating it is to work with early ethnography. The volumes on Chippewa music are rich repositories of Chippewa songs, a virtual time capsule of our past in silent poetry and music. Each song is accompanied by musical notation and Ojibway words, some translated into English. There are comments on symbolic meaning and, sometimes, mnemonic signs reproduced from birchbark scrolls. Ceremonies and the other contexts in which the songs are sung are summarized in short paragraphs labelled "Analysis," which include the tone, pitch, rhythm, melody, and occasional comments about the abilities and "personalities" of the singers—who are named—and the derivation of the songs or the cultural context in which they are sung. Densmore's 1913 publication includes seventy-five Ojibway songs from Lac du Flambeau, along with musical analysis and varied information about the singers, the events, or the stories associated with these songs. It is riveting to rediscover these precise, actual, affirming fragments of people and practices that are now submerged in the vagaries of our memories and unwritten histories. Densmore researched long before I was born, but I recognize this place and its people. I knew some of her informants, including my great-grandmother who died when I was eighteen, about whom she writes near her song entitled "Song of an Ambitious Mother," and her photograph:

> the Singer stated that this song was a memory of her earliest childhood, when she heard her mother sing it.... Mrs. Benjamin Gauthier (see pl. 30) who sang this song, is known also by her Chippewa name Bi'tawag-i'jigo'kwe (double sky woman). She is a granddaughter of Ginic'tano (wind-bound), who was chief of the Ma'nitowic' and Bimidjig'amag bands of Wisconsin Chippewa, and who several times visited Washington with tribal delegations. Mrs. Gauthier is a progressive member of the Lac du Flambeau village, but retains her interest in tribal traditions and customs. (Densmore [1913] 1972: 222)

This document of our past is an enormously valuable goad to our personal and public memories, but it is essentially a dictionary of historical songs—obscure, distant, and lifeless. In Densmore's report, there can be no smell of buckskin and woodsmoke, no soul-searing sound of the drums or piercing voices of the singers, no collective motion of the dancers. But beyond the absence of action, there is no analysis of the affective and ideological meaning of practice, ritual, or ceremony that embraces these songs and empowers the Chippewa in the experience of their daily lives. In fact, there seems no awareness that Indians *have* daily lives: personal, communal, historical, and cultural. A sense of social stasis envelops Densmore's photographs of posed Indians and their material objects. But this is all we have. Along with snapshots left by postcard photographers, these ethnographic images composed by Others form the photo albums that evoke and describe the past we lived in Lac du Flambeau.

In a section on "musical instruments," Densmore ([1910]1972: 10–11) includes two photographs of a Midé drum. This drum is more elaborate than the simple, hollowed-log drum that was at the tribal museum, but they are similar. The photograph of the man with the black hat and the midé drum that is in the Guthrie and Goc (1995) book appears between pages 35 and 36 in a section that details the construction of the Midéwigan, and is identified "Interior View" and "Midé Lodge." But in small print beneath this photograph and a second image of the Midéwigan encaptioned "Exterior View," Densmore ([1910] 1972: 37) writes, "These photographs were taken during a Midé ceremony at Elbow Lake, White Earth Reservation, May, 1909." The White Earth reservation is in Minnesota, a long way from Lac du Flambeau, Wisconsin.

This photograph of the drum and the drummer that records and retrieves an image of an actual Midéwiwin ceremony at the turn of the twentieth century is what Joanna Scherer (1992: 32) calls a "social artifact," an image that can become a primary ethnographic document through contextualized reading and interpretation. But if, in this image, the "incidental photographic closure of time and space" (Mydin 1992: 250) reduces the complexity of the Midéwiwin, this drummer, and the drum to a simplified, flat, and static representation, then the meaning of this image is neither evident nor fixed. This photograph of a Midé ceremony on the White Earth reservation in Minnesota originated as an illustration of Densmore's 1910 text. In the years since, the photograph has travelled on a journey of stories through time and space, a journey in which social interaction has changed its signification. For Indians on the Lac du Flambeau reservation in Wisconsin, this is now a photograph of our heritage—our ceremony, our drummer, our Old Village. This representation of a historically and culturally specific event has been released from its textual moorings to float in time and space as an isolated, transparent—and claimed—image, as generic as it is genuine.

Densmore's photograph of the drummer constitutes what Connerton (1989: 73) calls an "inscribing practice," a testimonial to past action that he contrasts with the current interaction of an "incorporating practice." These categories of action are revealing, but photographs conceal the sense of agency of the people they portray, and Connerton's categories

Midéwiwin member with drum in a Midéwigan, or Midéwiwin Lodge. From Frances Densmore, *Chippewa Music*, Vol. 1 (1910: 35–36), neg. 0595-c-1 (interior view of lodge, White Earth reservation).

of action are built upon differences related to time that photographs obscure and confuse. Images are powerful appeals to a mixture of the appropriated past and the active present for both Indians and Others. Photographs are especially important and insidious in relation to the ethnographic content of popular culture. In the guise of ultimate reality, authenticity, and authority, historical photographs bleed into current analysis and interpretation, reconstructing common phenomenological images of a culturally specific past for Indians and Others. This process of dislocating photographs in time and space is accelerated by the plethora of missing information—personal, lived, and local. Ethnographic photographs are contrived and constructed, but they reveal neither the context and conditions of their production nor the complexities of the experiences they seem to fix and transmit over time. From an ethnographic perspective, this evocative image portrays a significant relationship between an Indian and a Midéwiwin artifact. Densmore notes its location, but mentions no other details about the context of the photograph. I want to know what this seemingly transparent photo-graph—and most archival images of Indians—cannot tell me about the ceremonial or personal experience of the Chippewa man dressed in European clothes and the drum placed before him. Whose drum is this? Did he dream it, make it, or receive it from someone in his family, some-one who has walked on or another Midé? Does he use it only for Midéwi-win ceremonies or for personal prayers and songs? When he walks on, will it stay in his family, pass to another Midé member or be buried with him or elsewhere? Does every Midé member have a drum? Or only Midé priests? Who are the Midé drummers? And most importantly, who is he?

In the positivist rush to observe and document the songs and objects and actions of Indian ceremonials, early anthropologists adapted the methodological practices of the natural scientists who preceded them. Through fieldwork, ethnographers gathered impressive collections of material items that were often described, classified, and photographed in nameless, impersonal documents that are "undated, unplaced, almost unanchored" (Lippard 1992: 15). As Lucy Lippard (1992) writes:

> It is a curious experience to go through the photographic archives—files and dusty files of pictures of people, most of them now dead. So few of the subjects are identified—not by Indian name, colonial name, or even by tribal affiliation. They are like ghosts deprived of rest. The photogra-phers (they too are often anonymous) have put the subjects on the his-torical map, often falsifying forever a person's place in the world. (15)

As Lippard (15) adds, "There are many reasons for this—from the subjects' justified fears and resentments, to some photographers' igno-rance and indifference to scholarship. Many of these images are also propaganda—taken not only to record 'vanishing' indigenous cultures, but also to grease the wheels of assimilation." For Indians, photogra-phy's very "ellipse of language" and "condensation of the 'ineffable' social whole" that Roland Barthes (1973: 91) tells us "tends to spirit away politics," constitutes the camera a political weapon. From the perspective of research, anonymous Indian images and testimony are the underside of "Western scholarship, which looks to attribute words with great pre-cision to each particular speaker" (Ross 1996: ix). Both colonial gaze and social scientific method have left us these static, generic representations of individual cultural experience about which Allan Sekula (in Wees 1993: 42) writes, "Not only are the pictures in archives literally for sale, but their meanings are up for grabs." In addition, the collective roots of Native social identity and oral discourse encourage a certain individual anonymity, which contributes to the ambiguous meaning of photographs. Historically, Indians recognized that reality is experienced, mediated, and ambivalent. Even now, Native people often feel uncomfortable being photographed as isolated, named individuals speaking on behalf of others or expressing unequivocal information for tape recorders and notebooks. As Rupert Ross (1996: ix–x) points out, "There seems to be a widespread Aboriginal understanding that thought or information must be shared in ways that leave it open to the listeners to take whatever meaning they wish to find in what they have heard," and I would add, in what they have seen. But regardless of their intrinsic ambiguity, old photographs contain a sense of the strength of the people, and they can be used as tools to reconstruct the Indian past.

Because of the absences and openings in historical documents and the inevitable silences in Indian oral tradition, locating and identifying artifacts or objects is often happenstance, a matter of being in the right place at the right time and to see or hear a prod to the memory or imagination that can be validated in records, interviews, or photographs. This combination of serendipity and research is vital to the project of reconstructing Indian cultural history. In Lac du Flambeau, a large bib-like bag of solid beads called a "bandolier bag" recently found its way back home through just such a combination of chance discovery and archival evidence. The bandolier bag was in the back room of a shop that my brother happened to visit in Laguna Beach, California. The owner, Matthew Wood, had recently purchased two bandolier bags and after chatting with my brother, he invited him into the back room to see them. In the words of my brother:

> One had been identified as a Menominee bag from a piece of paper that was in the pocket, and I was pretty sure that the other was Ojibwe because of the typical floral design. I told Wood that our people made bags like that. There was a bow beaded into the pattern in the right hand corner that I had seen in old pictures. I knew that I had the picture at home on which the beadwork on the right hand corner looked the same as the bow in the right hand corner of the bandolier bag he showed me. (Laabs, 1997: 17)

Back in Lac du Flambeau, my brother thumbed through my father's albums and found the photograph he remembered. Bandolier bags are worn by men, but this was a photograph of a Chippewa woman wearing a bandolier with a similar—and common—pattern of floral designs on a white background. But in this photograph, the bandolier had a bow in the right-hand corner and next to it, beaded onto the bag, the initials "W.A." He telephoned Wood and learned that the bag in his possession, too, had beaded initials "W.A." near the bow. Wood sent the bag and when the photograph revealed that they were identical, my brother pieced together the bag's past from tribal records and memoried testimony in Lac du Flambeau. In his words, "The bag had belonged to William Americus. He was known in Lac du Flambeau as Rainbow. Born in 1889, he was married to Fanny Sun, who was known as a fine bead worker" (Laabs 1997: 17).

Fanny Sun is wearing the bandolier bag in the Lac du Flambeau photograph, and Celia Patterson, the niece she raised, is standing with her. Celia was about eight years old when the picture was taken and since she was born in 1910, the photograph can be dated about 1918. We will never know how this bandolier bag found its way to California, but the Lac du Flambeau tribal council purchased the bag and placed it on display in the museum. For Chippewa, what is important is that this beautifully beaded bag has returned home. We know who made it and who wore it. Rainbow's bandolier bag has reclaimed a place in the cultural history of Lac du Flambeau.

Photographs are vital evidence at the end of the research trail. But research sometimes begins with a photograph, an image of a frozen historical moment that can move the imagination. This was the experience of Maureen Matthews who followed the trail of "Fairwind's Drum" in her production of a radio program for the Canadian Broadcasting Corporation's series called *Ideas*. She explains:

> I first saw Fairwind's drum in a photograph. In the black and white print it sits suspended on four stakes, in the middle of a great pavilion.... Behind the drum stand three tall, serious-looking men.... I want to know about this. I want to know who these people are and what this drum means to them. But the drum was lost and the meaning has scattered like the pieces of a musical and cultural puzzle. To reconstruct the picture and what it means, we have to gather the pieces and figure out how each piece relates to the others. ("Fairwind's Drum" 1993: 1)

To "gather the pieces," Matthews and historian Jennifer Brown (1994) worked with Hallowell's ethnography—including a rediscovered manuscript—and his photographs of the Berens River area of northern Manitoba where Fairwind lived. Together, they reconstructed the pieces of the puzzle and built an interpretive framework through interviews with anthropologists who knew Hallowell, with local people, including Fairwind's relatives, and with a Mennonite schoolteacher named Gary Butikofer, who spent twenty years in the settlement of Popular Hill. Butikofer knew Fairwind before he died and recognized this drum's importance. In 1978, Butikofer bought Fairwind's drum from his grandson, Jacob Strang. The double drum skins were beyond repair and the drum's power was silent, but he kept it. When he left the area in 1990, he donated the drum to the Red Lake Museum. There, Matthews and Brown found Fairwind's drum at the end of a remarkable research journey that worked to renew the drum's value and visibility in local Ojibway cultural history, a project that began with the recognition that "a photograph is a passageway. Some photographs are dead ends. Others open into astonishing vistas and memories" (Lippard 1992: 17).

Midé Drums

The 1909 photograph taken at White Earth, Minnesota, and the texts inscribing Lac du Flambeau are blank pages compared to the thoroughly documented and richly textured narrative of Fairwind's drum, but I have begun to uncover what I can about Midé drums. Densmore ([1913] 1972: 11–12) writes that the drum she photographed was "purchased on the Red Lake reservation," and she describes in detail what the Midé water drum looks like and how it is constructed and decorated. She does not mention the painted circles that cover the bottom of the Lac du Flambeau drum, nor does she tell us whose drum it is, why he has it, or if this drum is private or communal property, a personal possession, or a legacy that can be passed on to others. Hoffman's (1891) 1885–86 account of the Midéwiwin in northern Minnesota is a lengthy, detailed, and important description of the preparation and enactment of curing and initiation ceremonies, including the beliefs and songs, cures and sacred objects, speeches and mnemonic scrolls of the Midéwiwin. But his discussion of drums is fully contained in the following informative but meagre description:

> The Midé drum differs from the drum commonly used in dances in the fact that it is cylindrical, consisting of an elongated kettle of wooden ves-

sel, or perhaps a section of the hollow trunk of a tree about 10 inches in diameter and from 18 to 20 inches in length, over both ends of which rawhide is stretched while wet, so that upon drying the membrane becomes hard and tense, producing, when beaten, a very hard, loud tone, which can be heard at a great distance. Frequently, however, water is put into the bottom of the drum and the drumhead stretched across the top in a wet state, which appears to intensify the sound quite considerably. The peculiar and special qualities of the drum are described to the applicant; that it was at first the gift of Ki'shi Man'ido, who gave it through the intercession of Mi'nabo zho; that it is to invoke the presence of the Midé Man'idos, or sacred spirits, when seeking directions as to information desired, success, etc.; that it is to be employed at the side of the sick to assist in the expulsion or exorcism of evil man'idos who may possess the body of the sufferer; and that it is to be used in the Midéwigan during the initiation of new members or the advancement of a Midé from a degree to a higher one. (Hoffman 1891: 190–91)

In Edward Benton-Banai's (1988) book, I discover both the imposing importance of the water drum and the validity of my memory of the small Midé water drum. There are actually two types of Midé drums made from hollowed-out logs. The larger drum, like the one at the tribal museum, has a deerskin head or drum skin, which is fastened with a wooden hoop. The smaller drum emerged later and contains seven stones, which are laced into the deerhide strips that hold the drum skin in place. These stones represent both Mother Earth and "the Seven Original Teachings that came to the Ojibway" (Benton-Banai 1988: 70). The Original Teachings are from the Seven Grandfathers, powerful spirits whose responsibility it is to watch over the earth's people (60). For the Midé, "all the gifts of physical well-being ... brought to the people from the Seven Grandfathers were symbolized in the Waterdrum. The Waterdrum represented all that was necessary for life. It embodied both the physical and the spiritual" (68).

Benton-Banai tells us how the water drum is constructed and what each part of the drum means; but he, too, writes nothing about the possession and descent of Midé drums. I could contact him to ask about this, but I am acutely aware of the impact that our conversation, generated in the name of research, can have on the issue of the disputed Midé drum. In the years that passed, my nephew had become the director of the tribal museum; the young women who dreamed the drum were occupied with other matters; the Midé Elder who asked for the drum had died; and the Midéwiwin itself was fragmented into competing camps with different leaders. No one had asked me about the drum. The allegiances to the conflicting positions had not dissipated, but the drum lay dormant in a shallow state of personal and collective silence. Since I have not determined the owner of the drum, is the information I will gain from this conversation worth the renewed anxiety and conflict that it may engender in Lac du Flambeau? Asking questions is not a simple, straightforward act in Indian communities. Questions forge a path of discussion and dissent that can diverge into misinformation, rumour, and reproach. Issues can absorb families, neighbours, enemies, and others in the turmoil of contention and opposition. I have decided to speak with a Lac du Flambeau friend who sometimes attends the Midéwiwin ceremonies.

My friend is neither a Midé nor deeply knowledgeable about its practices, but his memories resonate with what I seem to know or remember. Drums belong to individuals, but in the collective construction of Chippewa society, they can also belong to families and, if circumstances allow, they are passed on within families. Based on information in my father's files, this drum probably belonged to someone in one of fourteen families living in Lac du Flambeau.

My father's comments, labelled "Notes on Medicine Lodge from Conversations with Members in 1957," summarize brief discussions with six named Midé members, including a Menominee and a Chippewa living at Neopit and a Potawatomi living in Lac du Flambeau. The notes also name eight other Lac du Flambeau Indians who were active members of the Midéwiwin. His interest focused on the nature and extent of Midéwiwin religious practice on this reservation, and these few pages of notes sketch a picture of uneven cultural disruption and unmistakable institutional decline. One informant says that there are seven or eight Midés left in Lac du Flambeau, another estimates fifteen or twenty; but all six agree that no one here knows the entire ritual anymore, and no young men are in training to take over the Midé leadership. The most poignant comment is a note from my father which says, "Bridget Buckskin tried to sell me her otter medicine bag for $5.00 the day before this conversation, later for a 'half-jug' [of wine]. Have picked up and been offered literally dozens since then" (B. Guthrie 1957: 1).

From these interview notes, I learn that, in the late 1950s, there was a Midéwiwin "revival" among the Winnebagos at Black River Falls, Wisconsin, where they held a Midé ritual every weekend. There, young men who can recite the whole history of the Midéwiwin "stand in front of their fathers or grandfathers and 'they drum for them'" (B. Guthrie 1957: 1). But the revitalization of the Midéwiwin apparently did not spread to Lac du Flambeau.

In 1962, my father spoke with Viola Little Pat about the Midé. He wrote in his notes from that interview, "There is no longer a 'head man' left here since her father's death, but there are two 'old men' left at Neopit who can conduct the ceremony (B. Guthrie 1962: 1). My father's notes recall Hallowell's (1936) account of the decline of the Midéwiwin in the Lake Winnipeg region of Ontario. Reading between the lines, I realize why two of the "Flambeau drums" that were at Jim Bell's house went to Neopit. The drums passed to Benaise when Jim Bell died, and then somehow to a Lac du Flambeau man who moved to Neopit, probably because the ceremony was no longer held here. I regret not asking Benaise about all this. But these are not the drums that my father had, nor are they necessarily Midé drums.

Along the meandering path of researching drums, I learned that one of the two drums that are "gone" from Lac du Flambeau, according to the men with whom I spoke in the Old Village, was actually bought by a collector I knew who lived a hundred miles south of here, a man with a deep and an informed interest in Indians and artifacts. I passed the location of this drum on to a tribal council member, but the collector has since died and the drum has probably been released from its moorings forever. The drum was called a "Big Drum." The Big Drum is the name by which Lac du Flambeau Indians refer to the Dream Dance ceremonial, a distinct religious rite that Barrett (1911: 256) tells us "may be regarded as one form of the messiah cult and, though it is in reality a ceremony of modern origin, has spread over a wide area and is now practiced by many tribes." According to Barrett (261), the ceremonials of the Dream Dance or Big Drum, which originated with the Sioux and were passed to the Chippewa, centre on a large drum and a special pipe. If the objects and rituals associated with the Big Drum now represent tribal spirituality that is interwoven with the Midéwiwin, the Big Drum is a different and a more recent practice.

Neither Hoffman (1891) nor Benton-Banai (1988) nor my father speaks about "big drums" associated with the Midéwiwin. But Johann George Kohl ([1885] 1985: 42), who wrote an account of his 1855 travels in northern Wisconsin, describes Midéwiwin ceremonies in which a "big drum" is placed in the centre of the Midéwigan, a drum which he describes as "slightly different from the ordinary drum: it is longer, produces a more hollow sound, and has a special name, 'Midéguakik.'" Gerald Vizenor (1965: 94) writes about the Midéwiwin initiation, "As soon as the four midéwiwin leaders enter the midéwigan, they take up the mitigwakik, midé drum, and in unison commence to beat on it, while the leaders chant midéwiwin songs. The mitigwakik is covered with a head of raw deer hide, and when it is beat upon, it produces a weird and hollow sound that can be heard miles away." With only slightly different spellings, I know from the descriptions of these three authors, whose writing spans 130 years, that Benton-Banai's (1988: 68) "water drum," Vizenor's "mitigwakik," and Kohl's "big drum" are interpretations of the same Midé drum. But none of these accounts mentions possession or bestowal of drums. Even if I were able to follow the historical traces of the contested drum that was in the tribal museum to a particular family, the issue of disposition is complex and unclear.

Speaking about the Midéwiwin, Viola Little Pat (in B. Guthrie 1962: 1) told my father that the initiation candidate has a "helper who does the singing and drumming," and she suggests that many Midé members have drums, either their own or one shared among family members:

> During the initiation the headman passes down the line, each person singing a song. If the person knows the song, he can do his own drumming and singing; if not, the headman helps him, since certain songs must be sung. Viola always had her father or her husband drum and help her sing. (1)

These interview notes provide a basis for assuming that the disputed drum was purchased, probably about 1960, and that it is about sixty years old. But whose drum was it and who can claim it now? Does the disposition of a drum defer to Indians who wish to restore and revive its power, to those who follow the spiritual practices it mediates, or to other Indians who purchase it or who dream its existence?

Ethnographers and Indians agree that Chippewa knowledge and power are often acquired in visions or dreams. Writing in 1835, Henry Schoolcraft notes that dreams are an important religious experience for Chippewa because they represent direct communication with the spiritual world. More recently, Tom Boulanger (1971: 48–49) tells us about dreams among those he calls "Old Indian men," "When they dream of something they believe it. They sometimes dream of animals, and dream of different kind of roots, lakes, rivers ... winter birds and summer birds ... west wind, east wind, kinds of prayers, creatures and etc." In the traditional practice of vision quest, dreams render power and knowledge that are personal and private, like secret songs or guardian spirits. But dreams can also be shared in spiritual or healing ceremonies, like the Midéwiwin. The endowment of dreams can be passed on to others, and the power that dreams mediate can sometimes be purchased as property. Among Midé priests, the knowledge of medicines is considered private property, and those who train and inform Midéwiwin initiates are paid in material goods.

Writing on Ojibway sociology in 1937, Ruth Landes discusses "property," including spiritualized property. Her fieldwork among Minnesota and Ontario Ojibway both clarifies and confuses the disposition of the Midé drum. Like many earlier ethnographies, Landes's writing seems authoritative and absolute, with no possibility of discrepancy, doubt, or ambiguity. In contrast to common assumptions that, in the context of historical tradition, Indians had no concept of private property and, therefore, property was shared and communal, Landes ([1937] 1969: 87–88) states emphatically that among the Chippewa, "all property with one slight exception is held by individuals, not by groups." She explains the exception as a group of individuals who access an object or practice simultaneously; and she tells us that property is acquired not only through manufacture, purchase, and inheritance but also through dreams and visions. Her informants included men from Minnesota, but her primary respondent was Mrs. Maggie Wilson, a woman from Emo, Ontario, about whom she has written extensively. Like Grandma Gauthier, Maggie Wilson's knowledge and experience is that of a Christian, mixed-blood Indian woman. She "came from a long line of forebearers, on her father's side, who had served Scottish missionaries, spoke English, and wrote the missionaries' version of Ojibway and Cree" (i).

About the Midéwiwin, Landes ([1937] 1969: 132) writes that a Midé member's "equipment" includes the "sacred drum" and both "rattle and drum are appurtenances of the special offices." She concludes that "the material equipment from a Midé can be from two sources: first, acquired in the course of instruction, and secondly, bequeathed"—though not necessarily to family members; and she adds two caveats that concern the Midé drum. First, drums, like dances or songs, can be "secured through dream experience" (115), and secondly, "people sometimes have their paraphernalia burned after their death" or "they may abandon their possessions." She notes two cases in which Midé threw their sacred items "away" or "in the bush" because they were associated with "bad medicine" (132).

Landes ([1937] 1969: 43) also tells us that in the 1930s, "the elevated 'old' Midé shaman was taken to be the most evil of shamans." This association between the Midéwiwin and "bad medicine" is supported by Hoffman (1891), Densmore ([1910] 1972), Schoolcraft (1835), and Warren (1885), some of whom suggest that not only the knowledge to heal but also the knowledge and ability to bring about illness or death is acquired in the higher degrees of the Midéwiwin. Midé members were also associated with "Bear-Walkers," men who wander around villages in the form of a bear, sometimes robbing graves, sometimes using "bad medicine" to kill adversaries. More recently, Selwyn Dewdney (1975) writes that while there is no clear definition of the "evil" associated with the Midéwiwin, "bad medicine"

> was a tradition so deeply rooted in Ojibway society that a conflict persisted all through its history: menacing the good name of the Midéwiwin from its emergence, never purged from the cult even in its hey-day, and threatening to submerge it altogether in the later days of the Midé decline. (115)

Hallowell (1936: 35) reported that, in the Lake Winnipeg region of Ontario, the spiritual power of Midéwiwin medicine bags was recognized and feared, even after the ceremony was no longer practised.

Knowledge of "bad medicine" may be considered a personal asset among the Ojibway, a kind of property acquired by individuals, but Landes's writing on property represents a line of inquiry that Hallowell (1967: 241) tells us has long been misdirected toward issues of who owns property rather than the analysis of the kind of property rights, duties, and privileges that are exercised by Indians with respect to property. In fact, both Landes and Hallowell write about property from the abstract and analytical perspectives of anthropological analysis. In contrast, the Chippewa endowment of this drum is enacted in the nature and vigour of its ability to both mediate and assign power, knowledge, and authority; and this endowment is forged and expressed in relationships. For Chippewa, the rights and responsibilities articulated to these relationships—ceremonial and personal—are intertwined with the drum's ownership, with whose drum it is or was, and how they acquired it, whether through manufacture or bestowal, dissent, purchase, or petition. But in the end, it is the cultural, social, and spiritual meaning of the Midé drum that matters. In evocative words that move beyond the academic borders of analysis, Basil Johnston (1982) writes about the water drum:

> Only the drum possessed the special tones that would be suitable for the audience of the spirits. There was no sound, human or natural, to compare with it. What the drum imparted neither man nor woman could understand, for it transcended human comprehension, going beyond it in the form of an echo that could be heard only by the spirits. It was a mystery; and therefore, it was the best way for man to communicate with the spirit world. While he drummed, man chanted, so that his petitions were borne by the echo of the drum and transformed into the language of the spirits who dwelled above and below and beyond. Only the talk of the drum could gain the attention of the deities. (100)

Today, the silent voice of this water drum—dreamed and imagined and claimed—speaks to the "simulations of survivance in new stories" (Vizenor 1993: 11) that engage Chippewa identity, cultural continuity, and political possibility through the traditional prophecy of the Seventh Fire. In the Seventh Fire, the Oshkibimadizeeg or New People will return to the teachings of the Elders and, Benton-Banai (1988: 93) writes, "if the New People will remain strong in their quest, the Waterdrum of the Midéwiwin Lodge will again sound its voice." Like the ethnography, history, and testimony that encircle it, this drum has transcended the past to become absorbed in the cultural struggle of the present.

End of the Research Trail

I am nearing a narrow bend in this entangled research path. As Harold Hickerson (1970) describes it,

> The beginning of document research is going to the library closest to the area of interest and following your nose from there. If you travel a trail long enough, material takes shape and begins to make sense in terms of consistency. Depending on the scope of the problem, and assuming an adequacy of material, there is inevitably a point of diminishing returns reached, much as in fieldwork, and then research grinds to a stop. (4)

There are many more academic accounts of the Midéwiwin that discuss its origin, structure, and role in Ojibway society, but there is little more that I can learn about this drum from archival and ethnographic documents. Old photographs of drums and fieldwork reports of practice are invaluable, but they cannot tell me about the heritage, lived experience, or emergent meaning of this drum, or the efficacy of its disposition in Lac du Flambeau today. In fact, the distance and discrepancy in the writings of ethnographic analysis and the fragmented rememberings of Indian tradition only confuse the issues. Discussions with other people in Lac du Flambeau may tell me more about the presence and purpose of particular drums that are used in social or spiritual ceremonies today, but the meaning of this drum is constructed in the experience and discourse of the dreamers, the Elders, my brother, myself, and other members of the Lac du Flambeau community. Its placement is as complex as the cultural struggle over contested ideology and identity that reflects the Lac du Flambeau Indian community as a whole. This drum was neither "bequeathed" nor "thrown away," and Midé tradition suggests that the dreamers can claim it. Since it was most likely sold to my father forty years ago, the drum is probably dead, unempowered, and voiceless. But in Lac du Flambeau today, it can neither be displayed in the tribal museum nor placed in a labelled box to be held but hidden from view, a strategy that the University of British Columbia Museum of Anthropology has adopted for sacred objects. The Lac du Flambeau museum has built a "drum room," which now houses six Midéwiwin or Big Drums that are feasted, used in ceremonies, and inaccessible to outsiders. The drum can be returned to the museum or to the Midéwiwin, where it once raised its voice, to be repowered and speak again; but if there is concern about the ambiguous or sinister power that it might express or the personal medicine it might personify, the drum can also be buried. Even the issue of who has the right to make a decision about the future of the drum is contested. The drum remains absorbed in conflicting relations of ideology, family, identity, and power that are paralyzing.

My father could not have foreseen the future of this drum. He could not have known that this object would become entangled in a struggle over history and culture, over spiritual experience and political purpose—my own, my brother's, the Elders and dreamers, and others in Lac du Flambeau. Like the personal testimony, and the ethnographic and archival evidence that speak about drums, each of us reveals personal and partial truths. But within the diversity of ideologies and identities that are continually contested and negotiated in the formation of Indian community, there are common threads of collective memory and emerging meaning. In Lac du Flambeau, we wait for the drum to speak. In the words of Bren Kolson (in Perrault and Vance 1990: 134), "Stick of life, drum of hide, beating out / ancestral songs. Memories of life's defeats / and life's enduring will to go on and on and on."

≪ • ≫

Blood Borders:
Being Indian and Belonging

Jack Forbes (1987) writes, "I really resent white people trying to dissect us and tell us what makes a person a Native American."

> How much Indian blood do you have?
> What tribe are you?
> Oh, I never heard
> of that one. (121)

In an article entitled "Native by Nature?" Rick Harp (1994) writes about being Indian:

> How might I exist indeed? For me, a self-identifying Plains Cree—whose passport reads "Canadian," whose first and (currently) only language is English, whose mother is Native and whose father is not, whose entire life has been spent in urban environments, and whose education has been wholly obtained from non-Native institutions—the question is as immediate and urgent as it is profound. (46)

For as long as I can remember, blood borders and the conflicts of identity and recognition that spiral around them have been part of being Indian, and negotiating these borders has been a factor of daily life. In Indian Country, tribal or band membership matters, and it is entangled with Indian blood in a maze of ancestries and endorsements, rules, and exceptions. Indian blood and belonging are bound together in a knot of historical policies and current practices that are inevitably public and irrevocably personal. In my case, my father is a tribal member of the reservation where I was raised; my mother is non-Indian; my brother is a tribal member; and I am not enrolled.

The contradictions and anomalies of Indian blood borders are personally difficult and socially divisive. They are also politically significant. Issues of Indian identity and tribal membership cut to the core of Native resistance and empowerment in current struggles over the politics of difference and the pronouncements of sovereignty. The right to Indian identity has been controlled and curtailed by government policies since the formations of Canada and the United States. As a result, blood and belonging are knitted into the conflicts between Indians and Others over power and control, history and heritage, over acculturation, appropriation, and autonomy.

Indian membership policies are colonial codes that ricochet through time and space to cut across and construct Native identity and tribal affiliation. The codes that identify Indians in a matrix of blood or paternity circulate in conflicts over membership, in disagreements over who is an Indian, what signifies Indianness, and what being Indian means. This discord over blood and belonging is grounded in wider struggles over competing representations of nationhood that assert and contest the right of indigenous nations to represent, empower, and position themselves. In the wider political arena, the codes that determine who is an Indian also define the tribal borders of Native nations within nation-states and test the boundaries of Native self-determination. But like the colonial rules of Indian enrollment, Native membership policies based on blood quantum or paternal descent alone obscure or even erase the cultural and communal constructions of being Indian.

Being Different

If Cynthia Ann Parker had ever told her story, it would be characterized in populist literature as a "captivity narrative." In fact, her story is one of double captivity and transposed identity. The events as we know them seem almost imaginary, like the plot of an all-too-familiar cowboy-and-Indian film. Cynthia Ann Parker, blue-eyed and settlement-raised, was kidnapped by Comanches in 1835 at the age of nine. Twenty-five years later in 1860, married to the Comanche leader Peta Nocona and the mother of three children, she was captured again along with her infant daughter, this time by sixty Texas Rangers and volunteers who descended upon Peta Nocona's village. The relatives who kept Cynthia Ann Parker from returning to Comanche territory tried to dissolve the cultural affinity she felt for Indians, but the distance between her colonial past and Indian present was too great. Soon after illness took her daughter, Cynthia Ann Parker died. She never knew about the death of her son, the fate of her husband, or the fame of Quanah Parker, the son who survived. Years later, when his mother's remains were reburied in Oklahoma, the Comanche leader Quanah Parker began his speech at the graveside ceremony, speaking in halting English: "Forty years ago, my mother died. She captured by Comanche, nine years old. Love Indian and wild life so well no want to go back to white folks. All same people, God say. I love my mother" (in Vanderwerth 1971: 255).

That identity and difference related to race, gender, or nation are culturally constructed and historically constituted is widely recognized in the literature on cultural studies, feminism, history, and interpretive anthropology (Said 1978; C. Hall 1993; Carter 1998; Geertz 1973). For Native North Americans, these works create an opening to understand colonial experience, nationalist discourse, and identity politics as epistemological and representational knots. As Rick Harp (1994: 47) writes, "Colonialism isn't just about the forcible acquisition of control over land and resources, it is also—perhaps even more so—about a particular way of knowing and relating to reality." Like the Orientalist images in Said's (1978) analysis of Middle Eastern colonialism, North American's representations of themselves and of Indians are linked in articulation to ways of knowing and experiencing otherness. For newcomers, the otherness of Indians has been both fascinating and frustrating. Drawn in literature and art, social imaginaries emerge and recede, inscribing Indians as primitive and pagan, heroic and hostile, exploited and defended. These politicized images are woven into policies—colonial and current—that not only isolate and identify Indians but also construct and position Indian identity, creating unsteady circles of insiders and outsiders.

Identifying outsiders reveals and isolates those who are excluded. But recognizing insiders also builds connections among those who share both heritage and a sense of exile. Native encounters with newcomers affirm the oneness of indigenous nations, building bordered coalitions, constructing imagined communities of Indians who are yoked together in experiences and symbols of historical autonomy, culture and displacement that give rise to a common image of themselves. Michael Ignatieff (1993) writes about the imagined community that constructs a nation:

> You can never know the strangers who make up a nation with you. So you imagine what it is that you have in common, and in the shared imagining, strangers become citizens, that is, people who share both the same rights and the same image of the place they live in. A nation, therefore, is an imagined community. (144)

For Ignatieff (1993: 7–8), the imagined nationalism that emerges forms either a civic nation held together by laws or an ethnic nation held together by common, inherited roots; and neither configuration guarantees social cohesion or community. But if Native nations are understood as ethnic communities by outsiders, Indians themselves experience the lived reality of a cohesive nationhood that is impelled not only by roots and rules but also by the braided web of representations Indians build and enact. In Stuart Hall's (1993: 356) analysis, such national cultures are systems of representations, social collectivities held together in circulating images of seeming similarity that are rooted in history and culture. From this perspective, nation-states are a configuration of bordered communities, an aggregation of cultures that represent more than one nation. There is, of course, a difference between nations that share history and culture and a common image of themselves, and nation-states in which the history or culture that is shared or constructed is interwoven in institutional and legal frameworks of sovereignty and citizenship.

With respect to nation-states, Native nations are located somewhere in-between, in an ambiguous, conflicting formation of national dependence and tribal independence. As nations within nation-states, they are neither autonomous nor sovereign. Their special status as indigenous nations involves a knot of complementary, contested, and ultimate levels of authority. Tribal and band governments exercise substantial powers over the reservations and enrollees that construct and empower their national status. This sense of nationhood is an assertion of Native self-determination voiced in images of collective unity which allege that, among the multiple, mixed identities individuals express, "it is the nation that provides them with their primary form of belonging" (Ignatieff 1993: 5). "Belonging" to Native nations is a complex, conditional, and fundamental process because Indian identities are located in tribal nations. Native people are Mohawk or Cree, Ojibway or Ho-chunk, identifications that Mohawk writer Audra Simpson suggests are fused with nationhood: "'Mohawk' and 'nationhood' are inseparable. Both are simply about *being*. Being is about who you are, and a sense of who you are is arrived at through your relationships with other people—your people. So who we are is tied with what we are: a nation" (Simpson in Alfred 1999: 65, italics in original). The notion of the Native nation that Simpson invokes is constructed in the imagined unities of tribal heritage: experienced, attributed, and expressed.

Like the social alliances of the nation-states in which they live, Native nations reconstruct their historical hybridity as one continuous people in narratives that ignore the wars and adoptions, intermarriages, and displacements of lived histories; and these stories of oneness extend seamlessly into the mythic time of creation and migration. The oneness of Indian tribes or bands is built in shared stories and common meanings, in narratives that construct a particular heritage and a collective sense of experience and sacrifice, culture, identity, and empowerment. In the circulation of Indian narratives and the counter-narratives of nation-states, Native people retell and resist, building the oneness of different First Nations in tribal representations of identity and community, of blood and belonging. But the cultural differences of individual Native nations are also overlaid with a spreading sense of pan-Indianism.

Today, the narrative histories and emerging cultures of Native nations are interwoven in a variety of images, some tribal, some pan-Indian. Through the expression of shared stories and appropriated images, pan-Indianism can reinforce, transform, or even replace the lived histories and cultures of individual tribal groups. The stories that emerge to reconstitute and spread pan-Indian culture have raised questions about the authenticity of Indian history and experience. In writing that Ward Churchill (1992: 163) calls "the New Racism," James Clifton (1990: 42) suggests that Indian stories are "versions of a conventional narrative" that uphold a "cultural fiction," a trope that was invented by Europeans, sustained by North Americans, and manipulated by Native people themselves. Russell Means (with Wolf 1995: 116) writes about Lakota cultural ceremonies, "All those customs are gone now, along with the understanding of why we did such things. Today it's all backwards and upside down." But in his insightful writings, Chippewa author Gerald Vizenor (1994: 52) tells us, "Native American Indian identities bear the tribal memories and solace of heard stories. Postindian identities are inscrutable recreations, the innermost brush with natural reason, and, at the same time, unbounded narcissism and a rush of new simulations of survivance."

Ethnographic reconstructions of traditional culture wind through North American narratives of dominance, placing Native people in a time-distanced past that cannot be fully retrieved from the recesses of Indian oral tradition. Drawn in the histories and ethnographies of Others, Native cultures are commonly represented as "traditional," a conception that ignores the dynamic expressions of cultures that emerge, move, and fuse today in response to a changing environment, an environment which has given rise to the spread of pan-Indianism. Pan-Indian unities are built in expressions of transforming culture, in the contestation and commonality of reclaimed heritage and lived experience. There is a growing tension between Native people over expressions of pan-Indianism and possessions of tribalism. But despite the struggle over Indian appropriation and adaptation, the stories Native people tell are allied in a loose merger of collective memories and commemorated events. In the tension over monocultural expression of Indianness, the narratives that represent the traditions of other Native nations are sometimes claimed as common experience, sometimes rejected as tribally hybrid. Today, narratives that are remembered, created, and exchanged spiral in vague histories in which "what seems to take place is not just a simple recollection of an earlier day, but a virtual recreation of the feelings experienced then" (Ross 1992: 73). This sense of affectivity that rivets the past to the present in ideological expressions, which place and position, forges constructions of identity and nation that disrupt the national narratives of Others. In narratives of pain and empowerment, Native people construct both the unity of being tribal and the difference in being Indian.

Tribalism and pan-Indianism are rooted in a sense of *difference* that inscribes the relations between First Nations and the nation-states in which they have always been an anomalous presence. As Catherine Hall's (1993) historical analysis of English identity suggests, the position of Indians in Canada and the United States reveals shifting boundaries that distinguish Indians from Others. These mutable borders that define the nature of "imagined communities" of belonging and exclude those who do not belong (and may even threaten the imagined unity), construct and defend the cultural basis of communal groups (Gilroy in C. Hall 1993: 357). In North America, dominant cultures are built in shifting boundaries that unify and divide, absorb, and exclude. But the ongoing process of building, fortifying, and expanding cultural unities among those who represent difference in nation-states is always uneven and unstable. Colonial policies and practices reveal a constant tension between ideological approaches that exclude and contain those who are positioned as outsiders and approaches that forcibly remake outsiders into insiders through coercion or assimilation. Assimilation involves repressing old identities, in part by taking on new social memories. Those who are placed or overpowered by Others—who are excluded from or refuse to be absorbed into the cultural narratives of imagined communities—build their own collective subjectivities and social boundaries in a politicized process that expresses not only their resistance but also their cultural continuity.

For Native North Americans, the relationship between sameness, difference, and national formations has always been a precarious proposition. Displaced from their lands and lifestyles, and beset by the intrusion of conflicting cultural values, Indians have been disconnected, even isolated, from the social groups that dominate North America. Like other peoples of colour who are positioned outside the perimeters of dominant continental cultures, Indians battle historical projections of invisibility and exclusion that absorb the realities and specificities of their cultures. But because of their unique placement as indigenous peoples, the exclusion of Indians has always been an inevitable intrusion upon the "commonness" of cultural representations in North American nation-states. How can Canada or the United States construct a cultural basis for collective unity that excludes the original inhabitants, the First Nations, and Native American owners of the land? This contradiction lies deep within the nation-building projects of North American states, and it impels eliminating, absorbing, or containing Indians to legitimize the appropriation of their lands and resources and to build a basis for Canadian or American nationhood. The claims of imagined communities in North American nation-states that have represented Indians as different, inferior, and dispensable, have produced both the military operations to eliminate, confine, or restrain Indians and the institutional and legal policies that enforced their acculturation. These policies reflect the long-held assumption that "if Indians were an alien race because they had a different religion, language, social organization and political status than other Americans, they could be absorbed only if they became the same as other Americans" (Harmon 1990: 101). But recasting and absorbing Indians has not been easy.

Native people have countered the North American project to dominate, change, and absorb them with assertions of the very distinctions that disrupt and even threaten the imagined commonness of the dominant cultures of Canada and the United States: their Aboriginal status and culture. Indian resistance is sometimes confrontational, but more often, it is transformational, characterized by a progression of lateral movements of opposition that are grounded in cultural persistence. Like the folk hero Coyote, the trickster in Native narratives who shifts in form, position, and place but always survives adversity, Native North Americans manoeuvre around economic, political, and personal barriers, claiming the discourse that excludes them. Some Indians are cloaked in acculturation, as Jack Forbes (in Trinh 1994: 17) suggests in writing, "I could tell you how hard it is to hide right in the midst of White people. It is an art learned early because life depends on dissimulation and harmlessness." Acculturated Native people, too, proclaim the extent and nature of their difference in their struggles with North American nation-states over land and sovereignty, culture, and self-determination. This expression of strategic self-representation emerges from a sense of Indianness that draws upon the past to construct not only identity and community but also political possibility.

From their position of declared difference, Native North Americans continually rebuild the basis of their nationhood, realigning borders in blood and culture between themselves and Others that are perforated but not open. This assertion of aboriginality cuts across the imagined unities of the nation-states in which they live, compelling Others to define who Indians are in relation to who they are not. Indians are not newcomers or immigrants, not Euro-Americans or Euro-Canadians, and they do not perceive themselves as an ethnic group, an interest group, or part of the multi-cultural mix of North America. Aboriginality is represented in interwoven tribal unities that Indians and outsiders have constructed in interactions over time. However, the tribal unities and federal regulations that identify and demark Indians are riddled with borders that Native North Americans have erected among themselves.

Native solidarity is spliced with blood borders that sometimes spiral between tribes and within communities. This complex of Indian bloodism is prolonged and layered, and it engages issues of cultural, local, and personal identity and tribal membership that both unify and divide Native people. Today, the Native struggle to construct, represent and regulate tribal communities—and expressions of pan-Indianism—as blood-related unities is linked in articulation to tensions that are both historical and current. In North America, there is an unrelenting perception that Indianness is cultural but that being Indian is racial. Indians may share this perception today, but race has not always been a determining factor in the formation of Indian nations or tribal communities.

Like the nation-states in which they live, the heritage of Native nations and communities is not rooted in tribal or racial purity. Even before colonial expansion pressed Indian tribes into war with their neighbours, and relocation produced shared reservations of cohabiting tribes, Indians absorbed other Indians. Native adoption, assimilation, and intermarriage encouraged tribally hybrid societies and colonial contact opened Indian tribes to racial hybridity. Indians have not only fought with but have also married, captured, and claimed non-Indians since the 1700s. In many nations, expectations and privileges distinguished tribal adoptees from other tribal members. But even if the integration of tribal newcomers varied, the spread of Indian hybridity was certain. As Stuart Levine (and Lurie 1970) observed thirty years ago:

> Real "Indian-ness," by the way, is not necessarily measured on racial lines. There are tribesmen on reservations who number among themselves virtually no one who is a "full-blooded" Indian. Different tribes require different degrees of "blood" for membership; some have no such requirements at all, and among the millions of Indians living in the general population, the proportion of "blood" runs anywhere from four-fourths to infinitesimal. (11)

In the thirty-five years since Levine wrote his observations, the racial and tribal hybridity of Indians has increased, along with the seemingly contradictory constructions of one Native people and many different, blood-unified Native nations. For James Clifton (1989: 26), the sense of identity that unifies Indians is a reaction to their ascribed status and relative deprivation, and "the continuing tendency of thinking about Indians in racial terms, a form of thought regularly used by modern Indians." He (10) writes, "The idea of Indian blood is a culturally standardized figure of speech, a folk metaphor for biological ancestry, the old European root of thinking that something called *race* inherently determines the identities and characteristics of individuals and groups" (italics in original).

As they struggled with colonial practices that gnawed away at the cultural basis of Native identity and community, Indians may have appropriated the racial discourse of North America to determine membership; but the racial basis of Indian identity is neither agreed upon nor constant. The blood borders that both unite and divide Native people are overwritten with common meanings drawn from narratives of a distressing past and an uncertain future. In the representations that retell Indian heritage and peril, the shifting borders of unity are not built in a commonality of blood, or an appeal to nationhood based on "blood loyalty" (Ignatieff 1993: 9), but in the articulation of common ancestry, shared culture and similar lived experience. Paul Chaat Smith (1994: 38) writes about Indian unities, "What made us one people is the common legacy of colonialism and Diaspora." This perspective resonates with the rhetoric of inter-tribalism that has been a recurring political theme since Pontiac led his "Rebellion" against the British in the 1760s, Joseph Brant fought the Americans in the Revolutionary War of 1807, and Tecumseh commanded the Allied Nations in the War of 1812. The alliances that formed to resist colonial expansion never overcame the difficulties of sustaining inter-tribal unities; but like the Ghost Dance at Wounded Knee in the 1800s and the other nativistic religious movements that arose to reclaim culture and power in Indian Country, the shifting alliances forged for military purposes were precursors to the formation of national Indian organizations in the 1900s.

The roots of the pan-Indian movements that have gained momentum since the 1960s and 1970s reach back to the Society of the American Indians, a national reformist organization founded in 1912. Even this first Indian assembly, which was founded "to establish an identity beyond the tribe and within the American social order" (Hertzberg 1971: 300), faced problems of defining the relationship between Indian blood and culture and Native identity. In the end, the Society decided upon tribal affiliation and some Indian blood as a basis for membership, but the working definition of commonness placed importance on culture and heritage. While Others could be associate members, "full active membership was reserved for all Indians of the United States who had more than one-sixteenth 'Indian blood' plus Indians on tribal rolls who had less than one-sixteenth 'Indian blood'" (Hertzberg 1971: 81). This definition of Indianness reflects changes in identity brought about by intermarriage and acculturation, but it also speaks to shared heritage and experience built into the narratives of "survivance" (Vizenor 1994) and the issues of survivability. In stories of survivance, Indians speak of common culture and of shared experience that recalls, transforms, or sometimes simulates the traditional past. These vague expressions of Indian survivance intertwine with the lived experience of Native survival to voice the cultural, economic, and political strategies that Native people construct and adopt. Central among these strategies of Native self-determination and sovereignty is the control of tribal membership, which involves a move toward empowerment that is entangled in blood and bureaucracy.

In Canada today, Indians negotiate the issue of blood quotas in the back draft of revisions to the government's complex membership policy and the forward force of sovereignty and self-determination, land, and resources, all of which relate to land claims, administrative autonomy, and treaty rights. In the United States, Indians struggle over issues of land and treaties, sovereignty, and self-determination, all interwoven with gaming profits and per capita payments—real or potential—that pressure tribes to define and refine their membership. On both sides of the border, there are questions about the growing number of urban Indians for whom reservations remain "home," a cultural construct that they return to easily and often, and the spread of young Indians, removed or reclaimed, for whom reservations have never been home. At the same time, Indians recognize that traditional culture is increasingly inaccessible, fragile, and important, an insight that not only redeems Indian blood but also places value on the experience and knowledge of elders, whose age often resonates with bloodlines.

The current struggle over Indian blood ratios and tribal borders is further complicated by those Rayna Green (1988) calls "The Tribe Called Wannabe," non-Natives who, inspired by romanticism, spirituality, alienation, or conviction, reconstitute themselves as Indians. The most common claim may be that of a rediscovered Cherokee great-grandmother, but Indian history is engraved with examples of bloodless, self-designated Indians-in-disguise like the Englishman Archie Belaney, who became the internationally recognized Indian conservationist named Grey Owl, or "the glorious impostor" Sylvester Long, who transformed himself into the famous Indian performer Chief Buffalo Child Long Lance (D. Smith 1999). Belaney spoke and wrote for audiences in North America and Europe, where he was presented (in full regalia) to meet the Queen of England. Long, whose family was considered "coloured" but had some Indian blood, joined Buffalo Bill's Wild West Show at age thirteen. Belaney and Long were engaged in performances of "playing Indian," a practice adopted by an assortment of non-Natives who, having been befriended by Indians or honoured in ceremonial adoptions, believed that they had become Indians. "Playing Indian" invented personifications based on white imaginations and Native customs that confused the markings of Indian identification for outsiders and challenged the meaning of Native identity for Native people themselves. John Tootoosis (in Ruffo 1996) wrote about Grey Owl in 1936:

> An Indian can tell who's Indian.
> Grey Owl can't sing or dance,
> But he's doing good
> and when we meet
> I call him brother. (128)

But as David Foster (1997: 13A) writes about Native people in the United States, "Never mind the New Age pretenders who claim kinship to a Cherokee princess they saw in a dream. More nettlesome for the nation's 554 federally recognized tribes is what to do with their own sons and daughters." Foster notes that the number of people who identify themselves as Native American on United States census records has nearly tripled since 1970, but Native bloodlines are thinning. "One federal study estimated that the percentage of Indians who are full-bloods—sixty percent in 1980—will fall to thirty-four percent in 2000 and to three-tenths of one percent in 2080" (14A).

The trend toward an increased number of Native people and their decreased blood ratios is equally evident in Canada. Statistics Canada (2001: 1) reports that between 1951 and 2001, "the aboriginal ancestry population grew sevenfold, while the Canadian population as a whole only doubled ... the largest gain in the [aboriginal] population between 1996 and 2001 occurred among the Métis, whose numbers increased by forty-three percent." At the same time, Phil Fontaine, grand chief of the Assembly of First Nations, reports that, according to a Manitoba study "by 2050 there'll be no more Indians as we know ourselves, at least according to [the definition of Indians] in the Indian Act. By 2050, we will cease to exist in Manitoba" (Curry 2005: A4).

Native people manoeuvre through a minefield of tribal membership that reflects the perplexity of self-designation and the problem of uncoupling blood and belonging from tribal identities that are fragmented in the lived realities of today and simulated in the Indian stories and the dominant narratives of yesterday. The borders of bloodism between Natives and newcomers are fraught with illusory and real conjectures of identity and culture that have deep roots in the imagined nation-states of North America.

In the latter half of the nineteenth century, Indian blood and belonging became absorbed in "the heyday of dubious assumptions about race, based on a cluster of biological or historical speculations" (Carter 1998: 11) that not only collapsed race, culture, and character but also mapped their fusion in gradations of oppositional Otherness: Christian and pagan, savage and civilized. The evolutionary theories and racially based notions that emerged at the turn of the twentieth century to qualify and classify Indians, reflected concepts of racial purity and cultural authenticity that became entrenched in the legal systems of the United States and Canada, where they framed Native political and territorial dependence and defined Native people themselves. These definitions emerged in a period when Indians were first studied by social scientists and then "befriended" by reformers.

American Indian Blood

Indians became objects of interest at a time when the nation-state of the United States was already spliced by borders built on the assumption that blood can contaminate or ennoble. In the historical experience of African Americans, "just *one* drop of 'Negro blood' makes a man colored" (Hughes in Strong and Van Winkle 1996: 551, italics in original). Classifying Indians was more complex, but in the 1880s, the government was intent upon devising a system to define and control Native Americans. To procure Indian lands and resources for settlement and commerce, Indians were removed from their ancestral territories, relegated to reservations and placed in the charge of Indian Agents, whose authority included identifying and enlisting tribal members.

From 1880 to the 1920s in the United States, the "Friends of the Indian played a crucial role in the formation of twentieth-century ideas about who is an Indian" (Harmon 1990: 95). The "Friends of the Indian" was a network of reformist educators, clergymen, lawyers, journalists, and social scientists whose ideological positions on "the Indian problem" drew upon academic research. This alliance of specialists shared a common belief that, as Herbert Welch (in Harmon 1990: 97) wrote about Indians in 1895, "the solution to the problem lies in a natural and human absorption of the Indian into the common conditions of American life—annihilation for the Indian race, but a new life for the individual Indian." Their influence was instrumental in establishing two critical policies that were enacted to eliminate tribal Indians and to acculturate individual Indians. The first policy was the General Allotment or Dawes Act of 1887, which parcelled out reservation or public lands to individual Indians who, until 1906, became United States citizens upon accepting allotments. This move to transform Indian racial and cultural difference encouraged acculturation and allowed resource exploitation through the privatization and sale of Indian lands. The process of absorbing Indians and their lands was operationalized through a second policy that established a government registry of tribal members and Indian land allotments. Harmon (1990) writes:

> Between 1899 and 1911 the Board of Indian Commissions repeatedly called on the executive to complete tribal rolls and family records. Preparation of such rolls was difficult in part because Indians did not reckon kinship or take names in Christian fashion. As part of the effort to de-tribalize Indians, therefore, the reformers endorsed plans to rename Indians and to identify Indian family relationships according to the prevailing American kinship system. The enumeration of Indian families not only tended to fix the family member's Indian identity, it also confirmed ... that the total number of Indians is increasing, while the number of pure-bloods is diminishing. (105)

This endorsement of lineage, of identifying Indians in relation to lines of common descent, forced Native families—which included extended, adopted, and fictive relatives—into linear units based on bloodlines. As a result, a system of social organization was imposed upon Indians that not only ignored but also denied the social realities of their lived experience.

From the beginning, the codification of difference that identified American Indians was unequivocal about Indian blood. The authenticity of Indians was not only determined by bloodlines, it was measured in blood quantum. Between 1888 and 1897, the new policies recognized full-bloods as "real" Indians and excluded non-Native spouses from property rights, as well as "half-breed" children, because "mixed blood children could 'in no respect be deemed to be Indian'" (Harmon 1990: 105). But the interest in absorbing Indians led to a dilemma with respect to Indian acculturation and the exclusion of mixed-bloods. Non-Native reformers began to recognize that, along with changing the colour and customs of Indians, intermarriage increased Indian acculturation. In the end, the bureaucracy that expanded to record and regulate Indians facilitated the registration of mixed-bloods, but enrollment and allotment policies also established borders built in bloodlines. The Allotment Act of 1887 allocated 160 acres of reservation land to full-bloods and eighty acres to half-breeds.

In the late 1800s, the reformist debates about Indians focused on nature and nurture, heredity and environment, race and culture. But well into the twentieth century, Indians were defined by their attributes more than their relationships, and identified more by blood than belonging. As David Schneider writes (in Strong and Van Winkle 1996: 554), "Because blood is a 'thing' and because it is subdivided with each reproductive step away from a given ancestor, the precise degree to which two persons share common heredity can be calculated, and 'distance' can thus be stated in specific quantitative terms." Reducing Indian membership to a matter of measuring blood provided a prescription for implementing government policies to expropriate and privatize Indian lands and foster the acculturation of Indians. In the United States, the government established blood quantum as the criteria to identify Indians for land allotments, boarding schools, and tribal benefits.

In 1934, the Indian Reorganization Act was passed, which replaced the hereditary, traditional self-governments of Indian nations with tribal constitutions and local councils and which "defined tribal members and non-enrolled Indians through a mixture of descent, residence and 'blood'" (Strong and Van Winkle 1996: 555). In the new system of governance, federal administrators maintained their control of Indian communities and their membership. Tribal "descent" was measured in blood, and membership usually required genealogical proof of one-quarter Indian blood. Since 1934, Native Americans have been inching towards empowerment by enacting their own constitutional bylaws for tribal membership. Over the years, tribal bylaws have been written and amended in response to different interpretations of heredity, residence, and blood quantum. Today, tribal membership policies represent a range of criteria, producing entangled webs of membership with exceptions and anomalies that are asserted in the conflicting voices of those who are included as tribal enrollees and those who are excluded as Indian Others. Métis are among the excluded. Unlike in Canada, Métis communities, settlements, and culture never flourished in the United States and Métis status has never been recognized.

Canadian Indian Blood

The jurisdictional border between Canada and the United States is an arbitrary line for Native people, a boundary that not only assaults Native unity, but can also separate members of the same nation, confederacy, or family. Built upon a similar ideology of acculturating Indians and acquiring land, this invisible boundary delineates different government and tribal criteria that define who is an Indian in the two countries.

In 1850 and 1851—even before the British North America Act created the Dominion of Canada in 1867—Canadian acts were passed that pertained to the affairs of Indians. In 1876, federal legislation defined who was an Indian and the extent of the government's control over their lives. In accordance with the specifications of what became known as the "Indian Act," Canadian Indians were registered and given band numbers by the federal government. Although there have been amendments over the years in response to issues of federal concern, and challenges by Indians themselves, the Indian Act continues to regulate the obligations and benefits of First Nations today. In 1879, Métis were excluded from benefits should they withdraw from a treaty; and, in 1884, it became a criminal offence to practise the potlatch and other religious rituals or to incite Indians or "half-breeds" to riot. In 1884, too, a limited system of band governments was established but until the 1951 revision of the Indian Act, the Indian agent maintained full control over band finances.

Under the Indian Act an Indian is defined as "a person who pursuant to this Act is registered as an Indian or is entitled to be registered as an Indian" (Cardinal 1969: 19). In this circular wording of arbitrary power and colonial privilege, the government determined who would and who would not acquire Indian "Status" based on seventeen federal determinations of Indianness. The term "Status" derives from a sociological concept, about which James Clifton (1989) writes:

> Being an Indian means to occupy a particular social position (or status). Always, such social positions exist in some relationship with other statuses. Being Indian, therefore, is an aspect of the self, one that affects a person's rights and obligations, always in association with others occupying complementary social positions. (30–31)

When referring to Indians, this term assumed special meaning in Canadian legislation. Designating Indians as "status" emerged in the discourse about (and now, by) Indians because of the government's interest in defining the rights and obligations of treaty and trust "beneficiaries," or Indians who were removed from their lands and placed on reserves. To encourage acculturation, the government devised a method of identifying Native people that traced heritage by paternity, not blood. Native Canadians gained Indian Status on the basis of a father who was registered as an Indian and assigned a band number. If the patriarchal membership system embedded in the Indian Act seems more simple, straight-forward, and less divisive than blood quotas, it is not. This legislation designating who was a Status Indian established both a heritage of protection and a history of partition among Native people; and even with the sporadic revisions over the last 150 years, the Indian Act continues to regulate the identification and lives of Native Canadians, imposing rules that are supported by some Indians and contested by others. Registered Indians endorse the legal protections and fiduciary responsibilities entrenched in this legislation; but based on the Indian Act, Native people are divided between those who belong and those who are—or were—excluded from Indian Status, a distinction that included Ovide Mercredi, a former grand chief of the Assembly of First Nations, who became a registered Indian in 1985. Like thousands of other Native people in Canada, Mercredi would have been recognized as Indian under the federal system of blood quotas in the United States.

The divisions between different categories of Native Canadians that are historically embedded and legally empowered are unrelentingly confusing and conflictual. Native Canadians today are absorbed in a patchwork quilt of Status Indians and exceptions to the fundamental principles of both Aboriginal ancestry and paternal registry. The system of registration was adapted to provide benefits to Inuit, but Métis have always been excluded. At the same time, paternal registration constructs Indians as a culturally homogeneous group who can be separated from other Aboriginal people on the basis of male lineage, a judgment that disregards tribal traditions and the matrilineal heritage of some Native nations. Built upon this base, the registration of Indians not only confines the notion of aboriginality but also creates aberrations of membership among Aboriginal people.

First, Indians who were not initially registered for whatever reason—because they were checking a trapline, in hospital, or visiting in another village—became "non-Status" Indians, a recognized designation of exclusion that removed them from legal standing or benefits and that was automatically passed on to their children and grandchildren. Second, from 1880 until the 1951 revision of the Indian Act, Indians were—in an ironical expression of political rhetoric—"enfranchised" and lost their Indian Status for actions that reclassified them as legally non-Native, such as receiving government loans. Indians whose ancestors had not signed treaties or who gave up their treaty Status in exchange for rights that were historically denied to Indians—like voting or legal access to liquor—could apply for "script," which Harold Cardinal (1969: 19) defines as "a legal piece of paper proclaiming the victim's citizenship, providing a sum of money (it varied in different treaties) and a piece of land (the area varied)." Third, until 1985, when Bill C-31 was passed in Parliament revising section 12 (1) (b) of the Indian Act, registered Indian women who married non-Native men (or non-Status Indians or Métis), automatically lost their Indian Status and their children could not be registered. In contrast non-Native women who married Status Indian men became registered Indians and bore children with band numbers. Fourth, new and dissimilar tribal membership policies have emerged in response to a revision in the 1985 Indian Act that, in empowering tribes to determine their own membership, "defines seventeen different categories of Indian" (Mercredi and Turpel 1994: 88). On the basis of new federal and tribal membership policies, one can now be Indian but not affiliated with an Indian band, or be a band member and not be registered as an Indian.

Fifth, none of these provisions include the Métis, who are recognized as culturally distinct mixed bloods. Métis are entrenched in the historical development of Canada, and since 1982, have been recognized as Aboriginal people in the Canadian constitution, and, more recently, by Canadian courts. Since the late 1880s, Métis in the Prairie provinces have sustained communities or settlements that are characterized by a unique culture built upon their French and Indian heritage. A million Canadians can claim Métis blood and thousands have applied for Métis status. The recognition of who is and who is not Métis, however, is complicated by shifts in the meaning of the word "Métis" itself, which connotes both the specific collectivity of French and Cree descendants of Manitoba's Red River settlement who migrated to Alberta and Saskatchewan, and the general concept of mixed-bloods of French and Indian descent, largely located in Quebec. Sixth, current legislation in the Indian Act specifies that a child born into a family that has had two generations of marriage between a status and a non-Status person is not recognized as an Indian, a provision that Indians call the "double-grandmother clause." Finally, enduring boundaries have been established between Indians whose ancestors or current leaders signed treaties and other Indians, and between Indians and Inuit, who, in 1939, were included in the British North America Act but were excluded from the Indian Act. Today, there are federally registered Indians, tribal members, and treaty beneficiaries, and these categories sometimes coincide, sometimes compete.

In 1969, Fred Kelly (in Bowles, Hanley, Hodgins, and Rawlyk 1972: 25) wrote about the impact of Indian membership policies in Canada, "We have already been legislatively conditioned to consider ourselves in terms of treaty and non-treaty, registered and non-registered, Status and non-Status, Métis or Indian." Thirty-five years later, these divisions are even more complex. Superimposed over these mutable divisions are what Indians call "C-thirty-ones." This term refers to the Indian women and their first-generation children who, in 1985, regained or acquired the Status of registered Indians in a political move that precipitated a range of new and varied criteria for tribal enrollments under Bill C-31.

The revision of the Indian Act that folded particular non-Status women into the federal registry was a bittersweet victory for those who challenged the discriminatory application of the act in relation to the Canadian Charter of Rights and Freedoms, passed in 1982, along with the Canadian constitution. Their efforts toward reinstatement involved three decades of public pressure and two major court cases brought by Jeanette Lavell and Yvonne Bedard. The struggle of the women who lost their Indian Status by "marrying out" implicated not only the federal government but also Status Indian organizations. The National Indian Brotherhood of Canada (later renamed the Assembly of First Nations) argued in the public sphere of the courts that the Indian Act superseded subsequent legislation; and in the private terrain of the reserves, it argued that revising the Indian Act would provide a strategic opening for the nation-state's enduring interest in acculturating Indians. The statements of the National Indian Brotherhood resonated in reserve communities with the release of the 1969 *Statement of the Government of Canada on Indian Policy*, which called for the elimination of the special Status of Aboriginal people. The National Indian Brotherhood countered this *White Paper on Indian Policy* by adopting what became known as the "Red Paper," which represented Aboriginal Status as "Citizens Plus." By 1971, when the cases of non-Status women were meandering through the courts, the federal position was withdrawn. But by then, the White Paper had ruptured any residual sense of trust between Indian nations and the Canadian government.

When, in 1973, the Lavell and Bedard cases were heard by the Supreme Court of Canada, the high court ruled in a five-to-four decision that the Indian Act was exempt from the Canadian Charter of Rights and Freedoms. The issue festered in the political arena and, in 1977, women from Tobique, New Brunswick, raised the stakes by bringing the case of Sandra Lovelace to the United Nations. In 1981, the Human Rights Committee of the United Nations ruled in Lovelace's favour, finding Canada in breach of the International Covenant on Civil and Political Rights. Four years later, after Canada was publicly chastised for discriminatory legislation, the membership policy of the Indian Act was revised through the legislation of Bill c-31. But the wounds of rejection, resentment, and transgression have not yet healed. For reserves, new members bring new community, economic, and political pressures, including a nagging concern about an unintended challenge to the reserve system itself. The Lovelace case ruled against discrimination on the basis of sex and raised the issue of whether reserves discriminate on the basis of race. In the end, the Human Rights Committee recognized "cultural rights" and the "goal of tribal survival" (Saunders 1983: 22) in upholding Native rights to the irregular parcels of land that Indians reserved from territory that was surrendered or ceded through treaties. For Native Canadians, this reserve land is "home," whether ancestral or actual. But any sense of security that Indians might experience on these tracts of land is mixed with anxiety over external control and internal conflict. In reserve communities, there is a brittle awareness of external power and domination, and the uneasiness this fosters is linked to the fragile alliances among Indians who are divided into two classes of enrollment: federal Status and band membership.

The federal government has reregistered women who lost their Indian Status through marriage to non-Indians or non-Status Indians, as well as their first-generation children. But Indian enrollment is now a two-tiered process built into the federal rules of registration and the regulations of local Indian bands. Each Indian band has acquired the right to decide upon the criteria and the enlistment of its own band members. This long-overdue act of self-determination both supplements and cuts across colonial membership policies. Today, there are new inconsistencies in the membership criteria of Indian bands, new policies that qualify the commonness of being Indian. The complexities of membership—first federal and now tribal—affirm that "for the Canadian Indian, the question of identity bears heavily on the kind of life a native may live" (Cardinal 1969: 18). Among Indians, "not only has colonialism had a fundamentally pernicious impact on the way most members of the dominant Euro-Canadian see and act toward Native peoples, but more insidiously, on the way Native peoples look upon and act toward one another" (Harp 1994: 47).

Being Tribal

In *God Is Red* (1994: 220), Vine Deloria, Jr. writes that in Indian Country "no one will reject a tribal member as not belonging to the tribe. He [or she] may be viciously attacked as corrupt, as having assimilated, or as being stupid traditional. He [or she] is never disclaimed as a tribal member." If that were ever the case, it is not the case now. Battles over the representations of commonness and over blood borders can cut to the core of a community in tribal meetings on membership. And even among members, visible features of Indianness can build borders of heritage that sometimes disconnect and divide. David Foster (1997: 13A) writes, "Of course, legal membership doesn't guarantee social acceptance. In some tribes, light-skinned members aren't invited to sacred ceremonies."

Being tribal is an Indian identification for which meanings are layered and markings are not always visible, constant, or precise. Gerald Vizenor's (1994) analysis of Indian representations tells us that the meaning of being tribal is expressed in the narratives of dominance that Others have written about Indians and in the stories of tribal survivance that have emerged among Indians themselves. These representations of Indianness are interwoven through government definitions and Indian distinctions of who is a tribal member.

Native North Americans are registered with the federal government on the basis of blood ratio in the United States and parentage in Canada, but tribal membership can be based on additions, qualifications, and exceptions to the federal rules of enrollment. The result is a messiness that has grown more complex with the reclamation of Indian women and children through Bill C-31 in Canada, and the increase in intermarriage and Native urbanization in both countries. Bloodism permeates the definition of tribalism, but tribal membership reflects a mixture of criteria; and today, "Indian cards" that identify Status Indians or enrolled tribal members have gained added value. For those whose heritage, identity, or residence is marginal, tribal membership can become a weapon wielded in wars over tribal politics and economic enterprise. But current conflicts over tribal registries are more than intratribal squabbles. Battles about band membership are grounded in strategies of Native empowerment and struggles articulated to sovereignty, including the recognition of Native bands or tribes as nations that have the legitimate right to determine local membership. This struggle over identity and power confronts the legacy of Indian social imaginaries as simplistic, disorganized, and, most of all, dependent. Today, Native self-determination involves not only taking on economic and political independence but also taking back Aboriginal representations and the membership of Indian communities. This move is "a Herculean gesture away from the enframing efforts of the ... state, toward a place and a state of being that is our own" (Simpson 1997: 6). But reclaiming tribal empowerment involves identities and affiliations that are mired in the dominating representations of both Others and Indians.

Native nations, known to outsiders as tribes or bands, are social collectives, groups of Indians whose heritage is recognized by federal governments as culturally distinct, historically continuous, and politically separate on the basis of different decrees: treaties, land grants, statutes, executive or administrative orders, past practice, or current criteria. The rationale for recognizing Indian communities as tribes or bands, and the nature of their classification for benefits, varies on both sides of the border. In the United States, President Clinton signed an Executive Order on 14 May 1998, establishing Indian tribes as "domestic dependent nations under the protection of the United States." If the wording of the Order seems contradictory, the status of Indian tribes in the United States is equally ambiguous. Indians living as a tribe are sometimes recognized for one federal program or statute and do not qualify for another, and their access to the economic potential of gaming and casinos depends on state, not federal, legislation. Groups of Indians who have a historical claim and proof of Indian blood—like the Lumbees—can apply for tribal status. In Canada, communities of Indians must be registered or treatied to be recognized as bands (Métis and non-Status Indians cannot gain tribal standing), treaty benefits vary, and casinos are regulated by provinces and are rarely Indian-owned. But in both countries, bands and tribes hold land and receive designated benefits, exercise "sovereign" powers over members, membership and territory, and maintain a measure of self-government. Under Native control, membership is often restricted by legal and community decrees, and defended against the intrusion of Others. The current struggle over social protectionism is, in the end, a conflict over significations of tribal commonality—over the markings and meanings of tribal membership and the measures of Indian marginality.

In the United States, some tribes enroll all descendants of the land allotments granted through the 1887 Dawes Act, others require residence on the reservation for enrollment or for the exercise of tribal rights. Some tribal bylaws do not mention Indian blood at all; others contain membership clauses that require a blood ratio of 25 or 50 percent. Some reservations recognize any Indian blood, others recognize blood from other reservations of the same tribe, and still others require direct descent or blood ratios documented in the records of a respective band. The boundaries of tribal membership have always been movable, but today across Indian Country, individual tribal councils are redrawing the contours of blood borders. For instance, since 1987, the Cherokee nation has required no blood quota for membership, opening their tribal rolls of 50,000 people who can document Cherokee descent. In 1997, the Mashantucket Pequot tribe in Connecticut established a quota of one-sixteenth Pequot blood—the verification of which might require DNA testing—and proof of descent from the tribal census rolls of 1900 or 1901. In 1997, too, the Fort Sill Apache in Oklahoma reduced their blood quota from one-eighth to one-sixteenth (Foster 1997: 14A). More recently, the Navajo nation council voted down a resolution that would have lowered the blood quantum to one-eighth and increased the tribal roll from 310,000 to 600,000 members (Guidos 2004: 2). Other tribes have followed the example of the Miccosukees in Florida, who require 50 percent Miccosukee Indian blood for membership, or the Lac du Flambeau reservation in Wisconsin, where enrolled Indians with less than one-quarter Lac du Flambeau blood cannot be enrolled now and, if they gained enrollment in the past, cannot hold tribal council office.

The decisions taken by tribes across the country are valid and varied expressions of self-determination supported by the United States Supreme Court, which ruled in 1974 that "while there is a racial component to belonging to a tribe, the group identification is primarily political" (Carson 2002: 4A). The federal government now generally supports tribes determining their own tribal membership, even if band bylaws are mired in conflict that can be volatile. The Pequot, Cherokee, and Apache bands passed resolutions without incidents, but on many reservations across the country, membership is vigorously contested. There are "bitter membership feuds dividing tribes from the Maliseets of Maine to the Shakopee Midewakanton Sioux of Minnesota" (Foster 1997: 14A). These conflicts over membership that divide families and friends are also encircled by differences of political ideology. Some Indians favour limiting the number of tribal members to protect the value of benefits; some believe that political strength is measured in numbers, which are dwindling because of blood quantum requirements; some are concerned about being the only social group that defines membership in blood ratios; and still others conclude that tribal empowerment is related to the racial and cultural distinctiveness of tribal members.

Since the 1980s, tribal membership has become increasingly contentious in Canada as well. Federal Indian Status remains based on parentage, but since bands have begun to enact their own membership legislation, there are now two levels of membership: federal and tribal. In northern Quebec, Crees, who replaced the Indian Act with the Cree Act in 1975 through their modern-day treaty with Canada, have reclaimed their non-Status relatives and established residence rules for treaty beneficiaries. The situation for Mohawks in Kahnawake, near Montreal, is more complex. In 1981, the band council passed a membership code that requires 50 percent Mohawk blood for band membership, and charges all band members—male or female—to marry Indians or forfeit their band membership, along with the rights to live on the reserve, own land, hold office, or vote in tribal elections. The policy is not retroactive, but there have been sporadic efforts over the years—intense and conflictual—to expel residents who are not recognized as Band members. There have also been public court or band council challenges by those who cannot prove 50 percent blood, including the case of Peter Jacobs, a bloodless Indian, who was adopted and raised as a Kahnawake Mohawk but rejected for band membership under the 1981 policy.

Like the representations of Indianness that are contested elsewhere, the discourse on Indian blood in Kahnawake is interwoven with issues of history and heritage, traditionalism, sovereignty, and economics. But the deeper struggle over the borders of blood and belonging in Kahnawake emerges from an awareness that "Mohawk identity clearly has two components: culture and race" (Alfred 1995). As Gerald Alfred (1995) suggests, it is the ease with which blood-based race can be determined and the difficulty of defining and applying cultural signifiers that complicates the issue of tribal membership:

> The racial component of a person's identity is simple to determine once a standard is decided upon, and Kahnawake has decided upon a standard of a minimum of 50% blood quantum.... For persons possessing less than 50% blood quantum, status as a Mohawk is determined taking into account cultural and social factors. The cultural component ... is dependent upon nebulous factors such as values and participation rather than an easily measured factor like blood quantum. Certain factors are identified as indicators of whether or not a person is living life as a Mohawk—

pride in the Mohawk heritage, knowledge of the Mohawk culture and language, and participation and contribution within the Mohawk community. (171–72)

If the rules and regulations of blood and belonging are unsteady across Indian Country, they can be equally precarious for Indians crossing the border between Canada and the United States. While the United States government recognizes Indians on tribal rolls, the Department of the Interior and the Department of Immigration have different policies with respect to Indians. The 1952 Immigration Act defines North American Indians "as persons who possess at least fifty per centum of blood of the American Indian race"; and a 1986 court case upheld the Department of Immigration's right to request proof of blood quantum for entry into the United States (Deer 1996). Like the laws and policies that govern Indians, tribal identities involve a contingent blend of heritage, blood, and culture.

The boundaries of membership are exposed in the articulation between narrations of heritage—personal, physical, and cultural—and power relations within and outside Indian communities. Within communities, Indian alliances are forged between families and friends, memories and practices, spiritual beliefs and political positions. Threaded through the cultural webs of individual and tribal histories are the alliances that have been built and rebuilt in a tension linked to unstable political and economic forces outside the community. Because Native reality is built upon narratives of the past and experiences of the present, the imagined oneness of community is continually reconstructed in expressions of external domination and Indian resistance. The hierarchical power relations that emerge and shift move the borders of tribal recognition in a process that is local and tribally specific. But in Indian Country today, resistance is most often expressed in unstable but recurring alliances between traditionals and militants, between those who represent the "old ways" and those whose reconstructed knowledge of the past becomes a weapon of resistance in the present. Indian traditionals, who were once a conservative force on reserves, are now more often catalysts or cohorts for change. This is the case in Kahnawake, where the issues of Mohawk membership and the borders of imagined community are continually renegotiated in the discourse of historical narratives and the contingency of everyday life.

In 1990, when Kahnawake Mohawks became absorbed in what came to be known as the "Oka crisis," in Quebec they were enmeshed in a seventy-eight day confrontation between Indians and Others over land and treaty rights, sovereignty and self-determination. During the conflict, Mohawks on the Kanehsatake and Kahnawake reserves were drawn into a knot of old political grievances—imposed government, confiscated land and provincial government policing—that encircled a cultural transformation of Mohawk warriors, Indians whose positions on traditionalism, sovereignty, and self-determination were linked to casino gaming and cigarette smuggling. The divisions between Mohawk warriors and other Mohawks who opposed gaming and smuggling but supported sovereignty, self-determination, and land claims, criss-crossed tribal factions. Jagged fault lines appeared among elected band councillors and Mohawks who advocate traditional government, among those who followed different Christian religions and those who followed different canons of the Longhouse, and among kin and clans. But an unsteady alliance of traditionals and militants emerged in a rhetoric of resistance that linked external power and internal politics.

When this alliance led to a blockade of the bridge to Montreal that is located on reserve land, some non-Native residents of the surrounding towns turned from vocal protest to violence. The response of Kahnawake was characterized by a complex but perceptible unity in difference that moved the borders of this heterogeneous community beyond bloodlines. Mohawks with opposing positions on membership and governance, on economic development and religious practice, stood together against the threat of invading Others. This coalition of Mohawks, yoked to each other through common history and culture, may seem a predictable response to a social threat. But the alliances built in the narratives and representations of imagined community are never simple, straightforward, or static. At Wounded Knee in 1973, the barricades of the seventy-one day confrontation between Indians and Others were grounded in inter-tribal conflicts on the reservation of Pine Ridge, and the tenuous alliance between traditionals and militants was built, in part, on blood borders.

Like the Mohawk incidents at Kanehsatake and Kahnawake, the Lakota Sioux battles on the Pine Ridge reservation—including Wounded Knee—were linked in a chain of historical and current grievances that also engaged Indian warriors. In the 1970s, it was American Indian Movement (AIM) warriors who were summoned by reservation traditionals to intervene in Pine Ridge's strife over favouritism, corruption, and vio-

lence. They came in the shadows of 1876, when Lakota fought what outsiders call the Battle of Little Big Horn or Custer's Last Stand; and in
1890, when the Seventh Cavalry retaliated by killing three hundred Sioux
at Wounded Knee. They carried forth the Indian grievances related to the
treaty of Fort Laramie signed by the Sioux and the United States in 1868
and abrogated in 1871, after gold was discovered in the Black Hills. If the
presence of AIM warriors was contentious, "the chasm between the factions was not a new one at Pine Ridge" (Smith and Warrior 1996: 191).
Unlike the conflicts between Indian leaders and followers that occurred
in the nineteenth century, in the 1970s, inter-tribal power relations were
linked directly to external authorities. The accusations of violence, nepotism, and abuse of power involved the tribal chairman and the tribal
council, the Guardians of the Oglala Nation (GOONs), the Bureau of
Indian Affairs, the Federal Bureau of Investigation, and other law enforce-
ment agencies. These conflicts that allied traditionals and militants in
the name of resistance were entangled in tribal blood and belonging:

> During 1972, after Yellow Thunder's death, activists on Pine Ridge had
> formed their own AIM chapters, and they joined forces with traditionals
> in opposing the rule of tribal chairman Dick Wilson. Complaints against
> him were numerous, including his alleged favoring of the mixed-blood
> residents of the town of Pine Ridge Village at the expense of the full-
> blood Oglalas who lived in the outlying districts, his securing of jobs
> and services for his friends and relatives and to mixed-bloods generally,
> and shutting his opponents out of tribal government processes. (Smith
> and Warrior 1996: 191)

The national crises that divided Pine Ridge and brought Kahnawake
together are uncommon in Indian Country. More often, battles over tribal
membership take place on small, unknown reservations, where they are
invisible to outsiders beyond the border towns. In the silence of social isolation, the boundaries of communities are built and rebuilt in the emerging struggles over power and resources. On reserves, there are blood-ratio
battles over land, housing, and employment, over benefits and casino
profits; and the politics of blood and culture extend beyond reservations
to those who are "adopted out," "married out," or live as "off-reserve"
Indians. The circle of tribal membership can tighten to include only those
with 25 or 50 percent Indian blood or those who can prove direct band
descent, but some bands also require residence to participate in elections or to apply for benefits. Blood borders in Indian Country can

involve exclusion, nepotism, and control that can be manifested as suppressed, silent, or subtle responses to the hierarchical relations of power
in Native communities. But like the blood-related battles at Wounded
Knee, community conflicts over tribal power relations can be overt. The
oil-rich Sawridge reserve in Alberta presents an extreme example of
tribal authority gone awry, where once again the issue is the power and
politics of tribal membership.

At Sawridge, about twenty-seven people live on the reserve, and
almost all of whom are—like the chiefs for the past three generations—
members of the Twinn family. Two hundred and thirty Indians claim
membership, but enrollment is controlled by the band council of three
elected members of the Twinn family. Since 1985, when Bill c-31 restored
the Status of disenfranchised women and their children, only one person
has been reinstated as a band member. That person is the sister of the
recently deceased chief, who lost her Indian Status when she married a
Métis. Today, she is not only a band member, but the acting chief and
head of the tribe's economic enterprises, a position from which she and
two relatives control both the businesses and the membership codes of
the band. The Twinn family argue that their right to refuse the re-enroll-
ment of other Indians is entrenched in self-determination, self-government, and the reserve's constitutional right to determine its own band
membership. Other Indians maintain that their exclusion from membership constitutes a form of discrimination that is disallowed by Bill
c-31. Like the opposing voices that characterize other Indian communities, both sides are right. The membership of the Sawridge reserve will
eventually be decided by the courts, but neither court decisions nor DNA
testing will resolve the tribal struggle over the politics of enrollment,
which is far less extreme but as important on other reserves. Gil Oskaboose (1998: 2) writes in the guise of humour about power relations on
his tranquil reserve:

> It's election time again. Rumours are beginning to circulate—or be circu-
> lated—down at the band office about how "the new bunch" is going to
> take away all their cushy jobs and hand them over to their own friends
> and relatives. Band staff is busy forming the wagons into a protective cir-
> cle. Hasty alliances are being formed by people who wouldn't give each
> other the time of day in the past two years…. Family always votes for
> family, blood being "thicker" than water. Indian reserves are usually run
> by the largest families, who maintain their position by hook, crook, or
> sheer reproductive powers. (2)

Being Indian

I have Indian blood in my veins, am I not an Indian, too? Because you have more Indian blood than I, do you have the right to call me White, and then to call yourself, Indian?… In the veins of my grandfathers ran as much Indian blood as ran in the veins of your grandfathers. All my grandfather's blood was Indian (if there ever existed any such thing as "Indian blood") … I choose to be an Indian. That is my right, The right my grandfathers have given me…. My grandfather's past is your grand-father's past. If you are Indian, I am Indian, too. Though my skin is White, I too have a heritage in the past of our grandfathers. The past belongs to me as it does to you…. Our grandfathers were brothers. They made the past what it was together. We also are brothers.

(Guthrie 1973: 1–2).

Being Indian and being tribal—Status, registered, treatied, or enrolled—are not necessarily the same thing. In Canada, they have never pretended to be. In the United States, culture, heritage, and membership have not been synonymous since the rules and exceptions of land allotments were established in the 1800s. In both countries, blood borders have become the basis for battles over tribal membership in which Indians—tribal members and non-members—are claimed by some, disclaimed by others. But the articulation between Indian blood and identity is more complex than Strong and Van Winkle (1996: 555) suggest when they write, "'Indian blood'—and especially its more differentiated tribe-specific varieties—is a hegemonic discourse within and against which indigenous identity is defined." Tribal blood borders are boundaries of recognition based on ancestry that determine for tribes who is, and who is not Indian. Identifying as Indian and being recognized as Indian are knitted together in Indian Country, but they are different and mutable, reflecting a process that is not fixed in the names on tribal rolls or framed in some unchanging sense of the self. The colonial policies regulating Indians that fuse recognition and identification in the codes of tribal enrollment have displaced or erased the cultural criteria through which Indians have historically identified each other and themselves. Gerald Vizenor (1984: 107) writes about the Indian past, "The application of mixed-blood geometric scores was not a form of tribal cultural validation. Skin color and blood quantums were not the means the tribe used to determine identities." James Clifton (1989) remarks:

Originally, no native North American society subscribed to the idea of biological determination of identity or behavior. Indeed, the most common identity question asked of strangers was not, "What nation do you belong to?" or "What race are you?" Instead, when confronting unknown people, they typically asked, "What language do you speak?" They were disinterested in skin color, the standard Euro-American sign of racial identity. On the contrary, they stressed as criteria of group membership learned aspects of human nature: language, culturally appropriate behavior, social affiliation, and loyalty. (11)

Today, in the context of blood quantum, identifying who is an Indian is interwoven into the daily struggle over membership, meaning, and markers. Paul DeMain (in Guidos 2004: 2) tells us, "Only Indians, horses and dogs have pedigrees"; and Fort Sill Apache tribal chairwoman Ruey Darrow (in Foster 1997: 14A) remarks, "If we're stark white, we're still going to be Apache.... It's not so much blood as it is you know who you are, and you feel in your heart and your spirit that you belong to this group." For N. Scott Momaday (1975: 96), "an Indian is an idea which a given man has of himself. And it is a moral idea, for it accounts for the way in which he reacts to other men and to the world in general. And that idea, in order to be realized completely, has to be expressed." Being Indian may be harboured in the heart or the spirit, but it is experienced, enacted, and acted upon in a moving montage of historical, cultural, and racial representations. Indian identity is a cultural construction, not a structural location, an unstable blend of collective history and individual experience that is interwoven with Indian identification into the interactions of everyday life. Kim Anderson (2000) writes about her identity as a Cree/Métis woman:

> Those most critical of my Aboriginal status are, not surprisingly, white people, many of whom are quick to pronounce that I am "not really Indian," or inadvertently quantify my existence by asking, "Do you have Indian blood?" Some white people will question whether I am "really Native" because I didn't grow up on a reserve or in a Native community; some will call attention to the fact that I am "only half"; others will interrogate me about my urban status. (26)

Questions that position and place Indians may be asked more abrasively by non-Natives, but Native people are equally interested in the personal disclosures that locate tentative, contingent identities.

As Stuart Hall (1989: 72) suggests, "Cultural identities are the points of identification, the unstable points of identification or suture, which are made, within the discourses of history and culture. Not an essence but a *positioning*" (italics in original). Indian identity is personal and public, a prismal positioning, built in refractions of heritage, culture, and experience that continually relocate and redefine the conflicting representations and relations of Indianness. In reserve communities, issues of sameness and difference circulate within tenacious borders—geographic and interactional, imported and self-imposed. Alliances shift and overlap, exposing the autonomy, familiarity, and friction of interconnected, deeply rooted communities. In the words of Ojibway writer Calvin Morrisseau (1998: 57), "Community is more than a place. It is part of my history. It is part of me." Imposed through colonial control, blood quantum and paternity are part of this history, but the ratio of Indian blood and the specifics of blood heritage are facets in the unstable prism of features and factors that constitutes Indian identity. Richard Wagamese (1996) has experienced the prismal lens that locates being Indian:

> At that time I was wearing braids. I believed back then that the hair was a direct statement to the world about who and what I was. I believed that it defined me. One day I sat with one of the camp elders discussing various things and the subject of my hair and my identity arose. The Old One asked me if I truly believed that my hair made me an Indian. Of course, I answered in the affirmative. Too bad, was his only answer. (52)

Like Wagamese's braids, blood quantum consigns Indian identity to physical features. Stitched to tribalism, bloodism limits belonging to the colonial pattern of biological heritage. This prescription suggests gradations of Indianness based on quantum and colour, ignoring not only descent but also the range of cultural positionings that are linked to the ambiguity of lived representations and relationships, both Indian and Other. In the words of Cecilia Mitchell of the Akwesasne reserve (in Wall 1993: 143), "I am an Indian; I am close to my people, and I belong to their traditional beliefs, and I know medicine. I know a lot of things. I am like two people."

Indian identity and recognition emerge in the precarious discourses of history and culture and the expressed interactions of everyday life. As Audra Simpson (in Alfred 1999: 65) suggests, who we are and who is one of us are arrived at in relationships with other Indians. Personal identity and identification are not only socially constituted but also constantly shifting in "our involvement with others in a world of diverse and ever-altering interests and situations" (Jackson 1989: 3). Identities are enacted and expressed, and the relationships that situate our identities arise and move in the actions and exchanges of everyday life, in the conversations and conflicts, performances and practices that not only endorse identification but also negotiate the positionings of identity. Being Indian is negotiated in the arenas of discourse and interaction—the grocery store, the restaurant, the bingo halls, the band councils, the Native Friendship Centres—that are alive in the daily play of culture and heritage, power and politics, identity and community. Interwoven into the narratives and practices that emerge and circulate are the expressions of Indian traditionalism, both transformed and lived. In the ambiguity of the traditionalism that encodes Indian culture and history, the unstable points of suture that position Indian identification relate to two features of Native cultural formation that are seldom evident to non-Indians.

First, the objects and forces and even people with whom many Indians interact can be mutable, and their nature depends in large part on the relationship between a person and another presence—natural, spiritual, or human. The positionings of Indian identity can emerge in transformative and unpredictable relationships with people and practices and sometimes with animate and inanimate beings and the spiritual forces of nature. This invisible environment relates to a belief in mutability and anthropomorphic change that is drawn from the mythical past and knitted into the fabric of everyday life. The belief in transformation is a cultural code that can explain events of the past or even relationships in the present. For instance, a medicine person with special spiritual powers can produce fireballs, shake tents, or even change into an other-than-human form, becoming a bird or a dog. A rock or a drum or an animal skin is alive in some situations, dead in others, and the distinction depends upon the presence or absence of spiritual power. Similarly, a man can be an "uncle" or a "grandfather" in the presence of some younger people who are not family members, depending on how they relate to one another.

Second, because under certain circumstances, persons, objects and forces can change form or role as well as meaning in Indian cultures, "the focus seems to be less on the *characteristics of* things than on the *relationships between* things" (Ross 1996: 116, italics in original). Indian interaction—historical and current—takes place in a complex of *interdependencies* and *relationships* that are associated with particular privileges, petitions, and responsibilities. Even in small Native communities, where most people can be related by blood, custom adoption, or marriage, these positionings are not the static placements of social status in which the self is understood in terms of rights and obligations that relate to others in complementary social positions. Conversations and actions are coded in the claims and responses of experienced relationships, not the rules and regulations of ascribed positions or roles. Even now, with the imposed social organization of blood-related definitions of Indianness, Native communities and identities are built are on a scaffold of interdependencies and relationships. As Sasheen Gould (in Ross 1996: 129) says, "As a Mi'kmaq, I was born into a network of relationships and responsibilities. I am taught that these are to be the utmost priorities in my life. These include my family, my friends, my community and my nation."

For some Native people, building community can involve the customary process of adopting other Indians as family members, or the contentious process of adopting non-Natives. Creating relationships by "making relatives" through custom adoption, such as parenting nieces or nephews or grandchildren, is distinct from the relationships that non-Natives sometimes refer to as "blood brothers." Ed McGaa, also known as Eagle Man (1990: 113), writes about the distorted process of creating fictive relationships which is associated today with New Age spirituality: "Rainbow Crystal Woman, a Lakota Sioux, is my blood relative. Although we came into this world from different mothers and had different fathers, she is now my blood sister and I am her blood brother in the Indian Way." McGaa (1990: 8) adds, "The purpose of the *Hunkupi* (Making Relatives) rite is to create between two people a blood bond that is closer than a kinship tie … this ritual is to adopt one another into a new relationship."

Being Indian, being recognized as Indian, or being related by custom or imagination is entangled with people and practices that situate the positionings of Indianness in relation to two sites in particular: being "home" on the reservation or in other Indian communities, and being on a border, being displaced, or being ambiguous wherever one is in Indian Country. Even though thousands of Indians live in cities today, both these locations that situate the positionings of Indian identity and recognition relate to reserves, where, at least until recently, belonging has been more important than blood.

In reserve communities, being Indian and being recognized as Indian emerges in responses to questions that no one asks. No one asks if you bead or drink beer or make fry bread, if you go to church or spearfish or do sweat lodge, if you went to college or were in jail or supported the current tribal chair, or where you live or work or who your family is. No one asks about heritage, language, and craftsmanship; spirituality, land, and traditions; kinship, residence, and schooling; humour, sharing, and gossip; or about the cultural representations and relationships of Indianness. Everybody may not know one another, but everyone recognizes the positionings that identify them as Indians. Reservations are held together by what Wilfred Pelletier (and Poole 1973: 198) calls "community consciousness," an organic sense of individuality and collectivity about which he writes, "I'm not sure I can describe it except to say it's common ground, a kind of corporate consciousness that is shared by everyone in the community and used by everyone." For Shelley Niro, this sense of "common ground" emerges in extended community and is something Native people "share historically, cognitively, spiritually, even if—especially if—it's hard to agree on what that is." She associates this commonness with "'Reservation X' [which] cannot be identified by numbers, by ID cards, nor by a place on a map, but by something less measurable and more meaningful" (in Townsend-Gault 1998: 41).

For outsiders, Indian reservations have always been ambivalent places, socially marginal sites that provoke a certain fascination with the past and an uncertain fear with the present. For some outsiders, reservations represent historicized images where tribal values are intact, or assume the position of placements for ancient fantasies or New Age visions of "authentic" Indians who are the physical embodiment of the tribe, or historical residue for Indians who have left the reservation, seeming to reject not only the reservation but also the tribe. For others, reservations are prisons of poverty, where Indians are isolated from acculturation and entrapped in social problems for which the solution is leaving the reserve. Perceived from these contradictory perspectives or somewhere in-between, to most outsiders reservations are uncomfortable, unsafe, or unpredictable places, even in this era of Indian casinos and touristic enterprises. Yet these irregular pieces of land that represent a collective past and the prospect of an illusive future are homelands for Indians, regions where community signifies not only being home but also being grounded in the prospect of returning home, or just having a home. Beyond the poverty and problems, reservations signify the remembered, imagined, or lived communal experience, or as Renee Hallett (in Wall 1993: 156) expresses it, "It's just like a nest here at home. To us, family is everyone who comes through that door and everyone we meet as soon as we walk out of it. It's just like family to us no matter where we're at."

Reservations represent social spaces that map the cultural interdependencies of Indian identity onto the contours of territory. In representations of reservations, Native people—urban and reserve—enact and explore who they are in the context of heritage, lineage, and everyday life. Images of reservations as heritage or home are intertwined in the conversations, interactions, and practices in which Native people represent and recognize Indianness. In the reality of reservations—lived, remembered, or imagined—Indians are grounded in the heritage of the past and the power relations of the present that mark the land as "a place and state of being that is our own" (Simpson 1997: 6). Wilfred Pelletier (and Poole, 1973: 209) asks, "What's the meaning of that 'home' thing?" and then tells us, "All those thousands of Indian people who go back to the reserve every chance they get, even for a weekend, even for a day, you know what they say? 'This is where I like to be.' That's what they say, but what they feel is, 'This is who I am.'" In the words of Ovide Mercredi (and Turpel 1994: 19), "Being Cree is not having this skin—that is superficial. It is having a connection with the past, with the land."

Within reservation communities, relationships formed in compressed space and extended time have deep roots that are renewed in the recognition that "home is a placement to which we can always return" (McMaster 1995: 80). Returning home, as Gerald McMaster (1995: 81) writes, "does not mean a return to the margins, but rather a return to the centre, thus inverting and subverting the stereotype of reserves as somehow outside the core of the state." But many Indians today do not have a reservation home to which to return, and for those who do, returning home is rarely a simple process of celebrated oneness. More often, it is a sequential process of comings and goings that may eventually lead to staying. Vickie Downey (in Wall 1993) says,

> When I came back home, I would want to change things here. People weren't ready for that. So I would get frustrated and I would leave again. Then I would come back. It was like that for the longest time. Until finally now, I'm home and I feel good. I feel happy. I feel safe. And I deal with whatever problems we have here. I work with it. (8)

Little Star (in Nabokov 1992) writes about negotiating the cultural cleavages of moving back to the reservation, which is never a simple act of relocation:

The first thing that hits you when you go home—after you realize that you live there now, and you're not leaving in a few weeks—is that your college degrees don't give you the prestige on the reservation that you assumed they would. BIA people and some councilmen might be impressed, your own family may be proud, but people couldn't care less. You've been away for a long time and they study you for awhile.

Some try to prove themselves one of the people by drinking around alot, saying see I'm still one of you but the people trying to make up their mind about you wonder because we don't need more drunken Indians on the reservation, we have enough. Some miss their group at school, heads especially try to set up a copy of this little group on the reservation. They find they have to include whites, young vistas or public health people, there not being enough heads around the reservation that are past high school age. And the people hear rumors. Some go into a frenzy of activity to prove themselves, they get involved in everything, but miss the point because they don't really care about the people—they care American style about getting the job done. (388)

Reservations act like force fields, pulling Indians together even as the closeness resonates in struggles among themselves. Even when the allure of city jobs, education, and activities draws Indians away from the reservation, Native people find each other. Whether they live in common neighbourhoods or are dispersed throughout the city, Indians reconstruct heterogeneous forms of Native identity and community. Today, urban Indian communities that are built in a fluid mixture of tribes, bloodlines, heritage, and socialization are reworking the representations of reserves as they build urban organizations and services. There are Native Friendship Centres and women's shelters, youth groups and pow wows, all part of an increasing range of social, cultural, and community services. But despite the growing numerical and political strengths of urban Indians, home—whether based on heritage or experience—is still the lens through which most Native people view their presence elsewhere. The double-bind of physically moving away and emotionally being home may be more intense in the United States, where the contest over tribal membership involves not only tribal codes and practices but also per capita payments from casino profits. But on both sides of the border, Native people in cities complain that, because residents are given preference for housing and jobs, they are unable to move back to reserves and, in their absence, their privileges diminish. The divisions between reserve and urban Indians converge around tribal rights and resources, including voting in tribal elections. Tribal bylaws can refuse absentee ballots or remove the voting privileges of non-resident tribal members, a practice that was ruled discriminatory by the Supreme Court of Canada in 1999. As Native populations increase and reserve lands effectively decrease by remaining the same, the friction within imagined communities of Indians is becoming more acute.

Today, more than half of North America's Native people live in urban areas, including an increasing number of Indians who were not raised on reservations; and there are Indians who are continually on the move, an experience about which Mary Crow Dog (with Erdoes 1990: 72) writes, "If nothing else, my roaming gave me a larger outlook and made me more Indian, made me realize what being an Indian within a white world meant." In addition, interracial marriages, Natives adopted by non-Natives, and new tribal membership policies expose fractures of Indian identity, unity, and membership. For those whose absence, heritage, or bloodlines raise questions of descent, there are pressures to produce proof of genealogy and blood ratio. Even with tribal registries, "proving blood" can be impossible for Indians who were "adopted-out" in the "scoop" of the mid-1900s, when hundreds of Canadian Indian babies were adopted by non-Native families, many living in the United States. In the messy, mixed-blood, cross-acculturated world of Indians today, bloodism and Indianness produce mutually threatening Indian Others. Gerald Vizenor (in Trinh 1994: 17) writes, "So here we are now, translated and invented skins, separated and severed like dandelions from the sacred and caught alive in words in the cities." But in the cities across North America, Indians and bordered individuals redefine the parameters of the assertion that "my life is what Indian is, everything that I do. Everything that I do is based on my life as an Indian" (R. Hallett in Wall 1993: 160).

Living the borders of blood and belonging is a process of negotiating the changing positionings of Indianness. This negotiation takes place in the unstable borderlands between external representations of Indianness and Otherness and the internal perceptions of being Indian that circulate in unsteady codes of signification among both Indians and Others. While colonial and Indian legislation can create the borderland that Gloria Anzaldúa (1987: 3) speaks of as "a vague and undetermined place created by the emotional residue of an unnatural boundary," Indian borderlands are more often built in the actual ambiguity of blood and belonging. No matter how far removed from the lived experience of daily life elsewhere, that ambiguity refers back to the reservation.

In the cities across Indian Country, where so many Indians live, the questions that expose the boundaries of Indian identity and recognition are always the same: Where are you from? Who is your family? Do you speak "Indian?" Indian enrollment or even blood quota may be volunteered as responses, but they are rarely questions. The collision between the colonial imposition of blood-determined social status and the Indian experience of interconnected positionings makes the discourse of Indian identity difficult to locate, and to understand. Misunderstanding stretches to contemporary Native writing, in which references to blood sometimes express a seemingly racist appeal to Indian belonging and exclusion.

Native writers have both taken on and transformed the discourse of colonial blood quotas. Today, Indians write about "blood memory" (Van Winkle in Strong and Van Winkle 1996: 560), a literary reappropriation that may be inaccurate and incongruous, but is a powerful expression of shared heritage. For Indians, "cultural bloodism" represents an experienced past, both painful and joyful, about which N. Scott Momaday (1976: 22) writes, "Some of my mother's memories have become my own. That is the real burden of the blood." Momaday's allusion to "memory in the blood" reveals his perception that "the imagination that informs these stories is really not mine, though it exists, I think in my blood" (in Woodard 1989: 22). In this transposition of the knowledge and relationships that are encoded in oral tradition, Indian stories that travel through time "are experienced as transformations of a familiar pattern" (Ridington 1990: 138). This is not a case of retrieving recollections; it is a process of transforming memory. Memoried relationships with "grandfathers" and "grandmothers," with the experience and understanding of those who are elders or who have walked on, forge the imaginative basis for stories, including the contemporary narratives of dominance and survivance that transform ancestral knowledge and power. Blood imagery that expresses not only the presence but also the "goneness" of imagined communities resonates with the voices of other Indians, like John Trudel (Robertson 1998), who speaks of experiencing a trail of "genetic memory." For Indians, "memory in the blood" represents an affective bond to the past, built in the familiar patterns of relationships and the unsteady heritage of collective and personal alliances. For outsiders, the articulation of blood and culture, experience and ancestry—formed in Indian heritage and fixed in colonial policy—is wrapped in a naturalized perspective that is essentialist and racist (Van Winkle in Strong and Van Winkle 1996: 562). But if "blood memories" alienate Indians from Others in the imagined communities of North American nation-states, the endowment of blood relations both unifies and divides Indians themselves.

Like floating markers, blood borders that exclude or include weave through the words of Native North American writers. The expressions of personal experience are sometimes painful, sometimes celebratory, but always intense. Linda Hogan (1987: 235) says of a grandfather, "all his people are walking through my veins without speech"; Chrystos (1991: 70) speaks of her people "on both sides of the bloody borders"; Wendy Rose (1987: 34) writes, "I expected my skin and my blood to ripen not to be ripped from my bones"; and Shirley Flying Hawk d'Maine (1991: 135) sings, "I'm too red to be white; and I'm too white to be red; a half-breed, in-breed, no breed I'm called." These expressions of blood relations disclose the contested terrain of collective and personal Indian experience.

Disputes over being Indian and belonging are braided together with personal perceptions of bloodlines and the "perverse arithmetics" (Vizenor 1994: 12) of blood mixture. For Van Winkle (Strong and Van Winkle 1996: 552), Indian bloodism "destabilizes the concept of 'Indian blood' simply by taking it literally." He cites two voices of prominent activists, whose unenrolled tribal status has been an issue among Indians. The first is writer Ward Churchill (Jaimes in Strong and Van Winkle 1996: 551), who says, "I can report that I am exactly 52.5 pounds Indian—about 35 pounds Creek and the remainder Cherokee—88 pounds Teutonic, 43.5 pounds some sort of English, and the rest 'undetermined.' Maybe the last part should be described as 'human.'" In the second citation, Cherokee artist Jimmie Durham (Jaimes in Strong and Van Winkle 1996: 551) remarks, "The question of my 'identity' often comes up. I think I must be a mixed-blood. I claim to be male, although only one of my parents was male." But dismissing Indian bloodism in the guise of ironic humour ignores the predicament of tribes and the experience of individuals who live in the borderlands. In the end, Jimmie Durham (in McMaster 1995: 88) says, "I am not Cherokee. I am not an American Indian. This is in concurrence with the recent u.s. legislation, because I am not enrolled on any reservation or in any American Indian community."

Living in the Borders

In the writing of Native and non-Native artists and academics (McMaster 1995; Anzaldúa 1987; Falk 1994; Henderson 1995), there is new interest in social borders and the territories they mark. But even in texts that remap or remake boundaries and reveal the liminal experiences they locate, borders usually represent "a dividing line, a narrow strip along a steep edge" (Anzaldúa 1987: 3). This notion of borders as social barricades, as lines in the sand that designate who crosses the terrain they demark, places importance upon the territorial frames, the transgression of trespassing, and the experience of those who move between markers occupying the borderlands. These borderlands are not characterized as a "narrow strip," as an empty or barren place. Borderlands are contested spaces of cultural territory represented in social barricades that can challenge movement and consign positions. For Gloria Anzaldúa (1987: 3), borders not only designate places that are safe and unsafe, they are "unnatural boundaries," experienced by "those who cross over, pass over or go through the confines of the 'normal.'" But for those who live the boundaries of Indian blood and culture, borders represent the experiences of "being in" more than "moving through." These boundaries that mark a sense of movement represent the contradictory manoeuvres of a state—and a recognition—of being. Being "in-between" involves neither a permanent exclusion associated with stigma nor a touristic excursion reserved to choice. Travelling among borders is not a nomadic journey marked in recognized realities, nor a compelling pilgrimage to home or elsewhere that is aligned in signposts of identity. Indian borderlands are encircling regions of exposure—with walls which outsiders can find too high to breech—that mark the territory for Indian Others. In Indian Country, Indian Others continually manoeuvre an unpredictable montage of ambiguous borders and inevitable bridges. For those who engage them, Indian borderlands are open-ended, and negotiating the positionings of ambivalent identity and recognition is normal.

Social borders are moving markers, boundaries that shift according to the positionings we negotiate and build in discursive interaction, in the conversations and actions of social exchange. The boundaries between Indians and those sometimes perceived as Others by Indians not only move, they transform. Borders emerge and retreat in an interactional process that can confine or *redefine* the "normal." The markers that construct social positionings continually form, disintegrate, or blend, reflecting the prismal nature of borderlands and the experience they construct. Borderlands are always mixed environments, placements experienced by those in-between as imagined unities of culture, class, gender, or even blood. But this prism is not a deterritorialized domain, as Michel Serres (1994: 13) suggests in writing that "the border prism represents the symbolic vision of a deterritorialized world." Like those who live them, borderlands can be claimed, disclaimed, and reclaimed in a reflexive process that is always in flux. These places or placements are relational spaces that are constantly territorialized, deterritorialized, and *reterritorialized* in the adoption of the representations that emerge within them. Borderlands are sites of shifting identities and alliances that situate, challenge, and change in the positionings that insiders and outsiders negotiate.

Gerald McMaster (1995: 80) calls these locations that speak to both external and internal conditions "borderzones," in which social spaces intersect and "emergent social agents/subjects experience, interrogate and negotiate their conditions of existence." For this Native artist, the place/state in-between reterritorializes the cultural guardianship Indians associate with "home," expanding its range in a creative interchange, a prism of cultures and communities—Indian and even Other—that represent "highly contestable spaces, spaces that continually collide and mix" (88). Among Indians, the complex and unpredictable borderland positionings that inflect race, gender, and culture are encumbered with the ambiguity of blood and belonging. For those who move in this mix of borders and bridges, the struggle over reterritorialized spaces is implicitly a struggle over representations and expressions, over the dynamic positionings of identity and recognition that signify being "home" in Indian Country.

Those my brother calls Indian "insiders-outsiders," experience the bordered terrain of Indianness in shifting cultural representations and realities that are linked to race and culture, identity and recognition. Emily Hicks (in Serres 1994: 13) writes, "Border culture includes a deep fear, the fear of being seen/caught/asked for identification." But the anxiety of living on the border in Indian Country relates less to unpredictable demands for identification than to the unpredictability of identity that is presumed or proclaimed, but unrecognized. Indian insiders-outsiders live in a contestable personal space that is sometimes recognized as tribal, sometimes as Indian, sometimes as white. As Kim Anderson (2000: 29) writes, "The complex path of a mixed-blood individual can be greatly affected by factors such as one's appearance, loca-

tion and the political climate." Because the markers are never fixed, negotiating the moving borders of identity and recognition involves "devel-
oping a tolerance for contradictions, a tolerance for ambiguity" (Anzaldúa
1987: 79). In Indian Country, boundaries and the margins they erect are
complex, contentious, and unstable. The borders of Indian identity and
recognition move in a discursive dance of continuous positionings. Like
other Indian insiders-outsiders, I always expected that my mixed-blood
Chippewa experience would synthesize into some imagined unified
identity. I realize now that living on the borders lasts forever. There is no
synthesis of cultures or social resolution, just the prism of positionings
that empower being in-between.

Beyond Blood

Today, contests over Indian identity and tribal membership arise from
and reverberate in the experience and expressions of Native North Americans. As Ovide Mercredi and Mary Ellen Turpel (1994: 88) write, "We
must be the ones who determine who is and who is not a member of
our community, based on criteria accepted by our people." Their statement recognizes that, as Daniel Wildcat (in Foster 1997: 14A) says, "if
tribal sovereignty means anything, it means the right of a nation to determine who its members are." This long-overdue expression of Indian self-
determination and sovereignty is finally being written into band bylaws.
In the process of tribal empowerment and local politics, definitions of
membership are emerging that sometimes replace and sometimes renew
colonial codes. In an inevitable struggle over identifying markers of
tribal and Indian oneness, blood borders continue to fester, constructing
borderlands that are public, personal, and conflictual. But the efforts of
some nations resonate with the words of Marlene Brant Castellano (1970:
59), who wrote thirty-five years ago about resolving the colonial vestiges of Indian identity, "What is needed to translate this hope into experience is a new definition of what it is to be Indian, formulated not in
terms of white norms but in terms of what Indians value in their communal life. To have meaning, this Indian identity must be lived as well
as talked about."

Culture and relationships are recognized in the membership policies of the Dene nation in Canada's northwest, about whom Ovide Mercredi (Mercredi and Turpel 1994: 88) writes, "For them, membership

requires family connection, a knowledge of the Dene culture and language, and a commitment to the good of the people. For them, identity is not based on race but on culture and family; it reflects the Dene values." In Kahnawake, where Mohawks have battled over membership for twenty-five years and the band council has defied the government's legislation of Bill c-31 by "asserting its exclusive jurisdiction over membership matters" (Alfred 1995: 168), Mohawks are moving toward new membership policies that recognize not only blood but culture, language and contribution to the community. And both First Nations and Métis are currently engaged in discussions with the federal government that involve defining Aboriginal membership, Status, and citizenship (Curry 2005: A4).

There will always be contested borders and prismal borderlands between Indians and Others. As communities struggle over unities in difference, there will always be insiders, insiders-outsiders, and outsiders. But there is a growing recognition that Indian identity emerges in the prism of contingent lived relations that are interwoven into heredity, community, and culture. In the end, Indian identity and recognition are constructed, expressed, and negotiated in the continuity and contingency of All My Relations.

≪ • ≫

Conclusion:
All My Relations

He looks exhausted sitting alone in front of a white picket fence, one hand upon his stick. His face is gouged by time, unshaven, white hair unkempt, his medicine pouch barely visible beneath his shirt. Bearskin. I know the power of his name only through the storied memories of other Indians in Lac du Flambeau, but I've carried his postcard portrait with me for forty years. He sits near me now, beside Grandma Gauthier, looking weary with age, and old Mrs. Chen-gu-os-no-qua, who is posed in front of a screen door, her frail body covered by a bandolier bag, her head wrapped in a beaded belt perched like a hat. These images of my elders, whose suffering and strength stare across a century of change, walk with me wherever I go, prodding me to remember that we are all related.

The ancestors of Bearskin, Mrs. Chen-gu-os-no-qua, and Grandma Gauthier could never have imagined the entangled multiple identities and shifting alliances that we adopt, enact, and act upon today. Their lives were interwoven with the conflicts and politics of clans and ceremonies, trade and territory, adoptions and marriages. But their identity, authenticity, and practice of their culture were more familiar and less contested before the onslaught of Others: outpost traders, missionaries, lumber barons, and government administrators. Our ancestors never labelled their lifeways "popular culture," or spoke about "traditional," "transitional," and "modern" Indian lifestyles. In the years since, Natives and newcomers have appropriated the anthropologists' term "traditional" to speak about the popular culture that our ancestors once lived. This inscription of past practice, drawn from the histories and ethnographies of Others and the recesses of Indian oral tradition, is linked in articulation to authenticity, identity, and political possibility in current narratives of cultural struggle that divide Indians and Others and Native people themselves. In the words of Philip Deloria (2003: 407), "Defining oneself as an Indian in the twentieth century has meant walking a fine line between the domination and allure of American culture and the resistance and resilience of one's own tradition." He (402) writes about "one of the paradoxes of Indian country in the twentieth century: if Indians change, their culture is considered contaminated and they lose their 'Indianness.' If they do not change, they remain Indians, but are refused a real existence in the modern world."

Contemporary Native Culture

Today, Indians who represent the culture lived by Bearskin, Mrs. Chengu-os-no-qua, and even Grandma Gauthier are recognized as "Elders," old-timers," or "Chippewa traditionals." These contemporary Anishinabe, so appreciated for their knowledge of Indian heritage and their practice of Chippewa customs, are the keepers of emerging traditions that are instrumental codes to action knitted into the fabric of lived experiences in Indian Country. In texts that privilege old art and artifacts, customs and ceremonies, the stories told by scholars and image-makers sometimes suggest that traditional cultures have perished over time, or survived unchanged through periods of enforced acculturation that forbade religious ceremonies, Aboriginal languages, and hereditary chiefs. But the traditions that Native people enact and act upon today in the ambiguous play of power and identity neither disappeared nor remained intact.

McMaster and Trafzer (2004: 233) write about Indian culture, "Like a braid of hair, individual identity and community history are woven together with a philosophical system that gives meaning to the world. This braid is the tripartite link between our ancestors, our communities and individuals." But the strands of cultural meaning that are braided into Native identity, community, and heritage are not identical, immutable, or isolated. The social imaginaries of Natives and newcomers have long been intermingled in the narratives of history and culture that encircle Indian oral tradition and practices and circulate in literary, artistic, academic, and media expressions. The traditions that these narratives represent and express are continually transformed in memory, discourse, and meaning, continually attached, detached, and relinked to changing cultural, social, and political realities. As Stuart Hall (1981: 228) writes, traditions that appear to persist, actually change over time and come to stand in a different relation to the ways people live, define their relations with each other and Others, and relate to their conditions of life.

In Indian Country, traditional beliefs and practices continually emerged in periods of cultural invasion and social conflict, especially during the late 1800s and early 1900s. In these perilous years, Indians experienced the displacement, territorial transgressions, and cultural restrictions of reserves, the impact of Christianity and boarding schools, and the onslaught of commercial enterprise and government administration. The realities and lifeways of Indians continued to respond to new environments in the years during and after the Second World War, when Indians began to leave reserves for school, military service, or employment in the expanding cities. Indian experiences and lifestyles were always varied on reserves; but in urban areas, notions of "race, assimilation and individualism" (LaGrand 2003: 268) accentuated divisions between Indians and Others and similarities among different tribal cultures. And through all the unrelenting periods of cultural contingency and change, Natives and newcomers have been yoked together in narratives of dominance, survivance (Vizenor 1993), and survival: remembered and appropriated, imagined and experienced.

Today, the strands that form the braid of Indian identity, community, and heritage are interwoven with Others and with Indians in struggles over the politics of difference: rights and resources, art and artifacts, tribal membership and spirituality, stories and stereotypes. In communities built in the precarious power relations of shifting identities, alliances, and ideologies, Native people in cities and on reservations move back and forth across perforated borders, negotiating different— even opposing—discourses of emerging cultural and political possibility. Contemporary narratives of cultural struggle and political survival express ambiguous representations of Indianness that are articulated to heritage and traditionalism, land and spirituality, blood and belonging. But woven into transforming Native stories—collective and personal, lived and remembered, or imagined, expressed, and enacted—is the enduring sensibility of being Indian.

In Indian Country, some Native people speak about the prophecy of the Seventh Fire, predicting a time when we will return to traditional ways, relationships, and responsibilities. Some Elders say that this prophesy decrees that only Native people will be among the "New People," the Seventh Generation, who will return to the cultural teachings of Indian traditions. Other Elders say that non-Natives, too, are among those who will recognize the cultural ways that honour the earth and its people. For both, there is the promise that the Seventh Generation will lead us to the Eighth Fire, which embodies an eternal era of peace and kinship built upon the shared ideology of renewed wisdom and a new relationship among Indians and Others.

We are the Seventh Generation, and we are all related. Like the old Kiowa woman in N. Scott Momaday's (1966: 89) book *House Made of Dawn*, "our words are medicine; they are magic and invisible." And as Cherokee artist Jimmie Durham (in Smith 2004) tells us:

> It is necessary that,
>   with great urgency, we all speak well and listen well.
> We, you and I, must remember everything.
>   We must especially remember those things we never knew. (176)

≪ • ≫

References

INTRODUCTION

Cardinal, Harold. 1969. *The Unjust Society: The Tragedy of Canada's Indians*. Edmonton, AB: Hurtig.

Deloria, Vine, Jr. 1969. *Custer Died for Your Sins*. New York: Avon.

Hall, Stuart. 1989. "Cultural Identity and Cinematic Representation." *Framework* 36:68–81.

———. 1986. *Journal of Communication Inquiry* 10, 2. Special Issue on Stuart Hall.

Hodgson, Maggie. 1990. "Communities in Crisis: Healing Ourselves." Conference Report, June 6–8. Montreal, QC: Waseskun House.

Keeshig-Tobias, Lenore. 1992. "Not Just Entertainment." 98–101. In Slapin and Seale, eds. *Through Indian Eyes: The Native Experience in Stories for Children*. Gabriola Island, BC: New Society.

King, Thomas. 2003. *The Truth about Stories: A Native Narrative*. Toronto, ON: Anansi.

Momaday, N. Scott. 1966. *House Made of Dawn*. New York: Harper and Row.

Perreault, Jeanne, and Sylvia Vance. 1990. *Writing the Circle: Native Women of Western Canada*. Edmonton, AB: NeWest.

Redbird, Duke. 1975. Director. *Pow Wow at Duck Lake*. Montreal, QC: National Film Board of Canada.

Ross, Rupert. 1996. *Returning to the Teachings*. Toronto, ON: Penguin.

Slapin, Beverly, and Doris Seale, eds. 1992. *Through Indian Eyes: The Native Experience in Stories for Children*. Gabriola Island, BC: New Society.

Steiner, Stan. 1968. *The New Indians*. New York: Delta.

Swann, Brian, and Arnold Krupat. 1987. *Recovering the Word: Essays on Native American Literature*. Berkeley, CA: University of California Press.

CHAPTER 1 • LIVING THE HERITAGE OF LAC DU FLAMBEAU

Barnouw, Victor. 1950. "Acculturation and Personality among the Wisconsin Chippewa." *Memoir of the American Anthropological Association* 72.

Bartlett, William W. 1929. "Armstrong Reminiscences." In *History, Tradition and Adventure in the Chippewa Valley*. Eau Claire, WI: Wm. W. Bartlett.

Bokern, James K. 1987. "The History of Primary Canoe Routes of the Six Chippewa Bands from the Lac du Flambeau Region." Masters Thesis: University of Wisconsin.

Chicago Tribune. Chicago, IL.

Cleland, Charles E. 1985. *A Research Report on the Nineteenth Century Patterns of Resource Use and Economic Strategy of the Lake Superior Chippewa.* Odanah, WI: Bad River Band of Lake Superior Tribe of Chippewa.

Clifford, James. 1986. "Introduction: Partial Truths." In J. Clifford and G. Marcus, eds., *Writing Culture.* Berkeley, CA: University of California Press.

Daily News. 1986. 27 April. Rhinelander, WI.

Daily Press. 1987. 18 April. Ashland, WI.

Densmore, Frances. 1910. "Chippewa Music I." *Bulletin of the US Bureau of American Ethnology* 45. Washington, DC: Smithsonian Institution.

——. 1913. "Chippewa Music II." *Bulletin of the US Bureau of American Ethnology* 3. Washington, DC: Smithsonian Institution.

——. 1929. "Chippewa Customs." *Bulletin of the US Bureau of American Ethnology* 86. Washington, DC: Smithsonian Institution.

Fabian, Johannes. 1983. *Time and the Other: How Anthropology Makes Its Object.* New York: Columbia University Press.

Gauthier, Ben C. 1938. "Memorandum to Superintendent Cavill." In personal possession of the author.

Great Lakes Agency. 1944. "Wisconsin Program, Lac du Flambeau Reservation, Wisconsin: Part I—Basic Data; Section I—Resources." In personal possession of the author.

Great Lakes Fish and Wildlife Commission. n.d. "Chippewa Treaty Rights: Hunting, Fishing, Gathering on Ceded Territory." Odanah, WI.

——. 1988. "Data on Fish and Game Harvesting on Chippewa Ceded Territory." Odanah, WI.

Guthrie, Gregg. 1973. "Our Grandfathers." In personal possession of the author.

Hallowell, A. Irving. [1955] 1967. *Culture and Experience.* New York: Schocken Books.

Handrick, Philip. 1987. "A Chippewa Case: Resource Control and Self-Determinism." *Cultural Survival Quarterly* 2, 2.

Hoffman, William J. 1886. "The Midéwiwin or 'Grand Medicine Society' of the Ojibway." *Annual Report of the US Bureau of American Ethnology* 7. Washington, DC: Smithsonian Institution.

Hunt, W. Ben. 1954. *Indian Crafts and Lore.* New York: Simon and Schuster.

Kasten, Bob. 1987. *Special Report: Indian Treaty Rights.* Washington, DC: United States Senate.

Kimball, Art, Scott Kimball, and Brad Kimball. 1987. *The Fish Decoy.* Boulder Junction, WI: Aardvark Publications.

Klapper, Charles J., ed. 1904. *'Indian Affairs': Laws and Treaties,* Vol. 2, *Treaties.* Washington, DC: Government Printing Office.

Lakeland Times. Minocqua, WI.

Masinaigan: A Chronical of Lake Superior Ojibwe. Summer 2004. Odanah, WI: Great Lakes Fish and Wildlife Commission.

McBride, Elizabeth. 1987. "Wisconsin's Chippewa Struggle to Reclaim Old Ways and Resources." *Isthmus* 12, 4.

McKinsey, Shirley N. 1937. "An Economic Survey of the Lac du Flambeau Reservation of Wisconsin." In personal possession of the author.

Malhiot, François Victor. 1910. "A Wisconsin Fur-trader's Journal, 1804–5." In Reuben Gold Thwaites, ed., *Collections of the State Historical Society of Wisconsin.* Vol. 19. Madison, WI: State Historical Society.

Milwaukee Journal. Milwaukee, WI.

Milwaukee Sentinel. Milwaukee, WI.

Momaday, N. Scott. 1969. *The Way to Rainy Mountain.* Albuquerque, NM: University of New Mexico Press.

———. 1976. *The Names.* New York: Harper and Row.

Owen, David Dale. 1852. *Report of a Geological Survey of Wisconsin, Iowa and Minnesota.* Philadelphia, PA: Lippincott, Grambo.

Pratt, Mary Louise. 1986. "Fieldwork in Common Places." In J. Clifford and S. Marcus, eds., *Writing Culture: The Poetics and Politics of Ethnography.* Berkeley, CA: University of California Press.

Ritzenthaler, Robert. 1953. "Chippewa Preoccupation with Health." *Bulletin of the Milwaukee Public Museum* 19, 4.

Rutlin, Terry. 1984. "Fishing and Hunting Rights of Wisconsin Indians: A History." *Natural Resources* 6, 4.

US Senate. 1910. Hearings Before the Committee on Indian Affairs, US Senate on Senate Resolution 263. *Conditions of Indian Affairs in Wisconsin.* Washington, DC: Government Printing Office.

The September Outer's Book. 1917. Chicago, IL: Outer's Book.

Slabbaert, Lorraine. 1988. *The Enduring Ways of the Lac du Flambeau People.* Wisconsin Region Public Broadcasting System.

Soaring Eagle. 1986. Lac du Flambeau, WI.

Walkerdine, Valerie. 1986. "Video Replay: Families, Films and Fantasies." In V. Burgin, J. Donald, and C. Kaplan, eds., *Formations of Fantasy.* London, UK: Methuen.

Warren, William. 1885. "History of the Ojibways." *Minnesota Historical Collections,* Vol. 5.

Whaley, Rick with Walter Bresette. 1994. *Walleye Warriors.* Gabriola Island, BC: New Society.

Wausau Daily Herald. 1987. "Anishinabe: The Chippewa of Wisconsin." 1 November:9.

CHAPTER 2 • RIGHTS AND WARRIORS

Alfred, Gerald R. 1995. *Heeding the Voices of Our Ancestors.* Toronto, ON: Oxford University Press.

Atwood, Margaret. 1972. *Survival: A Thematic Guide to Canadian Literature.* Toronto, ON: Anansi.

Brantlinger, Patrick. 1998. "Forgetting Genocide: Or The Last of *The Last of the Mohicans.*" *Cultural Studies* 12, 1:15–30.

Benton-Benaise, Eddie. 1998. "The Ogichida Warrior." In *Masinaigan.* Spring. Odanah, WI: Great Lakes Indian Fish and Wildlife Commission.

Burgess, Marilyn. 1990. "The Construction of Gender in the Discourses Constituting a Canadian Western Frontier." Paper presented at the Doctoral Forum, Inter-university PhD Program. Concordia University, Montreal, QC.

Carey, James W. 1989. *Communication as Culture.* Boston, MA: Unwin Hyman.

Carpenter, Edmund. 1970. *They Became What They Beheld.* New York: Outerbridge and Dienstfrey/Ballantine.

Charney, Ann. 1995. "The Last Indian War." In *Defiance in Their Eyes: True Stories from the Margins.* Montreal, QC: Vehicule Press.

Clifton, James A. 1968. "Factional Conflict and the Indian Community: The Prairie Potawatomi Case." In Stuart Levine and Nancy O. Lurie, eds., *The American Indian Today.* Baltimore, MD: Pelican.

Coombe, Rosemary J. 1996. "Embodied Trademarks: Mimesis and Alterity on American Commercial Frontiers." *Cultural Anthropology* 11, 2:202–24.

Crow Dog, Mary, with Richard Erdoes. 1990. *Lakota Woman.* New York: Harper Perennial.

David, Joe. 1994. "How to Become an Activist in One Easy Lesson." *Semiotext(e) Canadas.* New York: Semiotext(e); Peterborough, ON: Marginal Editions.

Deloria, Philip J. 1993. "The Twentieth Century and Beyond," In *The Native Americans.* Atlanta, GA: Turner Publications.

Deloria, Vine, Jr. 1969. *Custer Died for Your Sins.* New York: Avon.

Deloria, Vine, Jr., and Clifford Lytle. 1984. *The Nations Within: The Past and Future of American Indian Sovereignty.* New York: Pantheon.

Goodleaf, Donna. 1995. *Entering the War Zone.* Penticton, BC: Theytus Books.

Green, Rayna, ed. 1984. *That's What She Said: Contemporary Poetry and Fiction by Native American Women.* Bloomington, IN: University of Indiana Press.

Hale, Horatio, ed. [1883] 1972. *The Iroquois Book of Rites.* Toronto, ON: Coles.

Hall, Louis Karoniaktajeh. n.d. "Rebuilding the Iroquois Confederacy." Monograph. In personal possession of the author.

Hall, Stuart. 1989. "Cultural Identity and Cinematic Representation." *Framework* 36:68–81.

———. 1985. "Signification, Representation, Ideology: Althusser and the Post Structuralist Debates." *Critical Studies in Mass Communication* 2, 2:91–114.

———. 1986. *Journal of Communication Inquiry* 10, 2. Special Issue on Stuart Hall.

Hazen-Hammond, Susan. 1997. *Timelines of Native American History.* New York: Pedigree.

Heinrich, Jeff. 2004. "A Struggle for a Cause Turns Nasty." *Gazette* (Montreal), 7 March: Insight, 1 and 3.

Henton, Darcy. 1990. "The Mohawk Warriors: Heroes or Thugs?" The *Toronto Star.* 24 November: D1 and D5.

Horn, Kahn-Tineta. 1997. "Traditional Culture and Community Competition: An Analysis of the On-going Struggle between the Great Law and the Code of Handsome Lake in Kahnawake." Master's research essay. Ottawa, ON: Carleton University.

Hughes, Ken. 1991. *The Summer of 1990: Fifth Report of the Standing Committee on Aboriginal Affairs.* Ottawa, ON: House of Commons Canada.

Ignatieff, Michael. 1994. *Blood and Belonging: Journeys into the New Nationalism.* Toronto, ON: Penguin.

King, Michael. 2004. "Article." *Gazette* (Montreal), 3 July: A7.

Kroker, Arthur. 1994. "The Mohawk Refusal." In Jordan Zinovich, ed., *Semiotext(e) Canadas.* New York: Semiotext(e); Peterborough, ON: Marginal Editions.

MacLaine, Craig, and Michael S. Baxendale. 1990. *This Land Is Our Land: The Mohawk Revolt at Oka.* Montreal, QC: Optimum.

Mauser, Gary. 1991. "Struggling to Control the Truth." *Adbusters Quarterly: Media and Environmental Strategies* 1, 4:12–13

Means, Russell. 1995. *Where White Men Fear to Tread.* New York: St. Martin's Griffin.

Moody, Roger, ed. 1988. *The Indigenous Voice: Visions and Realities,* Vol. 1 and 2. London, UK: Zed Books.

Parker, A.C. [1916] 1967. *The Constitution of the Five Nations or the Iroquois Book of the Great Law.* Ohswekon, ON: Iroqrafts.

Pindera, Loreen. 1990. Lecture. "The Oka Crisis." Concordia University, Montreal, QC.

Ruoff, A. Lavonne Brown. 1991. *Literatures of the American Indian.* New York: Chelsea House.

Steiner, Stan. 1968. *The New Indians.* New York: Delta.

Two Shoes, Minnie. 1998. "AIMster Gangsters from the Part." *Aboriginal Voices* 5, 3:28–29.

Vachon, Robert. 1993. "The Mohawk Dynamics of Peace." *Interculture* 26, 1.

Vizenor, Gerald. 1984. *The People Named the Chippewa: Narrative Histories.* Minneapolis, MN: University of Minnesota Press.

Wagamese, Richard. 1996. *The Terrible Summer.* Toronto, ON: Warwick.

Wallace, P.A.W. [1946] 1997. *The White Roots of Peace.* Ohswekon, ON: Iroqrafts.

Whaley, Rick with Walter Bresette. 1994. *Walleye Warriors.* Gabriola Island, BC: New Society.

Wilson, Edmund. 1959. *Apologies to the Iroquois.* New York: Vintage.

York, Geoffrey. 1990. *The Dispossessed: Life and Death in Native Canada.* London, UK: Vintage.

CHAPTER 3 • POSTCARDS OF MY PAST

Alexander, Don. 1986. "Prison of Images: Seizing the Means of Representation." *Fuse Magazine*. February/March:45–46.

Alfred, Taiaike. 1999. *Peace, Power, Righteousness: An Indigenous Manifesto*. Don Mills, ON: Oxford University Press.

Allen, Paula Gunn. 1986. *The Sacred Hoop: Recovering the Feminine in American Indian Traditions*. Boston, MA: Beacon.

Ames, Michael. 1987. "Free Indians from Their Ethnological Fate." *Muse*, Summer:14–19.

Asch, Michael. 1984. *Home and Native Land: Aboriginal Rights and the Canadian Constitution*. Toronto, ON: Methuen.

Atwood, Margaret. 1972. *Survival: A Thematic Guide to Canadian Literature*. Toronto, ON: Anansi.

Bacon, Bob. 1988. "Tourist/Home Movies." In Roger Moody, ed., *The Indigenous Voice: Visions and Realities*. Vol. 1. London, UK: Zed Books.

Bedard, Joanna. 1989. "Fluffs and Feathers: A Conference on Stereotyping, October 27–29, 1988." *Wadrihwa* 3, 1:2–3. Brantford, ON: Woodland Cultural Centre.

Begamudre, Ven. 1989. "On Cultural Justice and Cultural Revenge." *Blackflash*, Fall:11–13.

Bhabha, Homi. 1984. "Of Mimicry and Man: The Ambivalence of Colonial Discourse." *October* 28:125–33.

———. 1987. "What Does the Black Man Want?" *New Formations* 1:118–30.

Bulbulian, Maurice. 1987. Director. *Dancing around the Table* (I and II). Montreal, QC: National Film Board of Canada.

Canada. House of Commons. 1983. Issue 40. Minutes of Proceedings of the Special Committee on Indian Self-Government. Keith Penner, chair. 12 and 20 October.

Canadian Broadcasting Corporation. 1989. *Newswatch*. 21 February.

Cardinal-Shubert, Joane. 1989. "In the Red." *Fuse Magazine*, Fall:77–80.

Clifford, James. 1985. "Histories of the Tribal and the Modern." *Art in America*. April:164–77.

———. 1987. "Of Other Peoples: Beyond the Salvage Paradigm." In Hal Foster, ed., *Discussions in Contemporary Culture*, No. 1. Seattle, WA: Bay Press.

———. 1988. *The Predicament of Culture: Twentieth Century Ethnography, Literature and Art*. Cambridge, MA: Harvard University Press.

Coombe, Rosemary J. 1996. "Embodied Trademarks: Mimesis and Alterity on American Commercial Frontiers." *Cultural Anthropology* 11, 2:202–24.

Connerton, Paul. 1989. *How Societies Remember*. Cambridge, UK: Cambridge University Press.

Dirks, Nicholas B. 1990. "History as a Sign of the Modern," *Public Culture* 2, 2:25–32.

Dominquez, Virginia. 1987. "Of Other Peoples: Beyond the Salvage Paradigm." In Hal Foster, ed., *Discussions in Contemporary Culture*, No. 1. Seattle, WA: Bay Press.

Doxtator, Deborah. 1988. "The Home of the Indian Culture and Other Stories in the Museum." *Muse*, Autumn: 26–28.

Fabian, Johannes. 1983. *Time and the Other: How Anthropology Makes Its Object.* New York: Columbia University Press.

Fanon, Frantz. 1967. *Black Skin, White Masks.* New York: Grove Press.

Fisher, Robin, and Kenneth Coates. 1988. *Out of the Background: Readings in Canadian Native History.* Toronto, ON: Copp Clark Pittman.

Fusco, Coco. 1993. "Performing Culture." Lecture at McGill University, 6 April, Montreal, QC.

The *Globe and Mail*. 1989. Toronto. 4 March: C13.

Geertz, Clifford. 1988. *Works and Lives: The Anthropologist as Author.* Berkeley, CA: Stanford University Press.

Grossberg, Lawrence. 1988. "Wandering Audiences, Nomadic Critics." *Cultural Studies* 2, 3:377–91.

Hall, Louis Karoniaktajeh. n.d. "Rebuilding the Iroquois Confederacy." Monograph.

Hall, Stuart. 1981. "Notes on Deconstructing 'The Popular.'" In R. Samuel, ed., *People's History and Socialist Theory.* London, UK: Routledge, Kegan and Paul.

Hallowell, A. Irving. 1960. "Ojibway Ontology, Behavior and World View." In S. Diamond, ed., *Cultural in History: Essays in Honor of Paul Radin.* New York: Columbia University Press.

Hill, Richard. 1994. "The Old and the New: Different Forms of the Same Message." *Native American Expressive Culture* 60, 3/4:75–83.

———. 1992. "One Part Per Million: White Appropriation and Native Voices." *Fuse Magazine*, Winter: 12–22.

Hill, Tom. 1988. "The Pressures of Tourism." Paper delivered at a National Conference on Heritage Interpretation. Ottawa, ON.

Jacobs, Alex A. Karoniaktatie. 1986. "The Politics of Primitivism: Concerns and Attitudes in Indian Art." *Akwekon* 2/3:1–3.

Kinsella, W.P. 1983. *The Moccasin Telegraph and Other Stories.* Harmondsworth, UK: Penguin.

Lurie, Nancy Oestreich, ed. 1966. *Mountain Wolf Woman, Sister of Crashing Thunder: The Autobiography of a Winnebago Indian.* Ann Arbor, MI: Ann Arbor Paperbacks.

Marcus, George E., and Michael M.J. Fisher. 1986. *Anthropology as Cultural Critique: An Experimental Moment in the Human Sciences.* Chicago, IL: University of Chicago Press.

McLoughlin, Moira. 1990. "But I Saw It in a Museum, It Must be True!" Paper presented at the Twelfth Annual Conference of the Canadian Communication Association, Vancouver.

McMaster, Gerald. 1995. "The 'Injun-uity' of Aesthetic Tricks." *Cultural Studies* 9, 1:74–90.

Means, Russell. 1995. *Where White Men Fear to Tread: The Autobiography of Russell Means.* New York: St. Martin's Griffin.

Memmi, Albert. 1965. *The Colonizer and the Colonized.* Boston, MA: Beacon.

Momaday, N. Scott. 1976. *The Names: A Memoir.* New York: Harper and Row.

———. 1969. *The Way to Rainy Mountain.* Albuquerque, NM: University of New Mexico Press.

New, W.H., ed. 1990. *Native Writers and Canadian Writing.* Vancouver, BC: University of British Columbia Press.

Pearce, Roy Harvey. 1967. *Savagism and Civilization: A Study of the Indian and the American Mind.* Baltimore, MD: Johns Hopkins University Press.

Said, Edward W. 1979. *Orientalism.* New York: Vintage.

Spivak, Gayatri Chakravorty. 1988. "Can the Subaltern Speak?" In C. Nelson and L. Grossberg, eds., *Marxism and the Interpretation of Culture.* Chicago, IL: University of Illinois Press.

Townsend-Gault, Charlotte. 1998a. "First Nations Culture: Who Knows What?" *Canadian Journal of Communication* 23, 1:31–43.

———. 1998b. "Let X = Audience." In Gerald McMaster, ed., *Reservation X: The Power of Place in Contemporary Aboriginal Art.* Fredericton, NB: Goose Lane Editions; Hull, QC: Canadian Museum of Civilization.

Tribune Juive. 1989. "The Mohawk Nation, Kahnawake Territory," 6, 4. January–February.

Trigger, Bruce. 1988a. "Who Owns the Past?" *Muse,* Fall:13–15.

———. 1988b. "The Historian's Indian: Native Americans in Canadian Historical Writing from Charlevoix to the Present." In R. Fisher and K. Coates, eds., *Out of the Background: Readings on Canadian Native History.* Toronto, ON: Copp Clark Pittman.

Trinh, T. Minh-ha. 1989. *Women, Native, Other: Writing Postcoloniality and Feminism.* Bloomington, IN: Indiana University Press.

Vizenor, Gerald. 1994. *Manifest Manners: Postindian Warriors of Survivance.* Hanover, NH: Wesleyan University Press.

Vogel, Virgil J. n.d. "The Indian in American History Textbooks." Unpublished manuscript.

CHAPTER 4 • INDIAN COUNTRY

Andrews, Lynn. 1981. *Medicine Woman.* New York: Harper and Row.

Augustine, Stephen. 2004. "The Origin of the Mi'kmaq." Presentation at the Canadian Studies International Seminar, 17 August, University of Ottawa, Ottawa, ON.

Barnouw, Victor. 1950. "Acculturation and Personality Among the Wisconsin Chippewa." *Memoir of the American Anthropological Association* 72:1–151.

Bear, Chief Austin. 2004. "Healing Our Spirit Worldwide." Paper presented at the Pacific Region Conference, September 1–5. Cairns, Queensland, AU.

Benton-Banai, Edward. 1988. *The Mishomis Book: The Voice of the Ojibwa.* St. Paul, MN: Red School House.

Berkhofer, Robert F., Jr. 1978. *The White Man's Indian: Images of the American Indian from Columbus to the Present.* New York: Vintage.

Berland, Jody, and Jennifer Daryl Slack. 1994. "On Environmental Matters." *Cultural Studies* 8, 1:1–4.

Bevis, William. 1987. "Native American Novels: Homing In." In Brian Swann and Arnold Krupat, eds., *Recovering the Word: Essays on Native American Literature.* Berkeley, CA: University of California Press.

Boas, Franz. [1888] 1974. *The Central Eskimo.* Toronto, ON: Coles.

Boyarin, Jonathan. 1994. "Space, Time and the Politics of Memory." In Jonathan Boyarin, ed., *Remapping Memory.* Minneapolis, MN: University of Minnesota Press.

Brave Bird, Mary with Richard Erdoes. 1993. *Ohitika Woman.* New York: Grove.

Bredin, Marion. 1993. "Ethnography and Communication: Approaches to Aboriginal Media." *Canadian Journal of Communication* 18, 3:297–313.

Brody, Hugh. 1981. *Maps and Dreams.* Harmondsworth, UK: Penguin.

Brotherston, Gordon. 1979. *Image of the New World: The American Continent Portrayed in Native Texts.* London, UK: Thames and Hudson.

Came, Barry. 1995. "Coon Come Fights Separatists." *Maclean's.* 27 February:18–19.

Carter, Forrest. 1976. *The Education of Little Tree.* New York: Delacourte.

Castaneda, Carlos. 1968. *The Teachings of Don Juan: A Yaqui Way of Knowledge.* Berkeley, CA: University of California Press.

Castro, Michael. 1991. *Interpreting the Indian: Twentieth-Century Poets and the Native American.* Norman, OK: University of Oklahoma Press.

Chappell, E. [1817] 1970. *Narrative of a Voyage to Hudson's Bay.* Toronto, ON: Coles.

Chatwin, Bruce. 1988. *The Songlines.* Harmondsworth, UK: Penguin.

Churchill, Ward. 1992. *Fantasies of the Master Race: Literature, Cinema and the Colonialization of American Indians.* Monroe, ME: Common Courage.

Clifford, James. 1986. *Writing Culture: The Politics and Poetics of Ethnography.* Berkeley, CA: University of California Press.

———. 1988. *The Predicament of Culture: Twentieth Century Ethnography, Literature and Art.* Cambridge, MA: Harvard University Press.

———. 1994. "Diasporas." *Cultural Anthropology* 9, 3:302–38.

Cohen, Barri. 1994. "Technological Colonialism and the Politics of Water." *Cultural Studies* 8, 1:32–55.

Crow Dog, Mary, with Richard Erdoes. 1990. *Lakota Woman.* New York: Harper Perennial.

Cumming, P.A., and N.H. Mickenburg. 1972. *Native Rights in Canada*, 2nd ed. Toronto, ON: Indian-Eskimo Association of Canada.

de Certeau, Michel. 1986. *Heterologies: Discourse on the Other.* Minneapolis, MN: University of Minnesota Press.

Deloria, Vine, Jr. 1999. *For This Land.* New York: Routledge.

Deloria, Vine Jr., and Clifford M. Lytle. 1984. *The Nations Within: The Past and Future of American Indian Sovereignty*. New York: Pantheon.

Dorris, Michael. 1994. *Paper Trail: A Collection of Essays*. New York: Harper-Collins.

Eckert, Allan W. 1992. *A Sorrow in Our Heart: The Life of Tecumseh*. New York: Konecky and Konecky.

Erdrich, Louise. 1992. "The Names of Women." *Granta* 41:132–38.

Fedorick, Joy Asham. 1989. "Sense of Home." *Canadian Woman Studies/les cahiers de la femme* 10, 2/3:57.

Feit, Harvey. 1973. "The Ethno-ecology of the Waswanipi Cree: Or How Hunters Can Manage Their Resources." In Bruce Cox, ed., *Cultural Ecology: Readings on Canadian Indians and Eskimos*. Toronto, ON: McClelland and Stewart.

Fox, Chief Red. 1971. *Memoirs of Chief Red Fox*. New York: McGraw-Hill.

Geertz, Clifford. 1983. *Local Knowledge: Further Essays in Interpretive Anthropology*. New York: Basic Books.

Green, Rayna, ed. 1984. *That's What She Said: Contemporary Poetry and Fiction by Native American Women*. Bloomington, IN: Indiana University Press.

———. 1976. "The Pocahontas Perplex: The Image of Indian Women in American Vernacular Culture." *The Massachusetts Review* 16, 4:698–714.

———. 1992. "Rosebuds of the Plateau: Frank Matsura and the Fainting Couch Aesthetic." In Lucy R. Lippard, ed., *Partial Recall: Photographs of North American Indians*. New York: The New Press.

Grossberg, Lawrence. 1992. *We Gotta Get Out of This Place: Popular Conservatism and Postmodern Culture*. New York: Routledge.

Gupta, Akhil, and James Ferguson. 1992. "Beyond 'Culture': Space, Identity and the Politics of Difference." *Cultural Anthropology* 7, 1:6–23.

Hallowell, A. Irving. 1960. "Ojibway Ontology, Behavior, and World View." In S. Diamond, ed., *Culture in History*. New York: Columbia University Press.

Hamilton, Charles, ed. 1972. *Cry of the Thunderbird*. Norman, OK: University of Oklahoma Press.

Harjo, Joy. 1992. "The Place of Origins." In Lucy R. Lippard, ed., *Partial Recall: Photographs of North American Indians*. New York: New Press.

Hazen-Hammond, Susan. 1997. *Timelines of Native American History*. New York: Perigee.

Highwater, Jamake. 1981. *The Primal Mind: Vision and Reality in Indian America*. New York: New American Library.

Howard, Harold P. 1971. *Sacajawea*. Norman, OK: University of Oklahoma Press.

Johnston, Gordon. 1987. "An Intolerable Burden of Meaning: Native Peoples in White Fiction." In Thomas King, Cheryl Calver, and Helen Hoy, eds., *The Native in Literature*. Oakville, ON: ECW.

Keith, Michael, and Steve Pile. 1993. "Introduction Part 1: The Politics of Place." In Michael Keith and Steve Pile, eds., *Place and the Politics of Identity*. New York and London, UK: Routledge.

Lac du Flambeau News 8, 5, May 2000.

Limerick, Patricia Nelson. 1987. *The Legacy of Conquest: The Unbroken Past of the American West.* New York: W.W. Norton.

McLuhan, T.C. 1994. *The Way of the Earth.* New York: Simon and Schuster.

———. 1972. *Touch the Earth: A Self-Portrait of Indian Existence.* New York: Pocket Books.

McMaster, Gerald. 1995. "Border Zones: The 'Injun-uity' of Aesthetic Tricks." *Cultural Studies* 9, 1:74–90.

McMaster, Gerald, and Clifford E. Trafzer, eds. 2004. *Native Universe: Voices of Indian America.* Washington, DC: Museum of the American Indian, Smithsonian Institution in association with National Geographic.

McNickle, D'Arcy. 1978. *Wind from an Enemy Sky.* San Francisco, CA: Harper and Row.

Martin, Sandra. 2004. The *Globe and Mail.* 29 June: R1.

Massey, Doreen. 1995. "Places and Their Pasts." *History Workshop Journal* 39: 182–92.

Mercredi, Ovide, and Mary Ellen Turpel. 1993. *In the Rapids: Navigating the Future of First Nations.* Toronto, ON: Penguin.

Momaday, N. Scott. 1995. "Sacred Places." *Aboriginal Voices* 2, 1:28–29.

———. 1976. *The Names: A Memoir.* New York: Harper and Row.

———. 1972. "A Word Has Power." In Shirley Hill Witt and Stan Steiner, eds., *The Way: An Anthology of American Indian Literature.* New York: Vintage.

———. 1969. *The Way to Rainy Mountain.* Albuquerque, NM: University of New Mexico Press

———. 1966. *House Made of Dawn.* New York: Harper and Row.

Moody, Roger, ed. 1988. *The Indigenous Voice, Visions and Realities.* Vol. 1. London UK: Zed Books.

Morison, Samuel. 1971. *The European Discovery of America: The Northern Voyages.* New York: Oxford University Press.

Nofz, Michael P. 1987. "Treading Upon Separate Paths: Native American Ideology and Marxist Analysis." *Sociological Inquiry* 57, 3:223–36.

Parkman, Francis. 1908. *The Conspiracy of Pontiac.* New York: E.P. Dutton.

Ridington, Robin. 1990. *Little Bit Know Something: Stories in a Language of Anthropology.* Vancouver, BC: Douglas and McIntyre.

Rosaldo, Renato. 1989. *Culture and Truth: The Remaking of Social Analysis.* Boston, MA: Beacon.

Rothenberg, Jerome. 1972. *Shaking the Pumpkin: Traditional Poetry of the Indian North Americans.* Garden City, NY: Doubleday.

Said, Edward W. 1979. *Orientalism.* New York: Vintage.

Seattle, Chief. 1991. *Brother Eagle, Sister Sky: A Message from Chief Seattle.* New York: Dial Books for Young Readers.

Silko, Leslie Marmon. 1977. *Ceremony.* New York: Signet.

Simpson, Audra. 1997. "Paths Toward a Mohawk Nation: Radical Empiricism and Writing Culture in Kahnawake." Paper presented at the Conference of

Indigenous Rights, Political Theory and the Reshaping of Institutions. Humanities Research Centre, The Australian National University, Canberra, Australia.

Smith, Paul Chaat. 1994. "Home of the Brave." *C Magazine*: 32–42.

———. 1995. "Fables of the Destruction: Mistaken Identities and New Inventions." Public readings, 9 March, Oboro Gallery. Montreal, QC.

———. 1992. "Every Word Tells a Story." In Lucy R. Lippard, ed., *Partial Recall: Photographs of North American Indians*. New York: The New Press.

Speck, Frank G. [1915] 1972. "The Family Hunting Band as the Basis for Algonkion Social Organization." In Bruce Cox, ed., *Cultural Ecology*. Toronto, ON: McClelland and Stewart.

Stefansson, Vilhjalmur. 1947. *Great Adventures and Explorations: From the Earliest Times to the Present as Told by the Explorers Themselves*. New York: Dial.

Stump, Sarain. 1974. *There Is My People Sleeping*. Sidney, BC: Gray's.

Swann, Brian, and Arnold Krupat. 1987. *Recovering the Word: Essays on Native American Literature*. Berkeley: University of California Press.

Tanner, Adrian. 1987. "The Significance of Hunting Territories Today." In Bruce Alden Cox, ed., *Native People Native Lands*. Ottawa, ON: Carleton University Press.

———. 1983. "Canadian Indians and the Politics of Dependency." In A. Tanner, ed., *The Politics of Indianness: Case Studies of Native Ethnopolitics in Canada*. St. John's, NL: Institute of Social and Economic Research, Memorial University of Newfoundland.

Tilly, Charles. 1994. "Afterward: Political Memories in Space and Time." In Jonathan Boyarin, ed., *Remapping Memory: The Politics of TimeSpace*. Minneapolis, MN: University of Minnesota Press.

Viola, Herman J. 1981. *Diplomats in Buckskins: A History of Indian Delegations in Washington City*. Washington, DC: Smithsonian Institution.

Vizenor, Gerald. 1994. *Manifest Manner: Postindian Warriors of Survivance*. Hanover, NH: Wesleyan University Press.

———. 1993. *Summer in the Spring: Anishinaabe Lyric Poems and Stories*, new ed. Norman, OK: University of Oklahoma Press.

———. 1972. "Songs of the People (Anisinabe Nagamon)." In Shirley Hill Witt and Stan Steiner, eds., *The Way: An Anthology of American Indian Literature*. New York: Vintage.

Wagamese, Richard. 1992. *The Terrible Summer*. Toronto, ON: Warwick.

Warren, William. 1885. "History of the Ojibways." *Minnesota Historical Collections* 5. St. Paul, MN: Minnesota Historical Society Press.

Warrior, Robert Allen. 1995. *Tribal Secrets: Recovering American Indian Intellectual Traditions*. Minneapolis, MN: University of Minnesota Press.

Welch, James. 1979. *The Death of Jim Loney*. New York: Harper and Row.

Whaley, Rick, with Walter Bresette. 1994. *Walleye Warriors*. Gabriola Island, BC: New Society.

Wheeler, Keith, 1976. *The Chroniclers*. Alexandria, VA: Time-Life.

White, Richard. 1984. "Native Americans and the Environment." In W.R. Swagerty, ed., *Scholars and the Indian Experience*. Bloomington, IN: University of Indiana Press.

CHAPTER 5 • SACAJAWEA AND HER SISTERS

Albers, Patricia C., and William R. James. 1987. "Illusion and Illumination: Visual Images of American Indian Women in the West." In Susan Armitage and Elizabeth Jameson, eds., *The Women's West*. Norman, OK: University of Oklahoma Press.

Allen, Paula Gunn. 1988. "Who Is Your Mother? Red Roots of White Feminism." In Rick Simonson and Scott Walker, eds., *Multi-Cultural Literacy*. St. Paul, MN: Grey Wolf Press.

"An Altitude Super Card: Pauline Johnson." Banff, AB: Altitude Publishing.

Anderson, Kim. 2000. *A Recognition of Being: Reconstructing Native Womanhood*. Toronto, ON: Second Story. Now available from Sumach Press, Toronto.

Andrews, Lynn. 1981. *Medicine Woman*. New York: Harper and Row.

Anzaldúa, Gloria. 1987. *Borderlands/La Frontera*. San Francisco, CA: Spinsters/Aunt Lute.

Beam, Alex. 1995. "Walt Disney Meets, and Reinvents, Pocahontas." *Globe and Mail*, 5 June: A17.

Berkhofer, Robert F., Jr. 1979. *The White Man's Indian: Images of the American Indian from Columbus to the Present*. New York: Random House.

Billington, Ray Allen. 1981. *Land of Savagery/Land of Promise: The European Image of the American Frontier in the Nineteenth Century*. Norman, OK: University of Oklahoma Press.

Black, Nancy B., and Bette S. Weidman. 1976. *White on Red*. Port Washington, NY: Kennikat.

Brown, Joseph Epes. 1993. Advertisement for *The North American Indians: A Selection of Photographs by Edward S. Curtis*. Camp Hill, PA: Quality Paperback Book Club.

Canfield, Gae Whitney. 1983. *Sarah Winnemucca of the Northern Paiutes*. Norman, OK: University of Oklahoma Press.

Carter, Sarah. 1997. *Capturing Women: The Manipulation of Cultural Imagery in Canada's Prairie West*. Montreal, QC: McGill-Queen's University Press.

Colt, George Howe. 1995. "Who Was Pocahontas?" *Life Magazine*, July: 64–69.

Coombe, Rosemary J. 1996. "Embodied Trademarks: Minesis and Alterity on American Commercial Frontiers." *Cultural Anthropology* 11, 2: 202–224.

Dearborn, Mary V. 1986. *Pocahontas's Daughters: Gender and Ethnicity in American Culture*. New York: Oxford University Press.

Deloria, Vine, Jr. 1969. *Custer Died for Your Sins: An Indian Manifesto*. New York: Avon.

Donnell, Susan. 1991. *Pocahontas*. New York: Berkley Books.

Duncan, Dayton. 1987. *Out West: American Journey along the Lewis and Clark Trail*. New York: Viking Penguin.

Erdrich, Louise. 1984. *Love Medicine*. New York: Henry Holt.

———. 1992. "The Names of Women." *Granta* 41:132–38.

Francis, Daniel. 1992. *The Imaginary Indian: The Image of the Indian in Canadian Culture*. Vancouver, BC: Arsenal Pulp.

Fusco, Coco. 1990. "Managing the Other." *Lusitania* 1, 3:77–83.

Gray, Zane. n.d. *The Spirit of the Border*. Akron, OH: Saalfield.

Green, Rayna. 1992. "Rosebuds of the Plateau: Frank Matsura and the Fainting Couch Aesthetic." In Lucy R. Lippard, ed., *Partial Recall: Photographs of North American Indians*. New York: The New Press.

———. 1988. "The Tribe Called Wannabe: Playing Indian in America and Europe." *Folklore* 99, 1:30–55.

———. ed. 1984. *That's What She Said: Contemporary Poetry and Fiction of Native American Women*. Bloomington, IN: University of Indiana Press.

———. 1976. "The Pocahontas Perplex: The Image of the Indian Woman in American Vernacular Culture." *The Massachusetts Review* 16, 4:698–714.

Herten, Els. 1997. "Ban the "S" Word." Brussels, Belgium: KOLA.

Howard, Harold P. 1971. *Sacajawea*. Norman, OK: University of Oklahoma Press.

Kidwell, Clara Sue. 1992. "Indian Women as Cultural Mediators." *Ethnohistory* 39, 2:97–107.

Landes, Ruth. 1971. *The Ojibway Woman*. New York: W.W. Norton.

Lederer, Paul Joseph. 1982. *Manitou's Daughters*. New York: New American Library.

Lurie, Nancy Oestreich. 1961. *Mountain Wolf Woman: Sister of Crashing Thunder*. Ann Arbor, MI: University of Michigan Press.

Mallet, Kathy. 1992. "Isinamowin: The White Man's Indian." CBC Radio, *Ideas*.

McMaster, Gerald. 1991. "How the West Was Lost: An Artist's Perspective." In Greg Young-Ing, ed., *Gatherings*, Vol. 2. Penticton, BC: Theytus Books.

Mojica, Monique. 1991. *Princess Pocahontas and the Blue Spots*. Toronto, ON: Women's Press.

———. 1989. "An Invocation/Incantation to the Women Word-Warriors for Custom-Made Shoes." *Canadian Woman Studies/les cahiers de la femme* 10, 2/3:40.

Montour-Angus, Patricia. 1992. In *Everywoman's Almanac*. Toronto, ON: Women's Press.

Mulvey, Laura, Dick Snauwaet, and Mark Alice Durant. 1996. *Jimmie Durham*. London, UK: Phaidon.

Native Peoples Magazine. 2000. Advertisement for US Commemorative Golden Dollar Coin. 3.

Niro, Shelley. 1991. "Mohawks in Beehives" and "The Rebel." Photographs in the Collection of the Canadian Museum of Civilization, Ottawa, Ontario.

Paskievich, John. 1995. Director. *If Only I Were an Indian....* Montreal, QC: Zemma Productions, in co-production with the National Film Board of Canada.

Pronzini, Bill. 1994. "The Western Pulps." In Thomas W. Knowles and Joe R. Lansdale, eds., *Wild West Show!* Avenel, NJ: Wings Books.

Reiter, Joan Swallow. 1978. *The Old West: The Women*. Alexandria, VA: Time-Life Books.

Scriba, Jay. 1995. "Pocahontas: A Legend and a Tragedy." The *Milwaukee Journal*.

Silko, Leslie Marmon. 1977. *Ceremony*. New York: The New American Library.

Smith, Jack H. 1989. *Postcard Companion: The Collector's Reference*. Radnor, PA: Wallace-Homestead.

Sneve, Virginia Driving Hawk. 1987. "Remembering Minnehaha." *Country Living*. November: 72–74.

Solomon, Arthur. 1990. *Songs for the People: Teachings on the Natural Way*. Toronto, ON: NC Press.

Stedman, Raymond William. 1982. *Shadows of the Indian: Stereotypes in American Culture*. Norman, OK: University of Oklahoma Press.

Strong-Boag, Veronica, and Carole Gerson. 2000. *Paddling Her Own Canoe: The Times and Texts of E. Pauline Johnson Tekahionwake*. Toronto, ON: University of Toronto Press.

Todd, Loretta. 1992. "What More Do They Want?" In Gerald McMaster and Lee-Ann Martin, eds., *Indigena*. Vancouver, BC: Douglas and McIntyre.

Van Kirk, Sylvia. 1980. *"Many Tender Ties": Women in Fur-Trade Society in Western Canada, 1670–1870*. Winnipeg, MB: Watson and Dwyer.

Whaley, Rick, with Walter Bresette. 1994. *Walleye Warriors: An Effective Alliance against Racism and for the Earth*. Gabriola Island, BC: New Society.

Woodward, Grace Steele. 1969. *Pocahontas*. Norman, OK: University of Oklahoma Press.

CHAPTER 6 • DANCE ME INSIDE

Abley, Mark. 1997. "The Loss of Language." *Gazette* (Montreal), 10 August : D3.

Allen, Paula Gunn. 1987. "Bringing Home the Fact: Tradition and Continuity in Imagination." In Brian Swann and Arnold Krupat, eds., *Recovering the Word: Essays on Native American Literature*. Berkeley, CA: University of California Press.

Ashley, Kathleen M. 1990. *Victor Turner and the Construction of Cultural Criticism*. Bloomington, IN: Indiana University Press.

Augustine, Stephen. 2004. "The Origin of the Mi'kmaq." Presentation at the Canadian Studies International Seminar, 17 August. University of Ottawa.

Baktin, Mikhail. 1981. *The Dialogic Imagination: Four Essays*. Austin: University of Texas Press.

Barnouw, Victor. 1950. "Acculturation and Personality Among the Wisconsin Chippewa." *Memoir of the American Anthropological Association* 72:1–152.

Blundell, Valda. 1993. "Echoes of a Proud Nation: Reading Kahnawake's Powwow as a Post-Oka Text." *Canadian Journal of Communication* 18, 3:333–50.

Braroe, Niels Winther. 1975. *Indian and White: Self-Image and Interaction in a Canadian Plains Community*. Stanford, CA: Stanford University Press.

Burgess, Marilyn. 1993. "Canadian 'Range Wars': Struggles Over Indian Cowboys." *Canadian Journal of Communication* 18, 3:351–64.

Conklin, Abe. 1994. "Origin of the Powwow: The Ponca He-thus-ka Society Dance." *Native American Expressive Culture* 40, 3/4:17–21.

Corrigan, Samuel W. 1970. "The Plains Indian Powwow: Cultural Interaction in Manitoba and Saskatchewan." *Anthropologica,* n.s. 12:253–77.

Crow Dog, Mary, with Richard Erdoes. 1990. *Lakota Woman.* New York: Harper Perennial.

Dyck, Noel. 1979. "Powwow and the Expression of Community in Western Canada." *Ethnos* 44:78–98.

Eliot, T.S. 1932. "Tradition and the Individual Talent." *Selected Essays.* London, UK: Faber and Faber.

Geertz, Clifford. 1973. *The Interpretation of Cultures.* New York: Basic Books.

Gonzalez, Anita. 1998. "Powwow Dancing and Native Rap: American Indian Dance Patronage and the Politics of Spirituality." *Proceedings: Society of Dance History Scholars.* Eugene, OR: University of Oregon Press.

Green, Rayna. 1988. "The Tribe Called Wannabee: Playing Indian in America and Europe." *Folklore* 99:30–55.

Greyeyes, Michael. 1997. "Powwow: A Long Journey," *Aboriginal Voices* 4, 1: 28–33.

Grimes, Ronald L. 1990. "Victor Turner's Definition, Theory and Sense of Ritual." In Kathleen M. Ashley, ed., *Victor Turner and the Construction of Cultural Criticism.* Bloomington, IN: Indiana University Press.

Grossberg, Lawrence. 1992. *We Gotta Get Out of This Place: Popular Conservatism and Postmodern Culture.* New York: Routledge.

Haefer, J. Richard. 1982. "Foreward" in Thomas Vennum, Jr., *The Ojibwa Dance Drum: Its History and Construction.* Smithsonian Folklore Studies 2:12–13.

Hallowell, A. Irving. 1955. *Culture and Experience.* Philadelphia, PA: University of Pennsylvania Press.

Hassrick, Royal B. 1988. *The George Catlin Book of American Indians.* New York: Promontory.

Hertzberg, Hazel W. 1971. *The Search for An American Indian Identity: Modern Pan-Indian Movements.* Syracuse, NY: Syracuse University Press.

Hodge, F.W., ed. 1910. "Handbook of American Indians North of Mexico," *Bulletin of the US Bureau of American Ethnology* 11. Washington, DC: Smithsonian Institution.

Howard, James H. 1955. "Pan-Indian Culture in Oklahoma." *The Scientific Monthly* 81:215–220.

Johnson, Basil. 1976. *Ojibway Heritage.* Toronto, ON: McClelland and Stewart.

Kolson, Bren. 1990. "Celebration: Drum of Life." In Jeanne Perreault and Sylvia Vance, eds., *Writing the Circle: Native Women of Western Canada.* Edmonton, AB: NeWest.

Laubin, Reginald, and Gladys Laubin. 1977. *Indian Dances of North America.* Norman, OK: University of Oklahoma Press.

Lurie, Nancy O. 1971. "The Contemporary American Indian Scene." In E.P. Leacock and N.O. Lurie, eds., *North American Indians in Historical Perspective.* New York: Random House.

Mason, Bernard S. 1944. *Dances and Stories of the American Indian.* New York: A.S. Barnes.

McMaster, Gerald. 1993. "Tenuous Lines of Descent: Indian Art and Craft in the Reservation Period." *In the Shadow of the Sun: Perspectives on Contemporary Native Art.* Canadian Ethnology Service, Mercury Series Paper 124. Ottawa, ON: The Canadian Museum of Civilization.

Means, Russell, with Marvin J. Wolf. 1995. *Where White Men Fear to Tread.* New York: St. Martin's Griffin.

Momaday, N. Scott. 1969. *The Way to Rainy Mountain.* Albuquerque, NY: University of New Mexico Press.

Mooney, James. [1896] 1996. *The Ghost Dance.* North Dighton, MA: JG Press.

Morley, David, and Kuan-Hsing Chen. 1996. *Stuart Hall: Critical Dialogues in Cultural Studies.* London: Routledge.

Mukerji, Chandra, and Michael Schudson. 1991. *Rethinking Popular Culture: Contemporary Perspectives in Cultural Studies.* Berkeley, CA: University of California Press.

Nabokov, Peter, ed. 1991. *Native American Testimony: A Chronicle of Indian-White Relations from Prophecy to the Present, 1492–1992.* New York: Viking.

Nelson-Kennedy, Evelyn. 1990. "Our Modern Powwows." In Jeanne Perrault and Sylvia Vance, eds., *Writing the Circle: Native Women of Western Canada.* Edmonton, AB: NeWest.

Pearce, Roy Harvey. 1953. *Savagism and Civilization: A Study of the Indian and the American Mind.* Baltimore, MD: Johns Hopkins University Press.

Powers, William K. 1990. *War Dance: Plains Indian Musical Performance.* Tucson, AZ: University of Arizona Press.

Pow Wow Time. 1992. Program of the Toronto International Pow Wow 1,1:August. Hagersville, ON: Mississaugas of the New Credit First Nation.

Raybin, David. 1990. "Aesthetics, Romance and Turner." In Kathleen M. Ashley, ed., *Victor Turner and the Construction of Cultural Criticism.* Bloomington, IN: Indiana University Press.

Ritzenthaler, Robert E. 1953. "Chippewa Preoccupation with Health." *Bulletin of the Milwaukee Public Museum* 19, 4:175–257.

Ritzenthaler, Robert E., and Pat Ritzenthaler. 1983. *The Woodland Indians of the Western Great Lakes.* Milwaukee, WI: Milwaukee Public Museum.

Roberts, Chris. 1992. *Pow Wow Country.* Helena, MO: American and World Geographic.

The September Outer's Book. 1917. Chicago, IL: The Outer's Book.

Simpson, Audra. 1997. "Paths toward a Mohawk Nation: Radical Empiricism and Writing Culture in Kahawake." Paper presented at the Conference of Indigenous Rights, Political Theory and the Reshaping of Institutions. Humanities Research Centre: The Australian National University, Canberra, Australia.

Stump, Sarain. 1970. "Round Dance." In *Tawow: Canadian Indian Cultural Magazine* 1, 1:9–11.

Townsend-Gault, Charlotte. 1992. "Ritualizing Ritual's Rituals." *Art Journal* 2, 2:51–58.

Turner, Victor. 1969. *The Ritual Process: Structure and Anti-structure.* Chicago, IL: Aldine.

Vansina, Jan. 1985. *Oral Tradition as History.* Madison, WI: University of Wisconsin Press.

Vennum, Thomas, Jr. 1982. *The Ojibwa Drum Dance: Its History and Construction.* Smithsonian Folklife Studies, 2. Washington, DC: Smithsonian Institution.

Venza, Jac. 1989. Producer. "American Indian Dance Theatre: Finding the Circle." *Great Performances.* The Corporation for Public Broadcasting (PBS).

Wagamese, Richard. 1996. *The Terrible Summer.* Toronto, ON: Warwick.

Warrior, Robert Allen. 1991/1992. "The Sweetgrass Meaning of Solidarity: 500 Years of Resistance." *Border/lines* 23:35–37.

Wetelainen, Joanne M. 1982. "Out of Dreams and Visions." *The Ontario Indian* 3, 7:50–53.

Whipple, Catherine. 1995. "Powwow." *News from the Sloughs* 1, 1:1, 12.

Williams, Raymond. 1981. *Culture.* London, UK: Fontana Press.

CHAPTER 7 • DRUMMING THE PAST

Allen, Paula Gunn. 1986. *The Sacred Hoop: Recovering the Feminine in American Indian Traditions.* Boston, MA: Beacon.

Ames, Michael M. 1992. *Cannibal Tours and Glass Boxes: The Anthropology of Museums.* Vancouver, BC: University of British Columbia Press.

Ardener, Edwin. 1989. "The Construction of History: 'Vestiges of Creation.'" In Elizabeth Tonkin, Maryon McDonald, and Malcolm Chapman, eds., *History and Ethnicity.* New York: Routledge.

Barnouw, Victor. 1950. "Acculturation and Personality among the Wisconsin Chippewa." *Memoir of the American Anthropological Association* 72:1–152.

Barthes, Roland. 1973. *Mythologies.* St. Albans, UK: Paladin.

Benton-Banai, Edward. 1988. *The Mishomis Book.* St. Paul, MN: The Little Red School House.

Boulanger, Tom. 1971. *An Indian Remembers.* Winnipeg, MB: Peguis.

Brown, Jennifer, in collaboration with Maureen Matthews. 1994. "Fairwind: Medicine and Consolation on the Berens River." *Journal of the Canadian Historical Association*, n.s. 4:55–74.

Brydon, Diana. 1996. "The White Inuit Speaks: Contamination as Literary Strategy." In Bill Ashcroft, Gareth Griffiths, and Helen Tifflin, eds., *The Post Colonial Reader.* London, UK: Routledge.

Comaroff, John, and Jean Comaroff. 1992. *Ethnography and the Historical Imagination.* Boulder, CO: Westview.

Connerton, Paul. 1989. *How Societies Remember.* Cambridge, UK: Cambridge University Press.

Densmore, Frances. [1910, 1913] 1972. *Chippewa Music*, 2 vols. New York: DeCapo Press. Originally published as "Chippewa Music I" and "Chippewa Music II," *Bulletin of the US Bureau of American Ethnology* 45 and 53. Washington, DC: Smithsonian Institution.

———. [1929] 1979. *Chippewa Customs*. St. Paul, MN: Minnesota Historical Society Press. Originally published as "Chippewa Customs," *Bulletin of the Bureau of American Ethnology* 86. Washington, DC: Smithsonian Institution.

Dewdney, Selwyn. 1975. *The Sacred Scrolls of the Southern Ojibway*. Calgary, AB: Glenbow-Alberta Institute; Toronto, ON: University of Toronto Press.

Dorris, Michael. 1994. *Paper Trail*. New York: Harper Perennial.

Erdrich, Louise. 1993. *Love Medicine*. New York: Harper Perennial.

"Fairwind's Drum." 1993. CBC Radio, *Ideas*. Transcript.

Geertz, Clifford. 1973. *The Interpretation of Cultures*. New York: Basic Books.

Gooderham, Kent, ed. 1969. *I Am an Indian*. Toronto, ON: J.M. Dent and Sons.

Grossberg, Lawrence. 1997. *Bringing It All Back Home: Essays on Cultural Studies*. Durham, NC: Duke University Press.

Guthrie, Ben, and Michael J. Goc. 1995. *Reflections of Lac du Flambeau: An Illustrated History of Lac du Flambeau, Wisconsin, 1745–1995*. Friendship, WI: New Past.

Guthrie, Ben. 1957. "Notes on Medicine Lodge from Conversations with Members in 1957." In personal possession of the author.

———. 1962. "Questions on Midé." In personal possession of the author.

Guthrie, Gregg. 1996. "Notes on the Drum." In personal possession of the author.

Hallowell, A. Irving. [1955] 1967. *Culture and Experience*. New York: Schocken.

———. 1960. "Ojibwa Ontology, Behavior and World View." In S. Diamond, ed., *Culture in History: Essays in Honor of Paul Radin*. New York: Columbia University Press.

———. 1936. "The Passing of the Midéwiwin in The Lake Winnepeg Region." *American Anthropologist, New Series* 38, 1:32–51.

Hickerson, Harold. 1970. *The Chippewa and Their Neighbors: A Study in Ethnohistory*. Prospect Heights, IL: Waveland.

Hoffman, William J. 1891. "The Midéwiwin or Grand Medicine Society of the Ojibway." *Seventh Annual Report of the Bureau of Ethnology, 1885–86*. Washington, DC: Government Printing Office.

Johnston, Basil. 1982. *Ojibway Ceremonies*. Lincoln, NB: University of Nebraska Press.

King, Cecil. 1997. "Here Come the Anthros." In Thomas Biolsi and Larry J. Zimmerman, eds., *Indians and Anthropologists: Vine Deloria Jr. and the Critique of Anthropology*. Tucson, AZ: University of Arizona Press.

Kohl, Johann George. [1885] 1985. *Kitchi-Gami: Life among the Lake Superior Ojibway*. St. Paul, MN: Minnesota Historical Society.

Krupat, Arnold. 1992. *Ethno-criticism: Ethnography, History, Literature*. Berkeley, CA: University of California Press.

Laabs, Joyce. 1997. "Guthrie Makes Historical Discovery of LdF Bandolier Bag." *Lakeland Times*. March 21. Minocqua, WI: 17.

Landes, Ruth. 1968. *Ojibway Religion and the Midéwiwin*. Madison, WI: University of Wisconsin Press.

———. [1937] 1969. *Ojibway Sociology*. New York: AMS Press.

Leach, Edmund. 1989. "Tribal Ethnography: Past, Present, Future." In Elisabeth Tonkin, Maryon McDonald, and Malcolm Chapman, eds., *History and Ethnicity*. New York: Routledge.

Lippard, Lucy R. 1992. *Partial Recall: Photographs of Native North Americans*. New York: New Press.

Lurie, Nancy. 1991. Curator of Anthropology, Milwaukee Public Museum, Wisconsin. Correspondence in personal possession of the author. March 27.

Marcus, G.E., and M. Fischer. 1986. *Anthropology as Cultural Critique*. Chicago, IL: University of Chicago Press.

Momaday, N. Scott. 1975. "The Man Made of Words." In Abraham Chapman, ed., *Literature of the American Indian: Contemporary Views and Perspectives*. New York: New American Library/Meridian.

———. 1976. *The Names: A Memoir*. New York: Harper and Row.

Mydin, Iskandar. 1992. "Historical Images—Changing Audiences." In Elizabeth Edwards, ed., *Anthropology and Photography, 1860–1920*. New Haven, CT: Yale University Press.

Perreault, Jeanne, and Sylvia Vance. 1990. *Writing the Circle: Native Women of Western Canada*. Edmonton, AB: NeWest.

Ridington, Robin. 1990. *Little Bit Know Something: Stories in a Language of Anthropology*. Vancouver, BC: Douglas and McIntyre.

Ritzenthaler, Robert. 1953. "Chippewa Preoccupation with Health." *Bulletin of the Milwaukee Public Museum* 19, 4:175–257.

Rosaldo, Renato. 1989. *Culture and Truth: The Remaking of Social Analysis*. Boston, MA: Beacon.

Ross, Rupert. 1996. *Returning to the Teachings: Exploring Aboriginal Justice*. Toronto, ON: Penguin.

Scherer, Joanna C. 1992. "The Photographic Document: Photographs as Primary Data in Anthropological Enquiry." In Elizabeth Edwards, ed., *Anthropology and Photography: 1860–1920*. New Haven, CT: Yale University Press.

Schoolcraft, Henry R. 1851. *Personal Memoirs of a Residence of Thirty Years with the Indian Tribes on the American Frontiers*. Philadelphia: Lippincott, Grambo.

———. 1835. "Mythologies, Superstitions and Languages of the North American Indians," New York *Theological Review* 2.

Silko, Leslie Marmon. 1977. *Ceremony*. New York: Signet.

Van Maanen, John. 1988. *Tales of the Field: On Writing Ethnography*. Chicago, IL: University of Chicago Press.

Vansina, Jan. 1985. *Oral Tradition as History*. Madison, WI: University of Wisconsin Press.

Vennum, Thomas, Jr., 1982. "The Ojibwa Drum Dance." Smithsonian Folklore Series, 2. Washington, DC: Smithsonian Institution Press.

Vizenor, Gerald. 1994. *Manifest Manner: Postindian Warriors of Survivance.* Hanover, NH: Wesleyan University Press.

———. 1993. *Summer in the Spring: Anishinaabe Lyric Poems and Stories.* Norman, OK: University of Oklahoma Press.

Warren, William W. 1885. *History of the Ojibway. Collection of the Minnesota Historical Society* 5. St. Paul, MI: Minnesota Historical Society.

Wees, William C. 1993. *Recycled Images.* New York: Anthology Film Archives.

CHAPTER 8 • BLOOD BORDERS

Alfred, Gerald. 1995. *Heeding the Voices of Our Ancestors.* Toronto, ON: Oxford University Press.

Alfred, Taiaiake. 1999. *Peace, Power, Righteousness: An Indigenous Manifesto.* Don Mills, ON: Oxford University Press.

Anderson, Kim. 2000. *A Recognition of Being: Reconstructing Native Womanhood.* Toronto, ON: Second Story. Now available from Sumach Press, Toronto.

Anzaldúa, Gloria. 1987. *Borderlands/La Frontera: The New Mestiza.* San Francisco, CA: Aunt Lute.

Bowles, R.P., J.L. Hanley, B.W. Hodgins, and G.A. Rawlyk. 1972. *The Indian: Assimilation, Integration, or Separation.* Scarborough, ON: Prentice Hall.

Cardinal, Harold. 1969. *The Unjust Society: The Tragedy of Canada's Indians.* Edmonton, AB: Hurtig.

Carter, Sarah. 1998. *Capturing Women.* Montreal, QC: McGill-Queen's University Press.

Castellano, Marlene. 1970. "Vocation or Identity: The Dilemma of Indian Youth." In Waubageshig, ed., *The Only Good Indian: Essays on Canadian Indians.* Toronto, ON: New Press.

Chrystos. 1991. *Dream On.* Vancouver, BC: Press Gang.

Churchill, Ward. 1992. *Fantasies of the Master Race: Literature, Cinema and the Colonization of American Indians.* Monroe, MN: Common Courage.

Clifton, James. A. 1989. *Being and Becoming Indian.* Chicago, IL: Dorsey.

———. 1990. *The Invented Indian: Cultural Fictions and Government Policies.* New Brunswick, NJ: Transaction.

Crow Dog, Mary, with Richard Erdoes. 1990. *Lakota Woman.* New York: Harper Perennial.

Curry, Bill. 2005. "Ottawa, First Nations Seek to Redefine Indian Status." *National Post*, January 4: A4.

Deer, Kenneth. 1996. "Blood Quantam Required at Border." *The Eastern Door* 5, 7.

Deloria, Vine, Jr. 1994. *God Is Red: A Native View of Religion.* Golden, CO: Fulcrum.

Falk, Lorne. 1994. "The Border Prism." In Jordan Zinovich, ed., *Semiotext(e) Canada.* New York: Semiotext(e).

Flying Hawk d'Maine, Shirley. 1991. "Too Red To Be White—A Song." In Greg Young-Ing, ed., *Gatherings*. Vol. 2. Penticton, BC: Theytus Books.

Forbes, Jack. 1987. "Shouting Back to the Geese." In Brian Swann and Arnold Krupat, eds., *I Tell You Now: Autobiographical Essays by Native American Writers*. Lincoln, NB: University of Nebraska Press.

Foster, David. 1997. "Intermarriage Clouds Claims of Indian Ancestry." Associated Press and *Milwaukee Journal Sentinel*, 27 February. 13A–14A.

Geertz, Clifford. 1973. *The Interpretation of Culture*. New York: Basic Books.

Green, Rayna. 1988. "The Tribe Called Wannabe: Playing Indian in America and Europe." *Folklore* 99, 1:30–55.

Guidos, Rhina. 2004. "Defining Indianness Is a Double-edged Sword." *Salt Lake Tribune*, 10 May:1–3.

Guthrie, Gregg. 1973. "Our Grandfathers." In personal possession of the author.

Hall, Catherine. 1993. "'From Greenland's Icy Mountains … to Africa's Golden Sand': Ethnicity, Race and Nation in Mid-Nineteenth-Century England." *Gender and History* 5, 2:213–25.

Hall, Stuart. 1989. "Cultural Identity and Cinematic Representation." *Framework* 36:68–81.

———. 1993. "Culture, Community, Nation." *Cultural Studies* 7, 3:349–63.

Harmon, Alexandra. 1990. "When Is an Indian Not an Indian? 'Friends of the Indian' and the Problems of Indian Identity." *The Journal of Ethnic Studies* 18, 2:95–117.

Harp, Rick. 1994. "Native by Nature?" In Eleanor M. Godway and Geraldine Finn, eds., *Who Is This "We"?* Montreal, QC: Black Rose.

Henderson, Mae, ed. 1995. *Borders, Boundaries and Frames: Cultural Criticism and Cultural Studies*. New York: Routledge.

Hertzberg, Hazel W. 1971. *The Search for an American Indian Identity: Modern Pan-Indian Movements*. Syracuse, NY: Syracuse University Press.

Hogan, Linda. 1987. "The Two Lives." In Brian Swann and Arnold Krupat, eds., *I Tell You Now: Autobiographical Essays by Native American Writers*. Lincoln, NB: University of Nebraska Press.

Ignatieff, Michael. 1994. *Blood and Belonging: Journeys into the New Nationalism*. Toronto, ON: Penguin.

Jackson, Michael. 1989. *Paths toward a Clearing: Radical Empiricism and Ethnographic Inquiry*. Bloomington, IN: Indiana University Press.

Levine, Stuart, and Nancy O. Lurie, eds. 1970. *The American Indian Today*. Baltimore, MD: Pelican.

McGaa, Ed (Eagle Man). 1990. *Mother Earth Spirituality*. San Francisco, CA: Harper.

McMaster, Gerald R. 1995. "BorderZones: The 'Injun-uity' of Aesthetic Tricks." *Cultural Studies* 9, 1:74–90.

Means, Russell. 1995. *Where White Men Fear to Tread*. New York: St. Martin's Griffin.

Mercredi, Ovide, and Mary Ellen Turpel. 1994. *In The Rapids: Navigating the Future of First Nations*. Toronto, ON: Penguin Books.

Momaday, N. Scott. 1975. "The Man Made of Words." In Abraham Chapman, ed., *Literature of the American Indian: Contemporary Views and Perspectives*. New York: New American Library/Meridian.

———. 1976. *The Names: A Memoir*. New York: Harper and Row.

Morrisseau, Calvin. 1998. *Into the Daylight: A Holistic Approach to Healing*. Toronto, ON: University of Toronto Press.

Nabokov, Peter, ed. 1992. *Native American Testimony*. New York: Viking Penguin.

Oskaboose, Gil. 1998. "Ojibwe Voices: Send in the Clowns." *News from Indian Country*, August 2.

Pelletier, Wilfred, and Ted Poole. 1973. *No Foreign Land*. New York: Pantheon.

Ridington, Robin. 1990. *Little Bit Know Something: Stories in a Language of Anthropology*. Vancouver, BC: Douglas and McIntyre.

Robertson, Robbie. 1998. *The Underworld of Redboy*. Videocassette.

Rose, Wendy. 1987. "I Expected My Skin and My Blood to Ripen." In Beverly Slapin and Doris Seale, eds., *Through Indian Eyes*. Gabriola Island, BC: New Society.

Ross, Rupert. 1996. *Returning to the Teachings: Exploring Aboriginal Justice*. Toronto, ON: Penguin.

———. 1992. *Dancing with a Ghost: Exploring Indian Reality*. Markham, ON: Octopus.

Ruffo, Armand Garnet. 1996. *Grey Owl: The Mystery of Archie Belaney*. Regina, SK: Coteau.

Said, Edward W. 1978. *Orientalism*. New York: Vintage.

Saunders, Douglas. 1983. "The Re-emergence of Indigenous Questions in International Law." In Jean-Denis Archambault and R. Paul Nadine, eds., *Canadian Human Rights Yearbook*. Toronto, ON: Carswell.

Simpson, Audra. 1997. "Paths toward a Mohawk Nation: Radical Empiricism and Writing Culture in Kahnawake." Paper presented at the Indigenous Rights, Political Theory, and Shaping of Institutions Conference, Australian National University, Canberra, Australia.

Smith, Donald B. 1999. *Chief Buffalo Child Long Lance: The Glorious Imposter*. Red Deer, AB: Red Deer Press.

Smith, Paul Chaat. 1994. "Home of the Brave." *C Magazine*, Summer. 32–42.

Smith, Paul Chaat, and Robert Allen Warrior. 1996. *Like a Hurricane: The Indian Movement from Alcatraz to Wounded Knee*. New York: New Press.

Statistics Canada. 2001. *Aboriginal Peoples Survey: An Aborigial Profile*. Ottawa, ON.

Strong, Pauline Turner, and Barrik Van Winkle. 1996. "'Indian Blood': Reflections on the Reckoning and Refiguring of Native North American Identity." *Cultural Anthropology* 11, 4:547–76.

Townsend-Gault, Charlotte. 1998. "Let X = Audience." In Gerald McMaster, ed., *Reservation X: The Power of Place in Aboriginal Contemporary Art*. Fredericton, NB: Goose Lake Editions; Ottawa, ON: Canadian Museum of Civilization.

Trinh, Minh-ha, T. 1994. "Other Than Myself/My Other Self." In George Robertson, Melinda Mash, Lisa Tickner, Jon Bird, Barry Curtis, and Tim Putnam, eds., *Travellers' Tales: Narratives of Home and Displacement*. New York: Routledge.

Vanderwerth, W.C. 1971. *Indian Oratory*. Norman, OK: University of Oklahoma Press.

Vizenor, Gerald. 1984. *The People Named the Chippewa: Narrative Histories*. Minneapolis, MN: University of Minnesota Press.

———. 1994. *Manifest Manners: Postindian Warriors of Survivance*. Hanover, NH: Wesleyan University Press.

Wall, Steve. 1993. *Wisdom's Daughters*. New York: Harper Perennial.

Woodard, Charles L. 1989. *Ancestral Voice: Conversations with N. Scott Momaday*. Lincoln, NB: University of Nebraska Press.

CONCLUSION

Deloria, Philip J. 2003. "Part Five: The Twentieth Century and Beyond." In *The Native Americans: An Illustrated History*. Atlanta, GA: Turner Publishing.

Hall, Stuart. 1981. "Notes on Deconstructing 'The Popular.'" In R. Samuel, ed., *People's History and Socialist Theory*. London, UK: Routledge, Kegan and Paul.

LaGrand, James B. 2003. "Urban American Indian Identity in a US City: The Case of Chicago from the 1950s through the 1970s." In David Newhouse and Evelyn Peters, eds., *Not Strangers in These Parts: Urban Aboriginal Peoples*. Ottawa, ON: Policy Research Initiative.

McMaster, Gerald, and Clifford A.Trafzer, eds. 2004. In Gerald McMaster and Clifford A. Trafzer, eds., *Native Universe: Voices of Indian America*. Washington, DC: National Museum of the American Indian, Smithsonian Institution in association with National Geographic.

Momaday, N. Scott. 1966. *House Made of Dawn*. New York: Harper and Row.

Smith, Paul Chaat. 2004. "Season of Struggle." In Gerald McMaster and Clifford A. Trafzer, eds., *Native Universe: Voices of Indian America*. Washington, DC: National Museum of the American Indian, Smithsonian Institution in association with National Geographic.

≮ • ≯

Index

Page numbers in italics refer to illustrations.